3/-1-

DECISION MAKING IN
NATIONAL SCIENCE POLICY

DECISION MAKING IN NATIONAL SCIENCE POLICY

A Ciba Foundation and
Science of Science Foundation
Symposium

Edited by
ANTHONY DE REUCK
MAURICE GOLDSMITH
and
JULIE KNIGHT

J. & A. CHURCHILL LTD.

104 GLOUCESTER PLACE

LONDON W.I   1968

First published 1968
Containing 10 illustrations
Standard Book Number 7000 1340 7

Contents

Membership

J. Nekola	Institute for the Planning of Science, Academy of Sciences, Prague
A. E. Pannenborg	Director, Philips Research Laboratories, Eindhoven, Holland
A. Rahman	Scientist-in-Charge, Research Survey and Planning Organisation, Council of Scientific and Industrial Research, New Delhi
B. A. Rexed	Secretary-General, Science Advisory Council, Stockholm
J. Saint-Geours	Director of Planning, Ministry of Finance, Paris
D. Shimshoni	Department of Political Science, University of Tel-Aviv, Israel
A. Szalai	United Nations Institute for Training and Research, New York *and* Department of Economics and Law, Hungarian Academy of Sciences, Budapest
A. M. Weinberg	Director, Oak Ridge National Laboratory, Oak Ridge, Tennessee
J. R. Whitehead	Principal Scientific Adviser, Science Secretariat, Privy Council Office, Ottawa, Ontario

The Ciba Foundation

The Ciba Foundation was opened in 1949 to promote international co-operation in medical and chemical research among scientists from all parts of the world. Its house at 41 Portland Place, London, has become a meeting place well known to workers in many fields of science. Every year the Foundation organizes from six to ten three-day symposia and three or four one-day study groups, all of which are published in book form. Many other informal meetings also take place in the house, organized either by the Foundation or by other scientific groups needing a place to meet. In addition, bedrooms are available for visiting scientists, whether or not they are attending a meeting in the building.

The Ciba Foundation owes its existence to the generosity of CIBA Ltd, Basle, who, realizing the disruption of scientific communication caused by the war and by problems of distance, decided to set up a philanthropic institution whose aim would be to overcome such barriers. London was chosen as its site for reasons dictated by the special advantages of English charitable trust law, as well as those of language and geography.

The Foundation's many activities are controlled by a small group of distinguished trustees. Within the general framework of biological science, interpreted in its broadest sense, these activities are well summed up by the Ciba Foundation's motto, *Consocient Gentes*—let the nations come together.

1*

The Science of Science Foundation

The Science of Science Foundation was formally inaugurated in October 1964 on the occasion of the publication of *The Science of Science*, a volume of tribute to Professor J. D. Bernal issued to mark the twenty-fifth anniversary of the publication of his pioneer work on *The Social Function of Science*.

The purpose of the Science of Science Foundation is to promote the scientific investigation of science itself as a social phenomenon. That is to say, it exists to advance the study of and research into the sociology and economics of science; the psychology of scientists and of scientific work; the principles and philosophy of planning research; the analysis of the flow of scientific communications; the role and evolution of science in diverse types of societies including our own; and the relationships between science and technology and society.

The activities of the Foundation, guided by its distinguished Advisory Council, include seminars conducted by leading national and international figures and attended by members of government agencies, industry and the universities; it arranges an annual lecture at the Royal Institution; it has established a library of books, periodicals and documents relating to science policy at the University of Sussex; it issues a bi-monthly *Newsletter* with a world-wide circulation; and it organizes a lecture service for universities in the United Kingdom. The Foundation is planning to initiate and support research on the science of science and proposes to publish reports and books in that field.

The resources of the Science of Science Foundation consist of royalties on its publications, donations and grants from industry and foundations, and gifts and bequests from institutions and individuals wishing to advance the objects of the Foundation. The Foundation is registered as a nonprofit-making company limited by guarantee and as an educational charity.

Preface

Concern with national science policy is a comparatively recent phenomenon: it was only four years ago—in October 1963—that the Organisation for Economic Co-operation and Development held the first, historic ministerial meeting on science. This concern is largely based upon recognition of the contribution of research to economic growth, which has led governments in all countries to become major supporters of scientific activity. Most industrial countries spend between one and three per cent of their gross national product on research and development, of which about one-tenth is spent on basic research. In the OECD countries as a whole, the State bears at least one-third and sometimes more than two-thirds of the total cost of research.

The first report of the United Kingdom's Council for Scientific Policy in 1966 laid down in general terms the aims of a national science policy. They are: "to maintain the environment necessary for scientific discovery; to ensure the provision of a sufficient share of the total national resources; to ensure that there is a balance between fields and that others are not avoidably neglected; to provide opportunities for inter-fertilization between fields and between the scientific programmes of nations".

A national science policy has two aspects: a general one of co-ordination and a more basic one of priorities. It is not clear how best to determine what money should go to science as a whole nor how to distribute whatever money is available between the different branches of science.

Present practice represents not the use of rational criteria but the accretion of past empirical decisions. As one might expect, the pattern differs between industrial or medical research directed towards identifiable social needs on the one hand, and fundamental research on the other, in which the goals are internal to science. Again, the circumstances are by no means the same in Big Science areas—such as space research or nuclear physics, requiring large and long-term capital investment and possibly also international collaboration—and in many Little Science areas, say, of chemistry or biology, where costs are less and may be spread to provide a wide spectrum of endeavour.

The intention in convening this symposium was to discuss both the practice and principles underlying the selection of priorities and the criteria for allocating scarce resources, whether in men, money or materials, to scientific research.

The provision of qualified manpower is inseparable from the problems of investment in research, but it was decided not to discuss higher scientific education as a specific issue because it deserves an entire symposium in itself. It is also recognized—and repeatedly made explicit in the symposium—that the final decisions in the allocation of research resources are essentially political. This is to say, they involve other objectives of government and depend ultimately upon the goals and values of society; they are thus not purely scientific decisions but must involve the political process directly—in which, no doubt, scientists themselves should have powerful and persuasive voices.

In emphasizing the political nature of these decisions, however, it would be dangerous to conclude that the ultimate criteria are exclusively or even largely economic. Planning is clearly required, especially at the gross level of choice among fields, and also within the more expensive fields of research. But the criteria of choice are many. The possibility of economic return on investment is just one factor, and for so-called pure science not a particularly useful factor, because of the essentially unpredictable nature of the results of basic research. This indeed is the central problem of the economics of science—namely, the weakness of the feedback link between demand and supply, the absence of a market mechanism to regulate the economic support of fundamental research. If science is primarily supported to nourish technology and as an educational discipline, it must not be overlooked that science in itself represents one of the most characteristic and distinctive values of modern culture, not merely as a cumulation of knowledge and technique but also as an indispensable intellectual basis for industrial society.

A pluralistic society has many goals and values and identifying these may be philosophical problems beyond the reach of the science of science. But a true science of science built up brick by brick may be—whatever its philosophical limitations—the only way to inject quantitative assessment into decision making in national science policy. The stage has been reached when it is necessary to clarify the questions to be asked and the research to be done in order to develop the science of science. There is not so much a lesson to be learnt, as Bacon put it, as a task to be done.

It seemed appropriate at this time, therefore, for the Ciba Foundation and the Science of Science Foundation to collaborate in bringing together not only a number of key people concerned with advising on science policy, but also research workers in the new field of "the science of science". It is hoped that these proceedings reflect in some measure the rationale of science policy in a variety of countries, comparing mixed, planned and developing economies. Although the central theme is decision making at a national level, some attention is given to industrial decision making in the hope that this may afford comparative models, and also to the extension of national science efforts by international co-operation. From this symposium we sought not so much the answers as the questions, and we hope that from it may emerge some further understanding of the necessary and co-ordinated research that now requires to be undertaken by many disciplines.

It is a pleasure to record the thanks of the Ciba Foundation to Mr. Maurice Goldsmith, Director of the Science of Science Foundation, for the indispensable part he played in bringing this meeting about and for his collaboration with Mr. de Reuck in selecting the members, planning the programme and preparing the proceedings for publication; the costs of this symposium and of its members and of the associated social functions were defrayed by the Ciba Foundation, which provided the intimate seclusion of its conference room for the actual meeting. Both Foundations and all the members of the symposium are deeply indebted to Lord Todd for his congenial chairmanship of the meeting and the learning and experience that he brought to the guidance of these discussions.

CHAIRMAN'S INTRODUCTION

LORD TODD

THE fact that through the efforts of the Ciba Foundation and the Science of Science Foundation so many distinguished men from a variety of countries have been gathered together to take part in this symposium is itself evidence of the importance of science and science policy in the affairs of nations. I need not discuss here the reasons for this importance—we are all familiar with the rapid advances made in science and technology and the crucial importance of the latter to economic progress. It is perhaps less generally realized that these advances have had a profound social impact, and that, in my view at least, we have not yet come to terms with them either socially or politically. We still try to run a twentieth-century world dominated by scientific progress with nineteenth-century politics. Herein lies one part of the importance of science policy, for it could provide a way out of this difficulty, if it came to be accepted as a basis for political decisions; for we must remember that in government the ultimate decisions are political and not scientific.

Science policy is concerned with the deployment of financial, material and manpower resources over the whole field of scientific endeavour and impinges on a very wide range of activities, from higher education to industrial affairs. It cannot sensibly be considered save in the context of national industrial and economic planning, since it involves among other things choices between one area of science and another. Time was when science was a relatively inexpensive activity occupying few people and seemed to have little political relevance. But once it reached the point where it began to absorb a noticeable fraction of the national budget it was bound to run into trouble. Research and development have gone ahead with an exponential growth rate but the gross national product has not.

Scientific research—in the sense of activity directed to the pursuit of new knowledge without any relevance to either short or long-term economic objectives—is creative in character, and government should in a sense stand to it in the relation of a patron. It is, of course, impossible to differentiate between the various sciences or portions of sciences on this basis. One cannot say in any absolute sense whether radio-astronomy is

1

"better" than the comparative physiology of marsupials and I am sure that none of us would try to do so. All we could do perhaps would be to decide that Dr. A is a better and more imaginative scientist than his colleague Dr. B in the same field and that he is therefore more worthy of support. In other words, when it comes to pure science one can only back the man— and this is worth remembering when people talk of developing "centres of excellence" in various fields of science. Such centres, if they are to be successful, are built on men and not on massive budgets and imposing institutes.

Unfortunately, however, there is a limit to the amount of money which a government will be prepared to spend on scientific research aimed solely at extending the frontiers of knowledge. I would not care to put a figure on the amount it should spend, for I believe that it will vary from time to time and from place to place according to circumstances. But it is obvious that with the rapidly rising cost of research—already very large in certain areas—we are reaching the stage at which an individual country will have to decide whether it will devote its main effort to certain fields and have little to do with others, or spread its resources so thinly over every area of science that it makes no serious impact on any of them. So it is that, to my mind, the central problem of science policy in this area, as well as in the area of development, is the making of choices and the determination of priorities.

I have already suggested that such choices cannot be made on the intrinsic merit of one sector of natural knowledge as compared with another. It follows, then, that some other criterion must be applied. This must surely be the likely value to the national well-being of mounting a major effort in any given field. To assess this is very difficult indeed— anyone who has tried to quantify the contribution of the research effort in an industrial firm to productivity and profits can testify how difficult it is, even in that much more restricted context. But like Professor Weinberg, whose paper will follow, I believe that we can—and indeed must—make a shot at it. The making of such choices is not new; all that is new is seeking to make them after an objective appraisal of the bases of choice. After all, we have been making choices of this nature for a long time; the development of massive defence programmes has in fact stimulated some areas of science much more than others, and the British decision, taken shortly after the last war, to mount a massive effort in nuclear power production, as well as the American one to put a man on the moon, are other examples of choices made which have profoundly influenced scientific and techno-logical development. Whether these decisions have been right or wrong I shall not argue at this moment, but what is certain is that they were not taken on the basis of any coherent scientific policy. Yet such decisions have long-term effects. They can, by attracting a large proportion of our able young people into certain types of scientific work, create an imbalance which can be dangerous if it is not foreseen, and they can set the industrial pattern of a country for generations.

This central problem of choices and priorities in relation to economic needs must bulk largely in our discussions, but there are other aspects of science policy about which I hope we shall hear something. Should the main focus of fundamental research be—as I believe it should be—in universities, and should what has been called directed basic research be farmed out there (for example by contract) by government and industry? Should government research establishments be encouraged in developed countries in fields other than defence and certain public utilities? This last question is particularly important to the developing countries, about whose problems we shall also learn. It is clear enough that initially, government in such countries will have to bear the main brunt of research and development, but the pattern needs to be carefully thought out so that as industrial activity grows, a transition to the desired final pattern may be easily and smoothly effected. At least the developing countries should be able to avoid some of the mistakes that the rest of us have made. Closely bound up with this is the scale and form of technical aid which the developed can give to the underdeveloped countries, although this is a problem to which a whole symposium could be devoted—and perhaps should be devoted, since it is a major world problem of the greatest urgency.

Our symposium includes participants from both the Western and Eastern democracies, which differ considerably in their patterns of scientific and economic planning. Yet I believe that our problems are very similar indeed—priorities, the supply of and demand for scientific manpower, reduction of the time which elapses between initial discovery and practical application. We have been developing machinery for dealing with these problems each according to his own hunches, and different countries vary a good deal in their organization for the formulation and execution of science policy. I doubt if anyone here would claim that he or his country has yet found the perfect solution but I hope that as a result of our discussion and exchange of information we shall make some progress towards finding it. That I know is also the hope of the organizers of this symposium—The Ciba Foundation which I represent and the Science of Science Foundation.

SCIENTISTS IN THE ARENA

Sir Solly Zuckerman
Chief Scientific Adviser to H.M. Government

WHEN a revered public figure dies, a respectable interval usually passes before his house is marked by a plaque or, as in France, before a street is graced by his name. So it is with the stages of history. Regardless of the vast expansion of education and knowledge in the past few decades, no one yet calls the second half of our century "The New Age of Enlightenment"; nor, in spite of the apparent riches it has garnered, is it hailed as a new species of Golden Age. But however it may be viewed by future generations, we ourselves can see it only as a more tumultuous era than any man has known before—an age of atom bombs and of population explosion; of space exploration and of tormented nationalism; of immense new wealth and of widespread hunger. We live in a period of uncontrolled and accelerating change, an age in which technology has raced ahead, and in which hallowed social values have tumbled. Economic aid to under-developed countries is outstripped by military aid. Inadequate famine relief and fabulously expensive space rocketry march together. The most powerful state which the world has ever known, equipped with all the arms which modern technology can provide, finds itself pitted in seemingly endless conflict against a nonindustrialized opponent whose poverty in weapons is made up by a determination not to yield. We live in an age of paradox: an age in which the politician—to paraphrase a recent British Prime Minister—has been straining after the scientist and technologist, and in which the latter have been trying to understand the social consequences of the innovations to which their work has led. The world is clearly living through a period in which the aims of politics and the outcome of scientific endeavour appear to clash.

The great social changes of our times derive from the spread of education, from the proliferation of old and new media of communication, and from a background of political philosophy which itself is constantly transmuted as economic conditions alter. It is to factors such as these that we look when we seek the origin of the forces that have led, for example, to the end of colonialism and to the rapid multiplication of independent sovereign states over the past two decades, and to the world-wide diffusion of European concepts of social justice. But when we look at the major social problems of the post-war years, we can see that they have come about less as a result of clear-cut political decision than automatically from the unco-ordinated application of scientific knowledge. By multiplying the ends of production and by transforming the processes of production, science, using the term in its broadest sense, has transformed the politics of our times.

Many believe that we would be better able to control the speed and the directions of the growth of science if we knew more about the way it grows, and about the ways it affects social and economic affairs. Some do not share this optimistic view. They do not believe that a more detailed understanding of the way science has led to technology, and technology to production and wealth, would necessarily help the efforts of the politician to spread happiness and peace. But the proposition, nonetheless, contains two important admissions. The first is that scientists do not know much about the natural history of scientific growth; the second is that scientists as well as non-scientists are poorly equipped, if indeed equipped at all, to predict the social and political repercussions of the applications of science and technology.

Until recently, these were matters with which relatively few people concerned themselves. Today they are commonplace. In order to improve the organization and promotion of scientific activities, and in a presumed effort to understand the part which science and technology play in social and political change, practically all countries have their science advisory councils and their scientific advisers, and all industrialized countries—and also many under-developed countries now striving to develop their own industries on very primitive foundations—are intensifying their scientific and technological efforts. Ever since the end of the second world war, twenty years ago, we in the United Kingdom have been spurred on to increase the numbers of professional scientists and engineers in our working population, and to ensure that adequate resources go to research and development. This we have been encouraged to do by successive governments, basically because of a belief in the simple proposition—perhaps too simple a proposition—that both national security and the competitiveness of manufacturing industry, particularly in export markets, depend primarily on their scientific and technological backing. As a measure of the success of this effort to increase the volume of our scientific resources, the working population of scientists and engineers is approaching the record figure of 350,000, nearly treble what it is estimated to have been twenty years ago, and the amount of money which is spent annually on what is broadly called "research and development" (R and D) is nearly £1,000 million, compared with an estimated £10 million or so just before the start of the second world war. In the United States the most recent phase in the development of the nation's scientific potential has been even more aggressive. The volume of national resources which are devoted to research and development still goes on increasing at a fantastic rate. The Federal Government now provides 16 thousand million dollars for research and development (more than Britain's total expenditure on education and defence together), of which the bulk is spent by the Department of Defense, the National Aeronautics and Space Administration and by the Atomic Energy Commission. The scientific effort of the Soviet Union has also been greatly intensified over the period. So, too, has that of France, Germany and Holland, and of almost every other industrialized or industrializing country.

While some scientists still live and dream in ivory towers, the figures leave no doubt that the bulk of science and technology has moved to the public arena.

EVOLUTION OF THE UNITED KINGDOM NATIONAL ORGANIZATION FOR SCIENCE AND TECHNOLOGY

It is worth spending a moment outlining the nature of the transformation as it occurred in the United Kingdom, before I turn to the more important question of the confines within which so-called "science policy" operates, and of the limitations to its apparent influence. On this point there is more than a little confusion.

At the turn of the century, science in the United Kingdom was pursued with relatively little support from public funds, and politics went its way almost unaware that its preoccupations were going to be affected by the advances of scientific knowledge. The government Research Councils, which are at the heart of the British form of scientific organization, were created just before, during and immediately after the first world war, to ensure that adequate resources were made available for scientists to pursue their researches in medical, agricultural and industrial fields. The Haldane Committee, which was set up in 1917 to enquire generally into the responsibilities of government departments, and to advise how the "exercise and distribution by the Government of its functions could be improved", provided the blue-print for government action in relation to science (Cd. 9230, 1918). It recommended that the responsibility for our national research institutions should be placed "in the hands of a Minister who is in normal times free from any serious pressure of administrative duties" and who was "immune from any suspicion of being biased by administrative considerations against the application of the results of research". The Minister chosen for the task was the Lord President of the Council, and the recommendation soon developed into a presumed principle of scientific independence, which clearly helped the "pure scientist". But its effect was to create a series of autonomous Research Councils which pursued their work in quasi-isolation, and whose activities did little to influence the policies of those government departments which were concerned executively with related technological matters. In consequence, and contrary to what the Haldane Committee had intended, a vertical division developed between Research Council and university science on the one hand, and the executive activities of government departments on the other. This separation inevitably became associated with a widespread belief that the kind of work which was carried out in the universities and under the banner of the Research Councils was intellectually more exacting and worthy than the kind of scientific and technological work required and pursued by government departments and in industry.

The nation-wide mobilization of scientists and engineers in the second world war induced little permanent change in this attitude, or in the basic nature of our scientific organization. It did, however, point to the need for some central Advisory Council which would be charged, in the words of the Barlow Committee of 1946, with advising the Lord President of the Council "in the exercise of his responsibility for the formulation and execution of Government scientific policy" (Cmd. 6824, 1946). It was for this reason that an Advisory Council on Scientific Policy came into being at the beginning of 1947. One of the first problems which it debated was the place of science in government, and in particular the respective functions of government departments, of the Research Councils and of outside bodies in carrying out research (Cmd. 7465, 1948). The Council was divided in its views, but a compromise was reached on two general principles: first, that Departments of State with executive responsibilities should be responsible for identifying problems requiring research, stating their order of priority and deciding where to carry out the work, and how to apply the results; and, second, that the Research Councils, and particularly the old Department of Scientific and Industrial Research, should continue to initiate background research where they thought fit, free from administrative control of the executive departments and from considerations of day-to-day expediency.

While the Council was not inhibited when debating a variety of problems in which no other body had a particular vested interest—for example, questions such as the growth and deployment of scientific manpower, the scale of financial support for basic research, and matters concerning certain aspects of our overseas scientific relations—throughout its existence it not surprisingly found itself impotent when it came to advising either about the use of scientific and technological resources in executive Departments of State, for example, the Defence Departments, or about the programmes of the Research Councils. In spite of these inhibitions, it observed in its final Report (Cmnd. 2538, 1964) that the overriding issue by which it had been exercised during its seventeen years of life was the scale and balance of the national civil scientific effort. While it had failed to discover any way of deciding what proportion of any country's gross national product should be devoted to the advancement and exploitation of science, the essential task which it therefore passed on to its successor body, given that such a body was going to be provided with something approaching executive rather than just advisory responsibility, was to determine how much money should be devoted to science and technology, and the clarification of the priorities and criteria by which to decide how to divide the cake of our national scientific resources. This valedictory note was no confession of failure; it was merely an indication of the magnitude of the problems that needed to be solved. For it was plain to all that whatever the position which had prevailed before the start of the second world war, the United Kingdom no longer possessed the resources to engage freely over the whole front of science. Some fields, such as aerospace technology and high-energy physics, were moving well out of our national reach.

The way in which the old Council became transformed into its successor bodies, the Council for Scientific Policy on the one hand and the Advisory Council on Technology on the other, and the time this took, were determined first by the recommendations of the 1963 Committee of Enquiry into the Organization of Civil Science (Cmnd. 2171, 1963) and, second, from the departmental changes introduced by the present British Government when it took office at the end of 1964. Overshadowing the enquiries of the 1963 Committee was the soaring cost of certain branches of science, but the two essential questions to which it addressed itself were: first, the fact that the various agencies which were concerned with the promotion of civil science were not interrelated in a coherent and articulate pattern and, second, that the arrangements for apportioning resources between agencies were insufficiently clear and precise. The recommendations put forward by the Committee to deal with these organizational and administrative matters were in the end wrapped up in the changes which flowed on the one hand from the creation of the Ministry of Technology, which was immediately given responsibility for the larger part of the old Department of Scientific and Industrial Research, including several of its Research Stations, the National Research Development Corporation, and the Atomic Energy Authority, and on the other, from the shaping of the Department of Education and Science to its present pattern, which includes responsibility for most of the old Research Council structure (Medical, Agricultural, Science, Natural Environment and Social Science) as well as the University Grants Committee. These initial changes, made in accordance with the Science and Technology Act of 1965, were taken a considerable step forward when the Ministry of Technology took over, at the beginning of 1967, most of the functions of the previous Ministry of Aviation, and so became provided with the apparatus to help chart, and indeed determine, the future of a significant section of that part of British manufacturing industry which is based on advanced technology.

An inevitable change in the central science advisory structure followed these transformations of ministerial responsibility. The Council for Scientific Policy was established to advise the Secretary of State for Education and Science in the exercise of his particular responsibilities for the formulation and execution of government scientific policy but, as the Council recognized in their first Report (Cmnd. 3007, 1966), their mandate is primarily restricted to basic science, both nationally and internationally. At the same time, the Minister of Technology set up an Advisory Council on Technology to help in the evolution of his Ministry. And finally, and partly because the scope of these two advisory bodies relates to separate and limited parts of the whole field, in the same way as there is a vertical separation between the two departments to which they report, a Central Advisory Council for Science and Technology was recently established in order to help advise the government as a whole on the most effective use of our scientific and technological resources, whether in the civil or defence fields, or in the public or private sectors.

FUNCTIONS AND POWERS OF ADVISERS

The objectives and value of the scientific advice given by committees varies according to the circumstances of the moment and the executive responsibility of the authority which is being advised. This point may seem obvious, but it needs to be made because the issue has been greatly confused by writers who attribute to advisory councils, as well as to scientific advisers in general, far greater powers than they in fact possess. Even committees which are charged with the straightforward direction of programmes of basic research are far more limited in the exercise of a corporate wisdom than is often supposed. They can make judgments about the intellectual value and promise of work that may be proposed to them, and decide what degree of support it should receive. But encouraging or discouraging proposals is almost all they can do in the field of basic research, and even in that of inventions. Committees discovered neither the atom nor penicillin, nor did they invent jet engines or zip-fasteners. As C. E. K. Mees, an Englishman who for many years was vice-president for research of the Eastman Kodak Company, once put it, even if too vigorously: "the best person to decide what research work shall be done is the man who is doing the research, and the next best person is the head of the department, who knows all about the subject and the work; after that you leave the field of the best people and start on increasingly worse groups, the first being the research director, who is probably wrong more than half the time; and then a committee, which is wrong most of the time; and finally, a committee of vice-presidents of the company, which is wrong all the time." It is not without interest that we owe the resurrection of this adage to the Rand Corporation, a United States institution which is mostly associated in the public mind with the evolution of formalized processes for so-called decision making, and with rigid procedures for controlling research and development expenditures in the defence field.

This, however, is not the level at which the advisory bodies to which I have referred (the Central Advisory Council for Science and Technology, the Council for Scientific Policy, and the Advisory Council on Technology) operate. Their concern is primarily with general matters, such as the volume and scale of our national scientific resources, and with the criteria which determine, or which should determine, the way they are used. All experience has shown that this task is hemmed in by as many constraints and pitfalls as the difficulties which Dr. Mees had in mind when he spoke in 1935 about research itself being directed by committees. It is these constraints which determine the limits of so-called "science policy" when conceived of as a course of action which is laid down by bodies of independent scientists.

GROWTH OF SCIENTIFIC RESOURCES

Let us first look at the problem of increasing the numbers of professionally trained scientists and engineers. The original stimulus for embarking on this course in the United Kingdom came from the Barlow Committee of 1946 (Cmd. 6824, 1946), and was based on the very reasonable assumption that the problem of post-war reconstruction, and of maintaining, leave alone raising, our standard of living, depended upon a very rapid increase in the numbers of professional scientists and engineers in the working population.

Starting from the acceptance of this recommendation, a vast national programme was initiated to expand our universities and to up-grade technical education in general. This course of action was spurred by the advocacy of a succession of advisory committees, including the Scientific Manpower Committee which was established in 1950 (see Cmd. 8561, 1952) and which was somewhat more successful than industry itself in "guesstimating" the latter's likely future demand for qualified manpower, and by its successor body the Committee on Manpower Resources for Science and Technology. In 1939, just before the second world war started, the level of output of qualified scientists and engineers was of the order of 4,000 a year. Today it is 23,000. But while scientific advisory councils have been successful in urging the government to provide the resources necessary to allow of this vast rate of increase, they have been far less successful in determining what kind of subjects or what kind of science the students take up. Moreover, in spite of much propaganda, they have not been very successful in raising to the desired level the proportion of the brighter boys and girls in sixth forms who go in for science and technology. Regardless of national needs, hundreds of university places in departments of pure and applied science, and especially departments of engineering science, remain unfilled. This issue dogged the old Advisory Council on Scientific Policy in the same way as it does the present Council for Scientific Policy.

If their achievements have fallen short of the mark in these latter respects, the advocacy of these two Councils, coupled with pressure from the universities and Research Councils, was, however, highly successful in persuading successive governments to multiply the financial resources made available from public funds for science and technology in all its aspects—from pure research at one end of the spectrum, to development and production at the other. The propaganda which emanated from their efforts also undoubtedly helped to encourage private industry to intensify its own efforts in the field of research and development. In financial terms the results have been spectacular. In 1939 the total amount of money available in the United Kingdom for research and development was little more than a few million pounds. Today as we know, it is approaching £1,000 million which, even taking inflation into account, certainly means a very considerable increase. On the other hand, both the old Advisory Council on

Scientific Policy and the present Council for Scientific Policy have learnt from experience that the money which is made available by government for pure research is only with considerable difficulty reapportioned between one field of potential discovery and another. With new money limited, fashion and inertia play a much bigger part than rational decision in determining the pattern of research expenditure at any given moment.

No one need doubt that the advocacy of advisory councils was largely responsible for the fact that the amount of money made available for pure research has grown over the past ten to twenty years at a much higher rate than that of any other sector of public expenditure. But the situation is now changing. The claims of pure science for additional resources have to be judged within the same framework as claims for other national cultural activities. Scientists, however, can always make the special plea that without the new knowledge provided by pure science, there would be no new science to apply in all those fields of activity—manufacturing industry and agriculture for example—which help determine the rate of economic growth as a whole. Against this, however, it can be argued that new scientific knowledge is available to all, regardless of its national source, and that it is never as essential to provide it with such massive support as scientists customarily demand. I shall return to this point later.

It now seems to be generally accepted that the rate of growth of the resources made available for pure science in the United Kingdom has to start slowing down. This point is discussed in the first Report of the Council for Scientific Policy (Cmnd. 3007, 1966) where it is noted that in both the United States and in France, in contrast, it is still public policy to increase the resources for basic research by about 15 per cent annually at constant prices. If the same were done here, it would mean that by 1984 the Research Councils alone would dispose of about £500 million, which is eight times what they spend today. Such an increase would inevitably divert trained men from industry and would be out of all proportion to the expected growth in our scientific resources and our gross national product. What needs to be decided is how speedily levelling-off should be accomplished and on what criteria.

THE BRAIN DRAIN AND THE TECHNOLOGY GAP

The problems of the so-called "brain drain" and "technology gap", by which is roughly meant the gap between the general technological and industrial power of the United States compared with that of European countries, have also now moved to the centre of the science policy stage.

They are matters to which the old Advisory Council, as well as the present Council for Scientific Policy, also directed much attention. Generally speaking, we know the reasons why scientists and engineers who have been trained at great expense in the United Kingdom choose to go abroad, in particular to the United States. They leave in the hope of better status, higher salaries, lighter taxation, the promise of greater opportunities and of less frustration. And without doubt most of these hopes stem from the fact that the United Kingdom does not and cannot deploy such lavish re-sources as the United States in order to satisfy the appetites and release the potentialities of all our science and engineering graduates.

Diagnosis of the causes of the brain drain, which is only part of a much wider process, is relatively simple; it is the therapy which constitutes the problem. The term itself is something of a misnomer. In general, educated men throughout the ages have always moved from areas of lesser to areas of greater opportunity, where they expect to find better resources with which they can apply their talents. And there have always been areas of greater and lesser opportunity, both between countries and within countries. Culture has never spread evenly over the earth. We lose people to the United States; but we absorb large amounts of professional manpower from countries like India and Pakistan. Japan welcomed the scientific and technological culture of the West, in an age when it was taboo in China. In South Africa some parts of the population enjoy all the fruits of Western civilization, while the Bushman population live as primitive hunters and graziers in a stone-age culture. The United States refers to the movement of people from poorer to richer States as its internal brain drain. Before a monetary value was placed upon professional training, no one bothered about these things. No one noticed when a scholar from one country moved to another. It would have been thought odd if he did not. We accepted as natural that men like Rutherford and Florey should leave the countries of their birth to build up schools of science in England.

But in a period when scientific manpower is in apparently short supply in the United Kingdom, not surprisingly we take a different view.

The imbalance between countries of greater and lesser opportunity shows itself in other ways, every bit as important as the brain drain itself. One country's wealth inevitably throws into relief another's poverty. Every year in Britain we absorb into our hospitals, universities and industries, large numbers of professionally trained Indians and Pakistanis. But at the same time we give technical and financial aid to these countries, so that it becomes a moot question—as it is in the United States—whether what we give is as valuable as what we take. But beyond this lies another issue. We are not only increasing the numbers of professionally trained manpower in this country; we are also exhorting them to exploit their talents in manufacturing industry in order to improve our competitive position in overseas markets. We seek for innovations others have not devised, for the invention of new kinds of capital equipment, for the development of new products which overseas markets will absorb. In so doing we cannot avoid damaging the economies of poorer countries. For instance, jute is one of Pakistan's major exports. But in its end-uses jute is in immediate competition with certain synthetic substances which we manufacture for packaging materials and other end-uses. The better our chemical industry performs in this field, the worse, therefore, for Pakistan, so long as it remains under-industrialized.

The brain drain is part of an age-long international multi-faceted problem. Advisory councils might perhaps suggest measures which can minimize our own losses of trained manpower, but they cannot stop the differential growth of technologically based industry in the world at large, any more than so-called science policy can show how the widening gap between advanced and under-developed countries can be narrowed. The basic problem is that of enhancing opportunity where it is missing; and its solution is in the field of politics, not science. The concepts of the Common Market and of its reflection, a technological community of Europe, are concepts which carry with them the promise of wider and greater opportunity for the exercise of scientific and engineering talent. But they are not scientific; they are political and economic concepts. Scientific advisory councils and science policy have, as such, little to contribute to their formulation.

CRITERIA OF CHOICE

Let us turn to another problem on which advisory councils have focused attention. At the present moment the amount of money from all sources which the United Kingdom spends on research and development is, as I have said, approaching £1,000 million a year. This is very nearly 3 per cent of our gross national product, a percentage which is practically the same as that of the United States and higher than that of any other country except, perhaps, the Soviet Union. This money is divided between basic research, applied research and the prototype engineering development work which leads on to production, in the proportions of approximately 10 per cent, 25 per cent and 65 per cent. But the actual pattern of distribution between different fields of science and technology has been determined not on the basis of an up-to-date assessment of needs, but through a series of unrelated decisions taken in the past, many of them hardly explicit. Advisory councils, such as the old Advisory Council on Scientific Policy and the present Council for Scientific Policy, have dealt mainly with the amount of money which goes either to pure basic research or to objective basic research, the first constituting those enquiries which are carried out in order to increase scientific knowledge without any social or economic purpose in view, and the second those kinds of basic research which are deliberately undertaken in fields of recognized technological importance.

The criteria for assessing the relative merits of projects which fall into these two categories are necessarily different. Where pure basic research is concerned, judgments can be based only upon an intellectual assessment of the quality and promise of the work. Experience has shown that there is no objective way of deciding how much money should go to this kind of science. For where science is pursued simply as a cultural activity, its claims on resources have inevitably to be judged in relation to those of other cultural activities, although in this battle scientists have the advantage, as I have already indicated, that they can argue that without an adequate basis of pure science most other parts of the production process would suffer. In the case of objective basic research, the assessment of value has to take account of the social and economic purpose of the research, and of its cost, as well as of its merit from the point of view of scientific quality. The political object-ives underlying any sector of government, whether it be health, defence or transport, determine the volume of resources which is made available to that sector as a whole, and indirectly, therefore, the amount of money which can or should be devoted to the research and development necessary to sustain the whole operation.

There is an immediate parallel here with industry. The primary purpose of the research and development which is carried out by or for manufac-turing industry is not to increase the body of scientific knowledge, but to secure and maintain a high rate of productivity through technical innova-tion, and eventually to make greater profits. That which is spent on public services, such as health, agriculture, or defence, is directed to corres-ponding utilitarian, if not necessarily commercial, ends. Thus the criteria which determine the allocation of research and development resources for defence are fundamentally based upon an assessment of the needs of the armed services for equipment to carry out their defined tasks. The Services and their technical advisers determine their research and develop-ment priorities, and whatever the shortcomings in the way they are imple-mented, it is recognized that expenditure has to be controlled by rigorous procedures, beginning with the formulation of an operational requirement, and leading through a feasibility study and project study, to final production —given that the project can be realized within the limits of time and resources, and that what is being sought will still fill a justifiable need when it comes to fruition (Committee on the Management and Control of Research and Development, 1961).

Broadly speaking, the same kind of control should apply to applied research and development in all fields of public expenditure. Priorities need to be set on the basis of criteria which are partly technical, partly economic. The technical criteria relate to the feasibility of the project under consideration, to its level of technological sophistication, to the time it will take to complete the development, and to the likelihood that the project will be successfully completed in the face of competition from other countries. The economic appraisal demands as thorough an examination as possible of the financial costs of the project, of its expected financial return if sufficient capital is available to exploit it expeditiously and, in our case, of its impact on the balance of payments. The same kind of considerations apply, of course, to major industrial research and development projects and to projects which are carried out in collaboration with other countries.

RELATION OF RESEARCH AND DEVELOPMENT TO ECONOMIC GROWTH

Here we immediately run up against a limit in the powers of independent advisory councils. None of this kind of work falls within their ambit, for the good reason that in the case of industrial projects responsibility lies with industry itself, and for projects which are supported out of public funds, with the particular Minister concerned. But the problem of improving the efficiency of all activities which lead to economic growth, and in particular the efficiency of manufacturing industry, nevertheless lies at the heart of science policy. This was one of the basic arguments behind the call to multiply the numbers of qualified scientists and engineers. Those who are concerned with the formulation of science policy must necessarily have an interest, therefore, in the problem of applying the fruits of scientific research, even though they may not be directly concerned with the way this is done.

But here we are faced by the paradox that twenty years after the Barlow Committee used this argument to spur government action in this field, and in spite of any amount of literature on the subject, we still know very little about the true significance of research and development to economic growth. Of course, we all accept that if there were no new scientific knowledge to be exploited, the processes and products of manufacturing industry would soon become fixed in their present mould. Equally we know that broad international comparisons of research and development expenditures tell us very little that is significant about economic growth. For example, the United States and the United Kingdom stand high in the league of countries which devote resources to research and development, but their rate of growth has been remarkably low in comparison with that of Germany and Japan—two countries which have spent relatively little overall on R and D and practically nothing on R and D for defence. If we want to learn from comparisons, it will be necessary to undertake case studies of corresponding industries or, indeed, of corresponding firms in different countries; to the best of my knowledge, this has not yet been done except for parts of the electronics industry (Freeman, 1965).

Other factors which have to be taken into account are, of course, the productivity and educational level of labour, economies of scale, and qualities of management and marketing. Some estimates suggest that the knowledge which is gained through research and development, when translated by way of technology into innovation, contributes as much as 50 per cent to the economic growth of advanced technological countries. Others put the figure much lower. Analysis of statistics both in the United States and the United Kingdom also show that most of the money available for research and development, whether from government or industrial sources, is spent by a few large undertakings. For instance, in the United States, four giant companies alone account for a quarter of the total United States research and development expenditure, that is to say, for more than five thousand million dollars of R and D. In the main, the companies concerned are producers of aircraft and missiles, computers, radar and other electronic equipment, and, to a lesser extent, chemicals and machinery. Relatively little R and D is carried out in more conventional sectors of industry. From these analyses we also know that the large companies concerned employ more professional scientific manpower than do others in all sectors of employment, not only in R and D, and that they are usually powerful in overseas markets. The five United States industries with the strongest research effort account for over 70 per cent of the nation's export of manufacturing goods, although they are responsible for only some 40 per cent of the nation's total sales of such goods. Companies such as these begin to enjoy what is almost a monopoly position for their goods in world trade.

But when we are finished with observations such as these, we always seem to come back to the point that, other than the United Kingdom, most

European countries experienced greater annual increases of output per man-hour during the period 1950–1960 than did the United States. Does this mean, as some would argue, that the strength of a country's own R and D effort and the source of the technical information which it uses, have no particular relevance to the problem of economic growth? Japan, we are often reminded, has produced few innovations in the field of plastics but, nonetheless, is second now to the United States in their production, partly through the purchase of technical know-how and then through the operation of partly-owned subsidiaries of overseas companies. Or does it mean that these countries enjoyed this high rate of growth because they started at so low a level after the second world war?

What we can be sure of is that money spent on applied research and development, the results of which are not carried through to production, is money which is in effect wasted, and that in assessing the potential value of an R and D programme, it is essential for those concerned to assess lead-times and likely cost in relation to the resources the company commands, and the commercial returns which may result. This means, as several recent writers have pointed out, that it is necessary to differentiate between the scientific and technological work which leads to invention and that which is necessary to bring about the successful marketing of the end-product. This point is neatly illustrated in an official report on Technological Innovation which has recently been published by the U.S. Department of Commerce (1967). The authors were fifteen prominent Americans convened by the Secretary of Commerce, all of whom could claim some form of direct experience either of major research and development projects or of manufacturing industry. On the basis of their own practical experience, they differentiated between the process of invention, which they defined as the conception of an idea, and that of innovation, which they saw as the process by which an invention or idea is translated into something of economic value. Professor Quinn had the same notion when he talked of technology as constituting two phases of operation, first, one in which knowledge is "created for practical purposes", and second, a stage when that knowledge is "used and transferred for practical purposes" (Quinn, 1967). As he aptly put it: "a crude lathe in the hands of a skilled man can represent a sophisticated technological system" whereas "the most advanced computer in the hands of a savage jungle tribe is likely to simply be a rapidly rusting hunk of junk".

The authors of the report to which I refer soon discovered that such data as were available for their enquiry mainly concerned the amount of money that was going, or was said to be going, to research and development, and

19

that there were few figures which gave the cost of the complete process of innovation. A series of case studies was, therefore, made and it turned out that, on average, research and development accounted for only 5–10 per cent of the total cost; engineering design, 10–20 per cent; tooling and manufacturing engineering, 40–60 per cent; start-up manufacturing expenses, 5–15 per cent; and start-up marketing costs, 10–20 per cent. Basic R and D thus accounts for only a very small part of the efforts made by scientists, engineers, managers and market specialists in getting value out of new discovery. Obviously the inventive phase, if we can so call the stage of R and D, is vitally important, but its value, on the basis of this analysis, will not be realized by a firm unless it has something like nine times the resources which it devotes to R and D to spend on the rest of the process of innovation and production. Big, well-endowed companies which operate in accordance with technologically based management techniques will always be at an advantage. If they have been successful in diverse fields of production, and have already established close contact with markets for other goods, they will be all the more likely to hold their own. The "technological gap" about which we hear so much seems to be due less to differences in technological knowledge than to differences between European and corresponding American firms in the part of the innovation process which comes after the research and development has been done. British expenditures on research and development in advanced technological industry—aircraft, electronics and so on—are high in relation to those of most countries. The reason why they have not brought in their train all the rewards we should like is almost certainly that the bigger American firms against which they compete are better geared than we are to achieve commercial value out of what is discovered in the laboratory. They are better geared in the sense that the personnel they employ in all parts of the business are more technically orientated than ours, that they command greater financial resources than we do, and that they have a greater assurance of markets than we have.

These things cannot be changed just through the advocacy of advisory councils of independent scientists to different government departments. If they so decided, such bodies could, of course, recommend that less money be made available for basic research, and more for generalized scientific and engineering education, or that the former should not be reduced and the latter increased. But, as I have already said, widespread propaganda for people to go in for a scientific education has failed so far to fill all the places that have been made available in our universities for this purpose. And I am not sure that other forms of major advice about basic research or engineering education would have any greater immediate impact—and it is immediate impact with which we are so critically concerned.

DEPARTMENTAL TECHNICAL RESPONSIBILITIES

In the case of government departments which are concerned with technological matters, the responsibility for advising how resources can be used to best effect lies more at the door of the technical staff which the departments employ for the purpose than of independent advisers. Their task is always a formidable one, even when they have full accesss to all matters relating to the objectives of the departments to which they belong. Scientists and engineers who are members of departmental staffs almost inevitably fight for departmental interests. For example, the ill-fated TSR 2 aircraft project, which in the end was judged to be making too great a demand on public resources in relation to the military need it was designed to fill, was necessarily supported by those scientists and engineers in the Ministry of Aviation whose business it was to see that the project did not fail for technical reasons. To this extent, it could be claimed that they were supporting the vested interest of the Royal Air Force, which was the potential consumer. But it was their business to do this. Equally it could be said that independent scientists who felt that the project represented an unjustifiable strain on our resources lacked the necessary forum where they could make their views felt. There is always a difficulty in resolving con-flicts between departmental views and views which may be held outside. Dr. Skolnikoff, now at the Massachusetts Institute of Technology, and previously a member of the staff of the U.S. President's Special Assistant for Science and Technology, has recently published an interesting article (Skolnikoff, 1966) on this point, with particular reference to the difficulties of getting an overall scientific point of view to bear on United States foreign policy. According to him, the State Department's complete dependence on outside technical information, that is to say, on information provided by other Departments of State, and by external advisers employed by these departments, meant that on important issues of foreign policy the United States Government was "at the mercy of the technical judgments" of men who were concerned only with their departmental interests. He illustrates this conclusion by the difficulty which the State Department experienced in dealing with the numerous arguments put forward by scientists who were opposed to the conclusion of the Test Ban Treaty. "Each new technical concept for evaluation put forward by the agencies concerned appeared as a major problem, and the Department was unable to evaluate the practical feasibility of the concepts or their importance in the basic political equation"—which was achieving a treaty. Another illustration which he gives was the follow-up of President Kennedy's proposal in 1962 that the United States and the Soviet Union should co-operate in the expensive field of space technology. Naturally enough the agency which took the responsibility for putting forward proposals was the National Aeronautics and Space Administration (NASA) "whose technical judgment of the feasibility of certain classes of projects was inevitably affected by its own objectives, its concepts of what contributed most to American foreign policy, and its preferences with regard to international co-operation". Whatever the State Department may have wished, NASA "was ensuring that US–Soviet co-operation in space would be minor, involving little political risk but offering correspondingly little chance for political gain".

THE SCOPE FOR CENTRAL ADVICE

Every country conducts its business in its own way and in accordance with its own kind of political organization. In the Soviet Union the work of the Academy of Sciences is articulated with that of the State Committee on Science and Technology, and its members are paid by the State. France has its General Delegation for Scientific and Technical Research (DGRST), which reports to the Committee of Ministers. In the United States there are several executive and advisory agencies with one central Presidential body —the President's Scientific Advisory Committee, which is chaired by the President's Special Assistant for Science and Technology. The deliberations of this committee extend into all fields of government, military or civil. In general it has been more concerned to see that scientific knowledge is applied and new technology developed than to assure the growth of science itself—a task which it leaves to the National Science Foundation, the National Institutes of Health, the National Academy of Sciences and several other bodies. Because the President's Committee has the widest possible remit, it has concerned itself with federal expenditures for technical developments in both the civil and defence fields. In the words of one of its members, because of its past performance, the President's Committee serves "as critical adversaries of agency planners, to be convinced by them, so that it may provide to the President objective unbiased advice with respect to the quality and magnitude of on-going programmes and the plans of the science-using agencies and of inter-agency arrangements" (Handler, 1967).

The new Central Advisory Council for Science and Technology which has recently been established in the United Kingdom has the responsibility of "advising the Government on the most effective national strategy for the use and development of our scientific and technological resources". This responsibility will clearly be more readily discharged in the field of public expenditure on science and technology. But since the latter affects the deployment of all our scientific and technical resources, it will clearly need to direct some attention to the way resources are used in the private sector. Even if it is too soon to say how the Council will act, the responsibility is there.

INTERACTION OF PUBLIC AND PRIVATE RESEARCH AND DEVELOPMENT

Private, like nationalized, industry is concerned to make the most effective use of the scientific and technical resources at its disposal. How this is done is not the business of government. Nonetheless industrial innovations in the private sector all too frequently lead to major social problems, which in turn necessitate the use of governmental research and development resources. The multiplication of motor-cars leads to atmospheric pollution; but atmospheric pollution, not being the business of private industry, has to be dealt with by government. The introduction of pesticides and herbicides by manufacturing industry also has repercussions with which the government finds it necessary to concern itself. We have recently had an acute illustration of this kind of interaction between private and public technology in the foundering of the oil tanker *Torrey Canyon*. Giant tankers are obviously more economic than smaller vessels. But we now know from experience that their operation entails great public risks. The problem now is to determine how these can be reduced and how to deal with the consequences, given there is an accident. Technological development in the private sector can always have an impact on the way the scientific and technological resources which the government itself deploys may have to be used.

WHAT IS SCIENCE POLICY?

I return now to the question of science policy. Most of us think we understand what is meant by the phrase "foreign policy", "housing policy", or "educational policy". On the other hand, many of us— and I amongst them—find it difficult to use the term "science policy" with any precision. The bulk of the scientific activity of the country, whether measured in terms of manpower or money, proceeds independently of the deliberations of advisory councils on science policy. It takes place either in the laboratories and workshops of industry, or in government laboratories which are necessarily, and in my view rightly, controlled departmentally. Over the years, the preoccupations of those who have been concerned with science policy in the United Kingdom have, therefore, focused on our educational programmes, on the resources available for basic research and on schemes for international co-operation of the kind that the European Space Research Organization (ESRO) and the European Organization for Nuclear Research (CERN) represent. These matters relate to only a small part of the deployment of our scientific and technological resources, even though they are fundamental to the rest. They are the general problems of science. But the bigger part of our scientific activities, with which advisory councils concerned with policy cannot deal executively, is what produces the economic resources on which all else depends, as well as the problems which continually confound the world of politics.

Science is thus inevitably in the public arena, and decisions about the deployment of our scientific resources must in the end inevitably be political. Advisory bodies can only advise. In our system of government the power of decision rests with the minister concerned or with the Government as a whole, or with the boards of companies. Although we are learning fast, the scientist, as we stand today, not only does not have the responsibility for public decision, but also still lacks the apparatus with which to predict the repercussions of technological developments. It is the repercussions which more than anything else transform the sphere of politics—not straightforward decisions like that of increasing the size of the scientifically trained population. Science policy would have much greater meaning than it has if only there were fewer unknowns in the scientific and technological process. Since the scientist is in the public arena only as the expert worker and adviser, it is his employer, whether it be the government or the board of an industrial company, which commands his service and which has the responsibility for action. The decision whether to accept or reject his advice is theirs and theirs only. If the scientists who now advise want more than this, then they will have to become politicians, or if not that, then at least leaders of industry.

NOTE: This is the text of the Third Annual Lecture of the Science of Science Foundation, delivered at the Royal Institution in London on 10th April, 1967 by Sir Solly Zuckerman before an invited audience which included the members of this symposium. Sir Solly Zuckerman did not himself participate in the symposium.

REFERENCES

Cd. 9230 (1918). Report of the Machinery of Government Committee of the Ministry of Reconstruction. Chairman, Viscount Haldane of Cloan. London: His Majesty's Stationery Office.

Cmd. 6824 (1946). Scientific Manpower—Report of a Committee appointed by the Lord President of the Council. Chairman, Sir Alan Barlow. London: His Majesty's Stationery Office.

Cmd. 7465 (1948). First Annual Report of the Advisory Council on Scientific Policy. London: His Majesty's Stationery Office.

Cmd. 8561 (1952). Report from the Committee on Scientific Manpower. In Fifth Annual Report of the Advisory Council on Scientific Policy, 1951–1952. London: His Majesty's Stationery Office.

Cmnd. 2171 (1963). Committee of Enquiry into the Organisation of Civil Science. Chairman, Sir Burke Trend. London: Her Majesty's Stationery Office.

Cmnd. 2538 (1964). Annual Report of the Advisory Council on Scientific Policy, 1963–1964. London: Her Majesty's Stationery Office.

Bill 12 (1964). Science and Technology Bill. London: Her Majesty's Stationery Office.

Cmnd. 3007 (1966). Council for Scientific Policy. Report on Science Policy. London: Her Majesty's Stationery Office.

Committee on the Management and Control of Research and Development (1961). Report. Chairman, Sir Solly Zuckerman. London: Her Majesty's Stationery Office.

Freeman, C. (1965). Research and development in electronic capital goods. National Institute Economic Review, No. 35, pp. 40–91.

Handler, Philip (1967). Federal science policy. Science, 155, 1063–1066.

Quinn, J. E. (1967). Discussion on impact of government policy on technology and economic growth. In Technology and World Trade: Proceedings of a Symposium. United States National Bureau of Standards, Miscellaneous Publication 284.

Skolnikoff, E. B. (1966). Scientific advice in the State Department. Science, 154, 980–985.

U.S. Department of Commerce (1967). Technological Innovation: Its Environment and Management. Washington, D.C.: Superintendent of Documents, U.S. Government Printing Office.

THE PHILOSOPHY AND PRACTICE OF NATIONAL SCIENCE POLICY

ALVIN M. WEINBERG

Oak Ridge National Laboratory, Oak Ridge, Tennessee

THE debate on the allocation of resources for science is conducted on two separate planes. On the one hand there is the philosophical debate in the pages of *Minerva* or *Nature*—or even *Harper's*—which gives enjoyment, and I daresay employment, to a growing cadre of "social" philosophers of science. This debate is concerned, broadly, with the principles that *ought* to govern the allocation of resources to various scientific claimants. On the other hand, there is the practical debate, carried on within government agencies and congressional committees and the Bureau of the Budget, that leads to actual allocations. I propose to give a personal, and very oversimplified, view of the philosophical debate, and to examine the extent to which the philosophical debate has influenced the practical debate.

Both the philosophical and practical debates are conducted from two different viewpoints. There is first the whole question of scientific choice: how should one divide one's scientific resources among competing fields of science? And there is the orthogonal question of institutional choice: how should one divide one's scientific resources among competing institutions, particularly university and non-university laboratories? Since all government science is performed at either one or the other such institution, an allocation by institution implies some kind of allocation by field; and since science at every institution falls within some recognized field, allocations by field imply some kind of allocation by institution. Yet the two approaches can be recognized as being distinct, and I shall divide my discussion accordingly.

THE DEBATE BY SCIENTIFIC FIELD

Rational choices among scientific fields involve judgments of relative value. For example, before one gives more to high-energy physics than to orbital astronomy one decides that, in some sense, high-energy physics is "better" than orbital astronomy. To ask such questions *explicitly* in science is rather new, though implicitly they are asked by every scientific administrator. Ordinarily we are content to ask of a scientific activity, "Is this science true?", at least to the extent that the canons of the field in which the science is performed permit us to answer this question. But the allocation problem raises a rather different question—not the traditional, "Is this science true?" but the subtler, "Is this science worthwhile, more worthwhile than this other science?" This is a question of value, and any attempt to answer it in general terms amounts to devising a system of scientific value, or scientific ethics.

This question of scientific value underlies much more than the specific issue of the large-scale allocation of national scientific resources. For value judgments are at the root of the whole art of scientific administration at every level. Perhaps the quintessential job of the scientific administrator, no matter the extent of his responsibility, is to judge which scientific activity is the most worthwhile, given the aims that he has decided upon in advance. The best scientific administrator is the one whose taste and judgment is the most exquisite—the one who best senses what is more worthwhile and should be supported as well as what is less worthwhile and should be turned off.

I would go further and insist that some scientific value system is an important ingredient of the scientific activity itself. Every scientist, even the most individual, is in a sense an "administrator" as well as a "scientist". For every act of science consists of two parts: first, the decision to seek a solution to this problem rather than that; and, second, a technique for solving the problem one has chosen.

In performing the second part of his task—solving his scientific problem —the scientist is behaving like a scientist in the traditional sense. The bulk of a scientific paper usually describes how the scientist achieved his results, not why he chose to perform this experiment or calculation rather than this other. In deciding to do this particular science, the scientist is making an administrative judgment; he is estimating, usually implicitly, that allocation of his effort in this direction rather than in the other will better help him to achieve his aim.

The individual scientist, in making such choices—that is, in devising his scientific strategy—is motivated by both intrinsic and extrinsic factors. Intrinsic factors derive from the internal logic and force of the scientific situation. Thus, a scientist is often motivated by some essentially aesthetic feeling that drives him to seek more order. Or, perhaps more typically, the scientist may not necessarily be very curious about the *answer* that his

2*

activity will reveal, but is motivated simply by the belief that he can get *an* answer. Science is opportunistic; it exploits salients where it finds them, and, like a meandering river, it tends, as von Neumann said, to follow the path of least resistance.

Extrinsic factors derive from the scientific or practical matrix in which the particular science is embedded, from the desire to answer a question that is suggested to the scientist by his external scientific environment. An expert in neutron diffraction uses his technique to place an upper limit on the electric dipole moment of the neutron not because this quantity is relevant to neutron diffraction, but because its value is important to the high-energy physicists who have found evidence for the violation of CP symmetry. I suspect that in this sense much more of science is externally motivated than ordinarily is conceded by the scientist. The cue for what to do next often comes from a neighbouring science, or at least from a neighbouring branch of the same science, and therefore aims to answer a question put to the scientist from the rest of the world.

The ratio of extrinsically motivated to intrinsically motivated science undoubtedly varies from science to science. Those sciences, such as nuclear physics, whose theoretical structure is well developed, characteristically concern themselves with confronting a theory developed within a certain conceptual framework with experiments devised within the same framework. In this sense, nuclear physics is largely intrinsically motivated. By contrast, a science like chemistry, that has a looser theoretical structure, tends more often to be externally motivated—the physical chemist may receive his cues from the geochemist, the organic chemist from the biochemist, the analytical chemist from the metallurgist.

Of the two kinds of science, intrinsically motivated and extrinsically motivated, I would argue that the extrinsically motivated is apt to be the more "valuable". For in so far as science attempts to provide a coherent picture of the world, that science contributes most which adds most to this coherence, which shows connexions where none had been seen before, which has the widest range of applicability. The so-called scientific breakthroughs are those findings that have the most universal implication and that make the most difference to scientists, or practical people, outside the narrowly specific field in which the discovery was made.

It is on this account that in my calculus of scientific value (Weinberg, 1967) I have placed such emphasis on the external implication of a scientific activity. The three external criteria that I have proposed for assessing the worth of a scientific field I describe as technological merit, social merit and scientific merit. The first two are rather obvious, and in any case have evoked little criticism. The third is perhaps not so obvious: "The scientific merit of a field of science is to be measured by the degree to which the activity illuminates and interacts with the neighboring fields in which it is embedded." Thus, to quote an example I have used before, "The value of chemistry as a field can hardly be decided by the chemists alone; they must ask the biologists who need the results of structural chemistry to elucidate the genetic mechanisms of the cell; or they must ask the physicists who cannot probe nuclear magnetic resonances unless they understand how the chemical environment affects the details of their NMR signals; or they must ask the reactor technologist who needs the chemistry of protactinium to design a continuous purification system in a thorium breeder."

All the external criteria represent an underlying philosophical position that is as old as the Greeks: that no universe of discourse can be evaluated by criteria that are generated solely within that universe. Means are established within a universe of discourse: ends—that is, values—must be established from outside the universe. I call this the "embeddedness" of values, if one ought to give a name for an idea that is so old and so obvious. I believe that one way or another the embeddedness of values is implicit in the entire debate on scientific choice.

Has this philosophical debate had any effect on the actual allocation to various fields? At first sight one would be inclined to say no; for the most important scientific decision in the post-war United States, the decision to send a man to the moon by 1970, was taken by President Kennedy with almost no debate by the scientific community. Since every other allocation to science is relatively small in comparison with the decision to go to the moon, it is hard to avoid a kind of cynicism in the whole ensuing discussion of scientific allocation.

And yet I believe that we are witnessing a change. The most important scientific allocation to be decided upon in the United States now is what to do after Apollo. This decision is being taken in an environment very different from the one that prevailed at the time President Kennedy decided upon Apollo. We have had several high-level reports, the most recent being one issued by the President's Science Advisory Committee (Long, 1967), in which the merits of a manned mission to Mars are weighed. Many voices have now been raised publicly questioning the extrinsic motivation of the Mars mission: many of the points raised in the philosophical argument are being voiced in this very practical debate that is now raging.

But I believe that the philosophical debate may be having an even more pervasive effect. Scientific policy is made at every level: there are innumerable scientists, bureaucrats, administrators, each of whom is confronted with small decisions, and whose total activity constitutes "science policy". All such discourse requires a language. The philosophical debate has, by a rather mysterious social osmosis, imposed its language, and even its way of framing some of the questions, upon the debate. Many of the catch-words that were first raised in the philosophical debate—like Big Science, or Criteria for Scientific Choice (implying that such criteria can be formulated), or the National Science Foundation as a "balance-wheel"—have become part of the everyday language in the United States Government offices where decisions are being made.

The influence of the philosophical debate is perceptible in the many reports to the National Academy of Sciences assessing the problems, the promise and the needs of the various fields of science. For example, the Westheimer report on chemistry (1965) tried to answer the question, "Who besides the chemists are interested in the findings of chemistry?" (The answer, according to the Westheimer report, is just about everyone.) Or the Pake report on physics (1966), in setting up tasks for each of its subpanels, asked that they address themselves to establishing the merit of their subfields on a scale largely derived from that established in the debate on scientific choice.

These National Academy reports represent an attempt to bring the viewpoints engendered in the philosophical debate into the actual governmental decision process. In a way, these reports are forcing an unaccustomed simultaneity upon the confrontation among scientific claimants. Hitherto it has been customary to look first at material science, then at oceanography, then at astronomy, seriatim—largely because summaries of the various fields were not available at the same time. The realization that allocations tended to be pre-empted by the first claimant prompted the President's Science Adviser to ask that these reports be prepared more or less simultaneously for many fields of science. To be sure, many of the recommendations made in these reports have been ignored so far. For example, the suggestion in the Pake report that physics in the United States should receive an increase of 16 per cent each year has so far not been accepted; nor has the idea, presented in *Basic Research and National Goals* (Kistiakowsky, 1965), that the National Science Foundation become a "balance-wheel" to take up the slack left by the hard-hit mission-orientated agencies, been reflected in a corresponding rise in its overall budget. But these ideas are being discussed in the legislative and executive branches of the government, and such discussions may be a prelude to their adoption as government policy.

Yet something is missing. The debate so far has, so to speak, been too polite. There is a code of ethics (Cranberg, 1965) which states that criticism of one field of science by a practitioner from another is taboo; that every field of science must assume that every other field of science is as valid as itself, and that therefore criticism of scientific work or of scientific fields in the spirit of literary criticism is unacceptable.

Yet I think we shall have to accept and, in fact, encourage scientific criticism in this *genre*. For what is at issue is not a scientific activity's correctness, but its worthwhileness. And since this is not entirely a scientific question it can hardly be answered entirely by the scientists within the field being criticized. The reports of the National Academy of Sciences, whether they deal with physics, or chemistry, or ground-based astronomy, or botany, tend to be isomorphic: the field under review is very promising; its practitioners are excellent; and its needs are very great and expensive. I would think that such reports ought to be reviewed in sharp and critical, though responsible, vein by persons who are willing to serve as scientific critics.

René Dubos of Rockefeller University has recently urged that scientific criticism of this sort be encouraged (Dubos, 1966). The problem is to find scientific critics who at once know even enough to understand, let alone criticize, the other fellow's field and who are brave enough to stick their necks out on matters they understand imperfectly. In a sense, scientific critics are already at work—in the Bureau of the Budget, in the Office of Science and Technology, in the government agencies. What I would suggest is that some of the critical debate be made more public—for example, by commissioning serious reviews of these reports as they appear. The reports themselves are important contributions to both the philosophical and the practical debates; the reports will be made even more valuable by being criticized in the spirit prescribed by Dubos.

THE DEBATE BY INSTITUTION

I turn now to the debate by institution. Because government agencies and their laboratories are usually organized around social missions rather than scientific fields (atomic energy and space are notable exceptions), the allocation by institution in many ways is more congruent with the structure of government, and therefore more natural, than the allocation by field. In the final analysis, institutions are tangible and are able to receive funds, whereas fields are abstract and have no apparatus for receiving or spending money. The debate by institution may therefore in the long run prove more useful for practical science policy than the debate by field.

The debate by institution* has been rather less explicit than has the debate by field—perhaps, again, because institutions are tangible, whereas fields are abstract. If nuclear physics is said to be less worthy of support than space physics, there will be muttering among the nuclear physicists; if one of the National Laboratories is said to be less competent than another, the reaction from the management of the slighted laboratory will be swift and forceful.

Such debate as has been generated is to be found mainly in the various reports on basic scientific fields (such as the Pake or Westheimer reports), in the Seaborg report on *Scientific Progress, the Universities, and the Federal Government* (1960) and in the Kistiakowsky report, *Federal Support of Basic Research in Institutions of Higher Learning* (1964). In these remarks I shall touch upon two aspects of the debate by institution—first, the rivalry between universities and government laboratories for support of basic research, and, second, the redeployment of government laboratories that have outgrown their original missions.

The rivalry between university and government laboratory

That there is a conflict between the university and the government laboratory with respect to allocations for basic research is too evident to require much comment. In the United States the matter has come to a head, particularly in the field of low-energy nuclear physics. This field is pursued actively both at the government laboratory and at the university. The equipment is relatively expensive—about five million dollars for an isochronous cyclotron or a TU Van de Graaff machine—but not so expens-ive that it is obvious that the research should be centralized at a government laboratory. It is on this account that the competition has been so sharp. Or to take other examples, the Wooldridge Committee report on the National Institutes of Health (1965) all but concluded that basic research at the National Institutes of Health ought to be reduced in favour of basic research in the universities. In this respect the Wooldridge Committee echoed the recommendation of Sir Solly Zuckerman's Committee (1961) that free basic research had little place in mission-orientated laboratories.

Before one can rationalize any system of allocation between university and government laboratory, one must first answer the question, "What is

---

* See for example, Ritterbush (1966). Dr. Ritterbush is a member of the staff of the Smithsonian Institution, Washington, D.C.

the underlying purpose of these two different, but complementary, institutions?'' In this I take a rather extreme position: that the *primary* purpose of the government laboratory, except for those few established to pursue special areas of Big Science, like high-energy physics, or space exploration, is to exploit large-scale science and technology to solve what are ultimately *social* problems; whereas the *primary* purpose of the university is education.* This is not to say, for example, that the university's purpose does not include enlargement of human knowledge, nor that the government laboratory may not participate in education or basic research. Yet I would hold that where conflict exists, as it sometimes does, between separate purposes either in the government laboratory or in the university, precedence should be given to the primary purpose.

Once one has agreed on the primary purposes of government laboratory and university, then the question of how much basic research ought to go to the one or the other can be put: "How much basic research is needed at the government laboratory to achieve its mission—which is the solution of large problems set by the government; and how much basic research is needed at the university to achieve its mission—which is education?'' In the case of the government laboratory the answer is: "Some fraction, relatively fixed, of the budget allocated for the accomplishment of its applied end.'' This fraction is a matter to be decided between the laboratory management and the agency that provides the funds, and will surely vary from laboratory to laboratory. But the primary allocation is to the applied end. The basic research is somehow to be used as a means to the applied end, and in so far as the laboratory management is responsible for achieving the laboratory's purpose, it should have a strong voice in deciding on the fraction allocated to basic research.

I shall enlarge on the role of basic research in the mission-orientated laboratory. According to the usual view, basic research in the mission-orientated laboratory is justified because it eventually leads to applied breakthroughs. I see this more as a justification for basic research as a whole, not especially for its pursuit in the mission-orientated laboratory. No matter where it is performed, basic research can lead to practical results. I would rather claim that the unique interdisciplinary nature of basic research in the better large laboratories is a more important justification for its support in these environments. Some kinds of basic research are

---

* This latter view of the proper role of the university is well stated by President Kingman Brewster of Yale University: "The distinctive character of a university is its role in the transmission of learning and communication of the excitement of intellectual, aesthetic, and moral advance." (Brewster, 1966.)

simply done better in the interdisciplinary atmosphere of the large laboratory than in the individualistic atmosphere of the university. But my primary arguments for basic research in the mission-orientated laboratory are two-fold: basic research is a necessary window to the entire outside scientific landscape; and it provides the tone and standard that often falters in a narrowly committed applied laboratory. Basic research ought to be considered part of the whole institutional package; it is done in an applied laboratory in order to get on with the laboratory's entire purpose.

I would advocate, therefore, that basic research in the government laboratory be considered (and allocated for) separately from basic research in the university, since its purpose in the two instances is different. The sort of unnecessary conflict that can arise if this principle is ignored can be illustrated by an incident that occurred at my own laboratory a few years ago. We had been trying for several years to get an electron linac which was to be used to measure neutron cross-sections of importance to reactor technology. It was understood that the machine would also be used for other more "basic" research as well, but its contribution to reactor technology was its primary justification. At the same time a prestigious university requested a similar machine, to be used entirely for basic physics. The two proposals were viewed by the government as being competitive even though the purposes of the machines were very different. To my mind the issue should not have been between a linac for reactor technology at Oak Ridge National Laboratory versus a linac for basic research at the university; rather it should have been between a linac and, say, a critical facility, both for reactor technology; or between a linac at the university and a Van de Graaff at another university. (Actually the matter was resolved eventually by both institutions receiving their linacs.)

As for the university, there is a good built-in means for setting the desirable level of basic research, and this is the number of graduate students. This measure has the advantage, as Harvey Brooks says in *Basic Research and National Goals* (Kistiakowsky, 1965), of being susceptible to fairly quantitative estimates. It has the disadvantage that, as Harry Johnson implies (Kistiakowsky, 1965), assuring support to a field for every graduate student going into it can lead to a self-generating growth of the field whose limit is not clearly visible. Yet such concern may be exaggerated; the number of students going into physics in the United States in the past couple of years seems to be dropping even though support for basic physics at the universities, though by no means lavish, has not dropped correspondingly.

Such a pat resolution of the intrinsic conflict between university and laboratory is certainly oversimplified, and leaves out of consideration the very large basic scientific undertakings, like the 200 Gev accelerator, for which special government laboratories, either associated with or separate from universities, are set up. But these generally are not the areas in which the conflict between the two institutions arises: Big Science is conceded to be the province of the Big Laboratory, not the university. The issue of choice arises around Little, or Medium, Science, like low-energy nuclear physics, or biomedical research, which can be done in either environment. And here I contend that the matter is to be resolved by relating it to the institution's purpose. As long as the institutional purposes are sharply defined, and adhered to, the role of basic research in the institution and even its level should not be an impossible question to resolve.

I find this a relatively tidy way of looking at the whole question of scientific allocations. For the competition then is not so much between fields of science as it is between rival national purposes, like desalting, or developing nuclear energy, or sending a man to the moon, or, for that matter, education. Depending on how much importance a country attaches to each of these social purposes, the institutions set up to achieve these missions will receive a corresponding amount of support: and the amount of basic research required to support an applied mission will largely be set by the laboratory management's assessment of the importance of such basic research to the achievement of its institution's social purpose.

Redeployment of the government laboratory

But the tidiness is somewhat illusory, and here we come to what I consider a most important matter. Scientific or technological institutions set up to achieve one mission find it difficult to redeploy around new missions once their original mission has been achieved. Government laboratories usually work for a single government agency: what happens to the laboratory when the job of the agency is no longer as important as it was when the laboratory was established? If the government makes a commitment of support to its laboratories as institutions and delegates to the management the responsibility of allocating resources within the institution, it is natural that as the laboratory loses its sense of mission, the management will ensure survival of the institution by drifting into basic research. I believe that this is a phenomenon which one can see in government laboratories in many parts of the world. To some extent the bias against basic research in the government laboratories expressed by some university spokesmen may be a reaction to this tendency.

35

This drift toward basic research in a mission-orientated laboratory, if allowed to proceed unchecked, could destroy the laboratory's taste and capacity for getting on with practical missions. It is on this account that I believe that an urgent task of national science policy is to identify a backlog of important technical missions that can be parcelled out to existing national institutions, and to organize the national institutions so that they can redeploy around these tasks.

In the past couple of years a new twist has been added to this problem of redeployment. The government laboratories have, by and large, been organized to develop hardware—atomic bombs, or nuclear reactors, or radar, for example. But in the past few years, at least in the United States, we have begun to recognize many new problems that are traditionally *social* in character: disorganization of our cities, inadequacy of our transportation system, discord in relations between the races. Thus, there seems to be a mismatch between the predominantly technological, hardware character of the institutions that are available to the government for attacking its problems, and the "software", social character of the most urgent questions. The tantalizing thought articulated by Richard L. Meier in 1956 therefore presents itself: can one recast social problems to accentuate their technological character, and thus reduce them to a form that can be attacked by the existing, hardware-orientated government laboratories? (An attempt of this sort was made in California last year, when several aircraft contractors were called in to study air pollution, transportation and some aspects of city planning.)

I believe much more can be done in this direction than is ordinarily suspected, but to go into detail would lead me too far. Suffice to say that the proper instrument for the attack on such complex issues as the city or transportation or water is a coherent institution (of which I believe the atomic energy laboratories are models) that can develop coherent doctrines with regard to such issues. Since the problems have both social and technological components, I would expect that the existing laboratories, to deal with these questions, will have to add social scientists to their staffs.

One can visualize the government laboratories of the future as transforming themselves into socio-technological institutes which are aggressively deployed around "social" problems, and which use all the power of the interdisciplinary scientific and engineering laboratory, including "systems engineering", to bear on their solution. In such institutions a great deal of basic research will be done: but allocations to it will be largely at the discretion of the laboratory management. Characteristically these national socio-technological institutions will be mission-orientated; and the assessment and re-assessment of their mission will be the most important task of the laboratory management.

I see such a gradual redeployment of the world hardware-orientated scientific apparatus, meaning largely its government laboratories, as perhaps the most urgent question in world scientific policy. This is hardly a philosophical question; it is practical and it is urgent. What are needed are hard, specific tasks whose solution can plausibly lead to the resolution of social problems and which lend themselves to large-scale laboratory experiment—like identifying the biological sequelae of environmental pollution, or achieving water for agriculture from the sea, or developing a nuclear breeder and thereby providing cheap energy for mankind forever. We would all be more comfortable if we knew that these and other great questions were being worked on, coherently, in such national socio-technological institutes.

REFERENCES

Brewster, Kingman (1966). The strategy of a university. *Ventures* (Magazine of the Yale Graduate School), **6,** 6–10.

Cranberg, Lawrence (1965). Ethical problems of scientists—a summary. *Physics Today*, **18,** 51.

Dubos, René (1966). Science critics. *Science*, **154,** 595.

Kistiakowsky, George B. (Chairman) (1964). *Federal Support of Basic Research in Institutions of Higher Learning*. Report of Committee on Science and Public Policy, National Academy of Sciences. Washington, D.C.: National Academy of Sciences.

Kistiakowsky, George B. (Chairman) (1965). *Basic Research and National Goals*. A Report to the Committee on Science and Astronautics, United States House of Representatives, by the Panel on Basic Research and National Goals of the National Academy of Sciences. Washington, D.C.: United States Government Printing Office.

Meier, Richard L. (1966). *Science and Economic Development: New Patterns of Living*. (Second edn.) Cambridge, Mass.: Massachusetts Institute of Technology Press.

Long, Franklin A. (Chairman) (1967). *The Space Program in the Post-Apollo Period*. A Report of the Space Science and Space Technology Panels, President's Science Advisory Committee. Washington, D.C.: United States Government Printing Office.

Pake, George E. (Chairman) (1966). *Physics: Survey and Outlook*. Report of the Physics Survey Committee, National Academy of Sciences. Washington, D.C.: National Academy of Sciences.

Ritterbush, Philip C. (1966). *Institutions of Science*. A lecture given under the auspices of the Research Policy Program, at Lund University, Sweden.

Seaborg, Glenn T. (Chairman) (1960). *Scientific Progress, the Universities, and the Federal Government*. Report of the Panel on Basic Research and Graduate Education, President's Science Advisory Committee. Washington, D.C.: United States Government Printing Office.

Weinberg, Alvin M. (1967). *Reflections on Big Science*, p. 65 ff. Cambridge, Mass.: The Massachusetts Institute of Technology Press.

Westheimer, Frank H. (Chairman) (1965). *Chemistry: Opportunities and Needs*. Report of the Committee for the Survey of Chemistry, National Academy of Sciences. Washington, D.C.: National Academy of Sciences.

Wooldridge, D. E. (Chairman) (1965). *Biomedical Science and Its Administration. A Study of the National Institutes of Health*. A Report to the President. Washington, D.C.: United States Government Printing Office.

Zuckerman, Sir Solly (Chairman) (1961). *The Management and Control of Research and Development*. A Report of the Committee on the Management and Control of Research and Development. London: Her Majesty's Stationery Office.

DISCUSSION

Todd: I agree completely with Professor Weinberg's thesis that the scientist individually is a kind of administrator, in that he makes his own choices. Perhaps because I am a chemist, I also agree with the extrinsic character of most of the stimuli that make one decide which line to follow. The "art of the soluble" is the basic principle, as Peter Medawar has put it so well, but even within the realm of the soluble it is the extrinsic factor that so often drives the chemist, at least, to his choice. I believe that this may be true over a very wide field of science. However, when Professor Weinberg says that this is analogous to the overall problem of decision making in science, the problem is not straightforward.

The individual scientist makes his choice within an area where he has competence to assess the situation, but when one moves to the national scale, who is competent to make the assessment? Professor Weinberg mentioned the need for obtaining proper critical assessments of policy reports. This would be excellent, but it is still too "polite"; the scientists who would do this critical reviewing would perhaps in a majority of cases be too biased, in the sense that they would have an insufficiently wide knowledge of the whole group of fields under study, to be able to make the right assessment. So there is a difference between the situations.

Weinberg: This is perfectly right, but in spite of the difficulties, I believe that there are people who are in this position already. I have in mind the heads of large laboratories, who are obliged, as best as they can, to become sufficiently familiar with a broad range of science tasks, so that they can make such judgments. In many instances, large multi-disciplinary laboratories are run by people such as Robert Oppenheimer or W. B. Lewis or Francis Perrin, who possess an extraordinary grasp of many things, and do make judgments of this sort. So it is not as impossible as you perhaps make it out to be.

Todd: My point is that it is a different order of difficulty from that facing the ordinary scientist. The number of people capable of the kind of judgment required is small.

Weinberg: That is so, but the number of decisions that have to be made on the larger scale is perhaps also not too big.

Szalai: I want to take issue with the same point, but I want to put it more sharply. I do not see the situation repeated, no matter at what level, because in the present state of science, the macro-economics and micro-economics or the macro-planning and micro-planning of research effectively exist in two different worlds. On the macro-economic level, there is a certain orderly mechanism working. There is no doubt that if you invest heavily in zoology or atomic physics, unless you do it in a very silly way, there will automatically be an advance in that field, at any level of investment. However, on the micro-level, where research is actually done and where the individual scientist is making his choice of problems and taking decisions, to a great extent scientific research is one of the most unscientific activities in the field of science! In the present state of science, the micro-economics or micro-planning of research is very much an *art* (it should not be, but it is), although we know very little about this process because we have done little research on how research is done on the micro-level. But we are less poorly equipped in the macro-economics of research, at the national policy levels, where we see the semi-automatic consequences of overcapitalizing or undercapitalizing certain branches of science. Although there is obviously a connexion between the micro-level and the macro-level of decision, it is by no means true in practice that the transition from one level to the other can be made without large qualitative differences coming in.

Weinberg: The issue is not of deciding whether by pouring a lot of money into a field, that field will proliferate; of course it will. The issue is whether this is a worthwhile thing to do. The judgment of whether it is worthwhile is of the same *genre* as the judgment that the individual scientist makes when he decides on what his next step will be.

Szalai: You mean that it is unscientific too?

Weinberg: It is unscientific too, yes.

Bondi: May I make two points here. The first concerns Professor Weinberg's reference to the universities as having their *primary* purpose in education. There seem to be two possible attitudes in our thinking about universities, whose comparative validity should be clarified. There is what Eric Ashby calls the "mystique" of universities, which says that in a way nobody has quite measured, the best teaching is done by groups who are good at research. In order merely to teach their undergraduates well, university teachers have to be enabled to do research. The alternative attitude sees university teachers as hard bargainers who say to society: you want us to teach students, we want to do research—if you pay us to do research, we will do some teaching by the way. To discover how much research really is necessary for people to fulfil the social function of teaching university students (and how much for postgraduate teaching), would be a very worthwhile field of study.

As a small footnote to what has been said about the "micro-scale" of research and the importance of extrinsic factors in deciding choices, in dealing with research students and choosing problems for them, the extrinsic factors—how much time a student has left, and what would discourage him—play a very large role.

Rahman: My comments on Professor Weinberg's paper arise from the fact that *philosophical* treatment of the subject of scientific research tends to leave out historical and social factors that are built into the tradition of research, and vary greatly from country to country.

My first point is with regard to the role of the universities in research. I would illustrate this from the situation in India. The evolution of universities in each country is a part of its historical and social development. In India, scientific research has been limited to a few selected areas in which people had been trained abroad in the nineteenth and early twentieth centuries. For example, most research in botany is on the physiology, taxonomy, embryology and cytogenetics of angiosperms, and the taxonomy and physiology of fungi and the pathology of fungal diseases. And this limited field of study has been perpetuated, because younger people are being trained exclusively in it. Had the government not set up research laboratories, research would still be continuing almost entirely within such areas. The starting of national laboratories gave an impetus to new areas of research on the one hand and also to the training of people in new areas of technology, such as food technology, for which facilities were not available at the universities, on the other. As many universities began to realize the significance of these new areas, limited co-operation began, and some universities recognized the research staff as university research supervisors and awarded degrees to postgraduate students trained in the national laboratories. So this problem of the redeployment of potential scientific manpower and the role of the universities in it is built into the historical and social context of a particular country, and I feel that the philosophical approach leaves this out.

My second point concerns choice and decision making. In India, agricultural research is the oldest area of scientific research; but in terms of generating scientific outlook, and generating results that could be used for the development of agriculture, until very recently it had not been particularly effective. It must, however, be admitted that the question of the utilization of the results of research takes us into fields not limited to the technology of agriculture, since other social factors become involved.

The contrast is evident when we compare agriculture with the newer fields of research, like that of atomic energy, or the work of the national laboratories created by the Council of Scientific and Industrial Research. These two areas had a great impact in generating a new outlook and giving a dynamic attitude, as compared to the old-established branch of research. New techniques and new areas of research in agriculture became possible as a result of a major investment in atomic energy and industrial research and helped to revitalize it and to develop its organizational framework. This would not have been possible if a major decision had not been taken to develop new areas of research rather than a traditional one, which is also vital and significant for the problems of the country.

My third point, also connected with the historical background (again I can give only an impression; we are now trying to study this quantitatively), concerns the content of training. Most scientists in positions of responsibility in India have been trained primarily in the United Kingdom or in the United States, and they bring back with them the technology, the atmosphere, the social "frills" of those countries, and try to continue areas of research prominent there. This, rather than the inherent philosophical questions of choice or the detailed strategy of research, determines their scientific work. But the low level of technology in the country means that their researches may not yield results and their endeavours may remain superficial, scratching the surface of a problem rather than making an effective contribution. We did a study on electronics research and found that those areas which were in line with international development in the field were done by 41 per cent of Indian research workers in electronics, but this work was being done by them abroad; work in the remaining areas was done in India, but was not in line with international work on electronics because the built-in tradition over the period encouraged the taking up of problems that have become secondary problems in the major scientific countries.

Freeman: May I raise a point which may take the debate in a less polite direction, as Professor Weinberg suggested? The main problem in deciding on allocations between different fields of science surely is to identify fields which are worked out, where there will be diminishing or negligible returns from a big investment by society. It is much easier to identify new opportunities than to identify worked-out fields. For example, if I ask physicists whether the kind of work they are doing is likely to yield useful results, they all say that it is, otherwise they would not stay in the area. But is this true? In economics—my own discipline—I do not think that it is true. It is possible for economists to continue to cultivate a field long after it is likely to yield useful results. I wonder if the same is not true of other branches of science, and if so, whether it is not important for *outsiders* to be brought into the process of identifying worked-out fields—whether we *can* leave the judgment to the people within a field.

Weinberg: Decisions have been made in the United States, in science policy, particularly in physics, that imply that judgments of that sort are being made. For example, low-energy nuclear physics is in rather bad repute in the United States because people outside the field feel that nuclear physics is not as fruitful as it has been, although people within it disagree. The best policy that I can suggest is that the committees that assess a field of science should be peppered more liberally than they have been in the past with representatives from neighbouring scientific fields. A committee on nuclear physics might contain representatives from high-energy physics, possibly astrophysics and possibly solid-state physics. I suppose that it is because we are relatively so rich in the United States that we tend to be more polite than the English!

Carey: I agree. When constraints begin to tighten the whole system and resources level-off suddenly while the demand curve is rising exponentially, tensions are induced which bring out dissent and sharpen the debate on the margins, which tends to introduce one community or philosophy to another. As long as we can afford the inefficiencies of the present system, we shall go on with the inefficiencies. When we decide that we cannot afford them, we may become more rational.

Bernal: I want to raise a point arising from Professor Weinberg's definition of "worthwhileness" in research. There is another factor, namely the factor of time. Mr. Freeman raised the problem of knowing when a field is worked out; there is also the problem of the field where work would be premature. For instance, in molecular biology, my own field, we had to wait for a lot more chemistry to be known before significant advances could be made. This brings me to my second point. Professor Weinberg wants us to be science critics, but there are very few people who could do this effectively. A broader knowledge of science would be required than science teaching gives today.

Weinberg: The question of deciding when a field is ripe for exploitation is very clearly one of the most important *internal* factors that determines whether people should move into that field. It made no sense to try to develop nuclear energy until fission was discovered; then it made a great deal of sense. But that assessment is inherent in what every scientist does individually, and it is certainly very explicit in the discussions on a broad policy level.

EVALUATION OF RESEARCH PRODUCTIVITY

THE PRODUCTIVITY OF SCIENCE IN A SOCIETY

J. B. ADAMS

United Kingdom Atomic Energy Authority, Harwell Laboratory, Berkshire

INTRODUCTION

THE productivity of an activity is usually expressed as a ratio of an output generated by the activity and the relevant input which sustains it. Sometimes productivity is measured in incremental terms. But whichever definition is used, it is necessary to relate an input to an output, and the difficulty in applying this notion to science is that science, generally speaking, is part of some other activity whose output, although dependent on the investment input to the associated science, is also dependent on other factors. Therefore, in considering the productivity of science in society, it is first necessary to set forth those social activities in which science plays an important part, and then to relate the input to the scientific component of the activity to the output of the activity as a whole, either in absolute or incremental terms.

It is no doubt possible to divide and subdivide the activities of society in which science plays a part almost indefinitely, but for the purpose of this paper, which makes no pretence at a quantitative analysis, it is sufficient to take the very broadest of divisions and to consider science in industry, in universities and in government. Taking each of these main social activities in turn we need to determine its principal output, its inputs, particularly those associated with science, the relationships between the science input and the principal output, the criteria commonly applied to determine the scientific part of the activity, and finally the factors governing its productivity and the units by which it can be measured. Needless to say, the answers to this formidable list of questions are by no means common knowledge, if indeed they are known at all, and the main purpose of this paper is therefore more to encourage methical thinking about this problem than to review current thought.

Before embarking on this task, it is worth noting that this way of attempting to evaluate science as part of social activities makes the implicit assumption that science is a technique which the component parts of a society have found by experience to be useful, and sometimes essential, in order to achieve their aims. As society has developed it has constantly discovered new techniques and discarded old ones, but at the present time the technique of modern science is in the ascendancy, gradually displacing older techniques in ever increasing areas of social activities. For example, science, in the sense used in this paper, is a technique for finding out more about the natural world. It is useful, and occasionally essential, as a technique for improving the operations of industry, and nations now find it indispensable as a technique for achieving their ends and displaying to others their peculiar cultures.

A technique is not an end in itself, and this view of science as a means to the diverse ends of a modern industrial society rather than as an end in itself is only one aspect of science. It may be that as society develops it will find new techniques more effective than science for the achievement of its ends, or maybe society will change its aims and need less science to achieve them. Whether or not science, as a highly successful technique for understanding the natural world, will ever be surpassed, is perhaps more questionable, but then in its modern form it has been employed for only the last 400 years, and that is a relatively short time in the history of human societies. In this paper I shall discuss in turn the three social activities in which, at least at the present time, science is increasingly playing an important role.

UNIVERSITY SCIENCE

The unique output of universities is trained graduates and, since we are here concerned only with science, it is their output of trained scientists that is of interest. There is also an output of new scientific knowledge, and there is a wealth of existing knowledge maintained in the university system. The inputs to the system are money, mainly derived these days from governments, and school leavers coming from the lower levels of the education system. Just as the input of school leavers to the university system couples it to other parts of the educational system, so there are other feedback loops from the university system to the rest of the educational system—for example, university graduates becoming school teachers—which make it perilous to consider the university system in isolation from the rest. We are concerned here with a closely coupled system with feedback loops and natural time-constants which determine the speed and the manner in which it responds to external stimuli.

The output of trained scientists of the university system is absorbed by industry, government and the rest of society, and a part of it migrates to other societies, sometimes never to return. At the present time, because of the demands of the other parts of society, there is great pressure on the university system to produce more trained scientists. This, in turn, puts pressure on the school system to increase its output of school leavers opting to study science in universities, and even the output of school leavers going directly into society must these days be better trained in science. A pressure is then put back on the university system to produce more graduate scientists opting to become school teachers, and one of the loops in the educational system is completed.

The input of money to the university system can be divided into two parts —the teaching money and the research money. Increases in teaching money are necessary in order to increase the output of trained scientists, and improvements in the productivity (teaching money expended per trained scientist produced and teaching effort expended per trained scientist produced) also will increase the output for the same input. The input of research money is related to the output of knowledge, and it is generally recognized that this input of money also determines to some extent the output of trained scientists. This cross-coupling between the two inputs of money comes about firstly because university lecturers who produce the output of science graduates assert that they must engage in scientific research in order to teach at university level, and secondly because university science lecturers are usually appointed after a research period in the university system. Hence, more research money is needed to produce more university lecturers and further research money is needed to maintain them as competent lecturers. Therefore, in order to produce more science graduates not only must the teaching money be increased but also the research money. This process illustrates a feedback loop in the university system.

To complete this brief sketch of university science we come finally to the output of knowledge. Traditionally, knowledge gained in university science is published and is available to anybody who can make use of it. It does not therefore belong to the society in which it is generated and, since most societies these days behave in the same way, there is an input of new knowledge coming from all societies to any particular society which the other societies have paid for. Therefore, in contrast to the output of trained scientists, which is largely absorbed by the society in which it is generated, the output of knowledge is more in the nature of a contribution which a developed society makes to a commonwealth of knowledge of all societies and, perhaps for this reason, the input of research money which supports this output is often related to the relative wealth of a particular society. This free flow of new knowledge between societies is advantageous to the smaller societies, who gain most from the contributions made by the larger societies, their only restriction being their ability to make use of the new knowledge.

However, relating the input of research money to the wealth of the society in which the knowledge is generated overlooks the strong coupling, already mentioned, between the research money put in and the trained scientists produced. If the aim of a society is to produce more trained scientists for its own consumption, failure to increase the research money as well as the teaching money can result in a shortage of university lecturers, and hence an inability in the university system to produce more trained scientists. Indeed, it has been observed that lack of research money causes a migration of university scientists which further weakens the productiveness of the university system. What a society loses by this migration is not the new knowledge which the migrating scientists would have produced had they stayed (that they will produce anyway wherever they are going and they will publish it), but rather the new trained scientists they would have produced and the inspiration and guidance they would have given them.

The criteria applied to the ''new knowledge'' part of university science are the familiar internal criteria of scientific research, such as the ripeness of the field for exploitation and the availability of first-rate research scientists with creative ideas for making new advances in the subject. These are the criteria used by committees awarding research grants and are often referred to as the ''judgment by peers''. Publication of the research results and subsequent criticism impose other harsh judgments on the quality of this output. It is generally recognized that these criteria have maintained the quality of the output of new knowledge of universities in all societies at the highest levels.

The criteria applied to the output of trained scientists from university science are, on the one hand, another form of ''judgment by peers'', through the examination system which maintains the quality of this output and, on the other hand, criteria to do with the relevance of this output to the needs of society; it is the latter criteria which are being much discussed these days. The university system, and indeed the whole educational system, differs from other productive activities in a society in that the customers for its principal output do not directly pay for the goods they receive, and hence they influence the product only indirectly. Nowadays, it is governments who mainly finance the university system, and the trained scientists at graduate and postgraduate levels are absorbed by industry, government and the rest of the activities in the society. In terms of social engineering one should aim to match the output of trained scientists from university science to the current needs of the various activities of the society, and plan to keep it matched with the changing needs of society. The question is, who should control the output mix? Should it be the governments who largely pay for it, or the universities who produce it, or industry and the other activities of society who use it, or should it be some combination of all interested parties? At the present time it is the universities, responding to market pressures to a greater or lesser extent, who mainly determine the output mix, although it is becoming apparent that the personal choices of school leavers are also having a marked effect.

We come now to the productivity of university science and how it should be measured. As far as a particular society is concerned, the essential output of its university science is the trained scientist. In a modern industrial society this is the lifeblood of the society, and if it becomes insufficient in quantity, or lacking in quality, the survival of the society is placed in jeopardy. The new knowledge produced is of less importance in this respect, since if it were zero in one of the smaller industrial countries the total influx of new knowledge from all other societies to that society would hardly be affected. Nevertheless, the output of new knowledge is of vital importance to a society in that the input of research money that sustains it determines the quality and quantity of university teaching, and hence directly affects the quality and quantity of the trained scientists produced. Furthermore, the money for research, when divided into support for the different disciplines of science, offers a way of controlling the output mix of the trained scientists, and hence assists the matching of this output to the needs of society. For example, a society needing more physicists or more chemists in its industrial activities could make available to its universities more research money for these disciplines, leaving it to the well-tried internal criteria of science to determine how it was distributed.

There are two other respects in which the output of new knowledge from university science is relevant. First, a society in which little new knowledge is produced could become in the course of time unable to use the new knowledge generated by other societies, and, secondly, the ability to generate new knowledge is in itself a manifestation of the vitality of the society and of its cultural level and aspirations. Although one perhaps cannot quantify these matters, undoubtedly they affect the attractiveness of that society to its most creative citizens and to similar people from other societies. In a world which is rapidly shrinking, it pays a society to be as attractive as possible to creative people.

In measuring the productivity of university science, it seems then that the relevant output is the trained scientists and the input is the money for both teaching and research. The output mix of trained scientists should be kept in step with the needs of the society in which they are produced.

INDUSTRIAL SCIENCE

The inputs to industrial science are trained scientists from university science and money from profits made through the operations of industry. The outputs become manifest in improvements in the goods or services produced by industry, which produce more profit to the industry. Industrial science, in the sense that the term science is being used in this paper, affects all the operations of industry, from research and development through design and production to marketing and management. Therefore, improvements in goods or services due to industrial science can, and do, occur in all industrial operations. The difficulty in relating inputs to outputs is to trace an input through to a measurable output, since many factors apart from industrial science affect the final product and its saleability. Although several attempts have been made to relate input to output by historical studies of particular industries and products, there are at present only rough criteria available to industry. One general observation is that as time goes on, industrial goods and services steadily become more sophisticated scientifically and technologically, and this is reflected in increasing demands by industry for more trained scientists and more scientific training for all its employees. This trend seems to be built into the industrial competitive system, and it is accelerated by advertisement, which constantly stimulates consumers to demand increasing technological sophistication in the goods and services provided by industry.

All the loops in industrial activity seem to provide positive feedback, which increases the amount of industrial science and causes it to increase its demand on the principal output of university science. If industry had to pay for trained scientists this would provide some negative feedback, limiting the rate of increasing scientific and technological sophistication in industrial goods and services, but this is not the case. Nevertheless, this input is beginning to limit industry in all societies, not because the cost per trained scientist to industry is increasing, but because it is becoming difficult for university science to increase its output. Since it is governments which largely finance the production of trained scientists by universities, they effectively control the rate at which this output increases with time, and hence they determine to a large extent the competitiveness of their own industry, in so far as it is affected by industrial science rather than by other factors. Governments, in turn, derive their money from the society they represent, and the wealth of that society, if it is an industrial one, depends on the competitiveness of its industrial component. Thus, the loop is finally completed, but it is rather a long one.

In general, the criterion applied to industrial science is that it should increase the profitability of the industry. Where there are alternative ways of achieving that objective, industrial science must demonstrate that its way leads to the highest profits. In design, production and management the ways of industrial science are steadily gaining ground and "commercial criteria" can be applied, but in the research and development field it is more difficult to apply these judgments, and other relationships are being developed. For example, the amount of investment in research and development activity in an industry is related to the rate of change of its product with time. Those industries with a product which changes slowly with time need less research and development investment than those with a fast-changing product. This relationship enables an industry to use its research and development investment as a weapon in competition with other industries, either offensively to gain supremacy, or defensively to stay in business. There is, therefore, a threshold amount of research and development investment below which an industry cannot survive, and the level of this threshold depends on the particular products of the industry. Pooling research and development activity among like industries is effective only if individual industries can get their work done on a strictly confidential basis, otherwise they cannot use research and development as a weapon in competition. Furthermore, the fruits of research and development are a saleable commodity and can be bought by licence or stolen by industrial espionage.

These and other relationships are beginning to be understood these days, and it should be possible finally for an industry to determine the level of research and development appropriate to its products, its current competitive position and its strategy for the future. Whatever emerges from these studies, it is likely, however, that commercial criteria will always favour the shorter term research and development activity, where the effect on the product can most easily be traced back to the original investment. This means that long-term research and development aimed at, for example, a new power source for a society, or at a completely new communications system, must depend for its support on funds other than the profits of individual industries, unless of course single industries, by successive mergers, finally grow to the size of present-day nations. This suggests that the duration of research and development projects depends on the size of the organization, whether it is a society or an industry. The larger the organization, the longer term research and development projects it can attempt.

GOVERNMENT SCIENCE

The inputs to government science are trained scientists and money derived by the government from the society by taxation. The outputs are "missions", or national technological goals, and scientific and technological services required by the society or component parts of it. Thus, it is the function of government to determine the aims, ambitions and needs of the society it represents, and it is the function of government science to achieve them. Military missions were probably the first, and still are the dominant, scientific and technological goals of modern industrial societies, and they account for the biggest share of the investment in government science. However, new missions, not unconnected with military ones but not military in aim, have developed since the last war. Nuclear energy and space exploration are typical examples, and the civil parts of these technological programmes now account for sizable fractions of government science investment. Nowadays, new national technological goals are being considered and started that arise from aims and ambitions of societies quite different from military ones, such as the need for integrated transport systems and new transport methods for goods and people, and the interest in the natural environment, both to exploit it more fully and to protect it from the pollution of industrial societies. Benefit to the society as a whole, rather than profit to individual industries, is the criterion generally applied to these missions, although in the long term it is sometimes possible to show economic gains.

Government science is a self-limiting system, in the sense that the wealth of a society, both in manpower and money, must ultimately limit its aims and ambitions. Also, by absorbing part of the output of trained scientists from the university system—whether by employing them directly in government laboratories or indirectly in industry and universities by way of agency contracts—government science, especially when there is a shortage of trained scientists, appears to decrease the productivity of its industries and reduce the available wealth of industrial societies. However,

51

the effects of this negative feedback loop are balanced, some would say more than balanced, by the positive effects of government science on industrial performance and competitiveness. National technological goals of the kind mentioned above are difficult and challenging scientifically and technologically, and the stimulus they have given to industry has been immense. In some cases, completely new major industries, which now account for a large part of the employment in modern societies, have come into existence. Even more important, industries, new and old, have been able to establish production facilities for new and improved products to satisfy the demands of government agencies so that when commercial markets for these products finally emerged these industries have been able to sweep in to satisfy them. Thus, in those societies with more ambitious goals, industries have not only been stimulated to make rapid technological changes, but have also acquired considerable lead-times in production which have greatly improved their competitiveness, whereas similar industries in less ambitious societies have found their competitive position correspondingly worsened. Furthermore, it has turned out that ambitious national goals attract scientists and technologists from other societies, thus further weakening the competitiveness of the industries in those societies. A solution to this dilemma for the smaller industrial societies is for them to join together into societies of a size comparable with the largest, so that they can support equally ambitious and exciting, but not necessarily identical, technological goals. This is not a question of keeping up with the Joneses for reasons of national pride or dignity, but a question of economic survival in the long term.

Government science, especially the mission-oriented part, can be either carried out, in whole or in part, in government laboratories, or contracted out to industry and to the universities; but whichever method is adopted for the research and development component, the manufacturing part of the mission is normally undertaken by industry. Societies differ in the amount of research and development done in government laboratories. In America, the practice is to use industry and universities for a large part of this work, whereas in Europe, and particularly in Britain, more is done in government laboratories. The advantage of using industry for this work is that the research and development flows naturally through into design and manufacture, and any commercial "fall out" from the work can quickly be taken up by the industry. Similarly, the advantage of using universities for government research and development is that the young scientists, by partaking in this kind of work while at university, are more familiar with the work they will be asked to undertake when they take up employment in the society. The disadvantages of using industry and universities are that the criteria appropriate for government missions ("agency criteria") are very different from the commercial criteria of industrial science, and from the criteria of university science. By imposing agency criteria on the other two bodies, governments can distort the proper functioning and the productivity of those bodies, and make them too dependent on agency contracts, and too mindful of agency criteria, to the detriment of their own. It is a nice question whether the advantages of governments contracting industry and universities for mission-oriented research and development outweigh the disadvantages.

In concluding this commentary on government science, it is worth emphasizing that the criteria of government science are essentially political in nature. Decisions such as putting an American on the moon are taken by politicians for political reasons, and it could hardly be otherwise. Productivity in government science is measured in terms of the cost in manpower and money expended to attain the mission. If the aim of the mission is economic in character then cost-benefit analyses can be used, provided the time-scale of the mission is not too long.

CONCLUSION

By dividing the activities of society in which science plays an important part into three broad areas, and by discussing the role of science as a technique in each area, it has been possible to trace some relationships between the inputs, usually trained scientists and money, and outputs of the three activities. The outputs of each area of activity are different, and the criteria used to judge the performance of science in each area are also different. It has also been possible, in a rough way, to suggest measures of productivity, and again they are different in the three areas. Particular emphasis has been laid on loops in the systems, both within the particular activities and those coupling the three activities together. The importance to the whole system of whether the loops are feeding back positively or negatively has been discussed. If it were possible to develop a computable model of the three activities, as is now being done for complete educational systems, and relate it to an economic model of the whole society of which they are a part, one could learn better how the complete system works and experiment with changes in the feedback loops. Lacking such a model, one can only observe and analyse the existing system and try to deduce what effect possible changes might make. Such a procedure can hardly be called a science, since real experiments are impractical and without them theories cannot be checked. Furthermore, the time-constants of the system and its component parts are very long—several years, even decades—so that controlled experiments, even if practical and tolerated by society, would be extremely difficult. Nevertheless, a methodical approach to the problem is probably better than wild surmise.

Some general comments about the coupling between university, industrial and government science and the society in which they are embedded may be appropriate in conclusion. A scientist looking at these different activities of society in which science is playing such an important role and observing the feedback loops between them naturally wonders what is driving the whole system. There is a tendency these days to think that science somehow is the driving force, and this finds popular expression in the current anxieties about science budgets and the way they are increasing exponentially with time. But, if science is a technique and only a means to an end, something other than science must be determining the ends. Undoubtedly science is a very popular technique and a very successful one, but if we could, for example, find out more about the natural world and at less cost by means other than science, it is very likely we would be using them. Similarly, if industry could manufacture goods and provide services and sell them profitably to society without using science, or by employing a different and cheaper technique, commercial criteria would insist that it did so. And if governments found a cheaper non-scientific way of satisfying the aims and ambitions of the societies they represent, clearly less science and fewer scientists would be required. Whatever is said about science lobbies and their effect on governments, science cannot be the primary driving force in the system. Rather it seems that the drive comes from society itself and from its latent ambitions, which science now enables it to realize. Probably all societies have similar aims and ambitions, but the larger and more wealthy societies can realize the most, and they can tackle the most challenging and exciting missions. If there were no interactions between societies, or if the ambitions of a society did not affect the competitive power of its industry and attract to it essential elements of the population of other societies, the behaviour of one society might invoke jealousy or envy in another, but it would not affect it economically. However, these couplings do exist, and the smaller industrial societies are learning to pay serious attention to them.

In any society, whatever its size, there must ultimately be a limit to the amount of science used. If science continues to be a most successful technique for improving industrial profits, for increasing the wealth of a society and for satisfying its aims and ambitions, science budgets are not likely to be the real limit. It is more likely that scientific and technological manpower will finally set the bounds since, however efficient the educational system, there must be some limit to the natural abilities and aptitudes of a population. When these are fully realized in a particular society, it can proceed further only by attracting this essential manpower from its neighbours, and even this becomes economically questionable if, in the long term, the most attractive societies find themselves having to support the rest.

SUMMARY

An attempt has been made to analyse the role of science as a technique in three activities of a society—the universities, industry and government—in all of which it plays an important part. The function of science in each activity is examined with the aim of relating an investment input associated with science to the characteristic output of the activity. Productivity is discussed in each activity as the ratio of this investment input to the final output, so far as these can be directly related. It is shown that each of these three activities is closely coupled with the others by feedback loops which can either increase or decrease the activity, depending on whether they are positive or negative. Furthermore, the three activities are part of the society and interact with it, and nowadays industrial societies are themselves closely coupled together so that the behaviour of one affects the others. Some of the implications of these coupling loops are discussed.

DISCUSSION

Todd: Dr. Adams, would you agree that so far as university research is concerned, it is not simply putting money into particular areas of science that can distort the picture, but publicity can have just as big an effect? One can invest considerable sums in a particular area of, say, biology, but there will not be much effect unless one also turns on the public "propaganda" machine, to encourage people to go into that area.

Adams: Provided that the internal criteria of science are satisfied, putting more money into a particular field of research should increase its output. One of these criteria is that there are enough scientists engaged in the research of sufficient quality to permit an expansion. I suppose that turning on the public propaganda machine will increase the flow of scientists into a particular research field, especially if it is made clear that more money is going into it too.

Todd: The effect of publicity would certainly be difficult to define exactly. I recall the great boost which for some reason forestry received in Great Britain in the late 'twenties. Within a few years we had three or four times the number of forestry experts that we have ever had before, and we did not know what to with them. They eventually drifted off into other fields and the forestry schools collapsed.

Adams: I am sure that public propaganda is effective, but there have recently been signs that university entrants do not seem to be responding to the national calls for scientists and technologists. Perhaps the discipline of science is becoming too severe in comparison with other studies at universities.

Szalai: Dr. Adams' interesting paper has one major deficiency, to my mind. He spoke of the visible or easily measurable inputs and outputs of research, but they cannot really be discussed without also taking into account the invisible inputs. It is not true that you get anything out of research solely by putting in money and people. First of all, you must draw on a lot of existing scientific information—partly accessible in documents but partly only in the minds of people. When you take on your staff, you have access to a lot of "know-how" incorporated in their professional experience, and without that they could not even make use of documentary knowledge. In the same way, it is not true that documents published and people taught are the only output of research. In some branches, the essential customers for the "goods" produced are the people who themselves produce them. For instance, there is a very strong feedback of mathematical results into mathematics. The results by and large recycle within the system. Thus the major customer for someone's research results might be the universities, who will include them at some point in their teaching. There is another "invisible" channel: some results filter through innumerable communicating capillaries into the general state of art. There is also some dissipation of results into the general culture. Without a certain overall level of science and a certain general cultural level in the material sense, one cannot raise the level of research beyond a certain point. So it is how far those invisible outputs are measurable (and they are not as immeasurable as Dr. Adams suggested) that is important for our understanding of the whole system, with all these feedbacks and general outlets. Without them, you may get a very incomplete collection of inputs and outputs.

Adams: I am not sure how one would measure invisible inputs or outputs. However, sometimes an output is invisible because one is looking for it in the wrong place. I tried to emphasize the importance of feedback loops. To take your example in university science, it is quite possible that there is very little output at the university level, but because of the unity of the whole educational system the output may be at an earlier stage in the educational system, for instance at the level of school leavers entering society without going to university. They are taught by science graduates who are trained in the universities, and even if all these graduates were used up in keeping the university part of the system going and in providing school teachers, the input money to the universities could still be justified.

As regards the output of knowledge from university science, my point was that this output is a contribution to the commonwealth of scientific knowledge of all societies. It does not belong to the particular society in which it is generated. A small society gains more from the contributions of other societies than it does from its own efforts. This is what makes it difficult to use this output as a guide to investment in university science.

Krauch: Is the model you describe adequate when actual data are put into it? And to what extent do you use "educated judgment"?

Adams: I am afraid that the model that I presented is not yet a quantitative one. My point in presenting it was to show, in the simplest form possible, the differences between the three main branches of scientific activity and the couplings between them. If one could put real figures into such a model it would be possible to understand better the effects of the feedback loops, and if we had a computable model it would be possible to break some of the loops and see what happens. This is the only way of checking some of the assumptions that are built into any science system. For example, I have assumed that university staff must carry out research in order to teach at university level, and this assumption, which is a common one (and to which Professor Bondi referred earlier, p. 39), determines some of the feedback loops in the educational system and hence its performance.

I hope that the simple model I have presented convinces people that the criteria of the three branches are really quite different, because there is a strong tendency these days to talk in terms of total science budgets, which to my mind are meaningless because they ignore the very different purposes of the investments.

Weinberg: A significant point in relation to Dr. Adams' paper concerns the distortion of the pattern of output of the universities in reaction to government support. This is not a philosophical question, but rather a practical one. There is evidence—certainly in the United States, and I would not be surprised if this were so also in the United Kingdom and other Western European countries—that government support of research at the universities has converted them into self-sustaining, self-contained universes. The spin-off from the universities in the way of trained people, to government or to industry, may be much smaller than the government, which put the money into them in the first place, may have expected.

Adams: Our two countries differ in the way government agencies carry out the research and development for their missions. In the United States, these agencies rely heavily on contracting universities and industry to carry out the research and development. In Britain we make more use of government laboratories for this work. I know that there is criticism in the United States that your system interferes with the proper functioning of universities and industry, and in my paper I attribute this to the incompatibility of the criteria of government agencies and those of university science and industrial science. In Britain at this moment, some people are arguing that more government research and development should be done in universities and in industry and that government laboratories should be run down.

Freeman: As I understand the reports on Project Hindsight, which was a study undertaken by the Department of Defence of the United States to examine the sociological history of a number of important developments, tracing them back to their origins in basic research and seeing the extent to which basic research actually culminated in development, it appears that the output, so far as one can measure it, of the federal laboratories working on weapon systems was a good deal higher than that of either private industry under contract to government or of the universities. This conflicts with what one had been led to believe about the efficiency of government research, and suggests that in this area at least, government laboratories have been highly productive. (See Sherwin, C. W., and Isenson, R. S. [1967]. *Science*, **156**, 1571–1577; Sherwin, C. W., and Isenson, R. S. [1966]. *Project Hindsight, First Interim Report*, October 1966. No. AD 642–400. Springfield, Va.: Clearinghouse for Federal Scientific and Technical Information.)

Adams: Mr. Freeman's example seems to confirm my point that each branch of science has its own particular criteria which tends to optimize its output. If one branch tries to impose its criteria on the other two, then it is likely that the productivity in those branches is reduced.

Todd: The conclusions on differing productivities of Project Hindsight may be irrelevant for the field of science policy as a whole, because the government institutions that had such high productivity were highly mission-orientated institutions working strictly on defined lines that were virtually the same as industrial lines. One cannot therefore generalize from this to the whole of science.

Weinberg: This image of the inefficiency of government laboratories did perhaps originate in the university community, and was not necessarily ever highly accurate. There is some feeling that Project Hindsight did not fully reflect the impact that the university system has had, even in the development of industrial and military devices; there are innumerable less tangible impacts, such as the spin-off of trained people, consultancies and so on, which Project Hindsight did not take into full account.

Carey: I agree. The main dividend of Project Hindsight was the soothing of states of nerves about the utility of basic research, and I think it succeeded at least in doing that!

Weinberg: Project Hindsight reinforced an obvious point, but one that needs re-stating—that basic research which is closely coupled to application and is done next door, so that people can rub shoulders, has a way of paying off very directly.

King: In the United Kingdom much of the criticism of government laboratories comes not from universities but from government itself, concerned with the lack of close correspondence between mission and performance—the mission probably not having been sufficiently clearly defined or perhaps requiring redefinition after a number of years of work during which both technical advance and the changing nature of the problems have blurred the correspondence.

Todd: This question of the nature of the institutions in which scientific research is best carried out is a major one. Dr. Adams has pointed out that there appear to be two systems operating: in the United States there is little in the way of support for government institutions, but a lot of money is fed into industry and the universities. In the United Kingdom, the universities have less, and most money goes into government institutions. My feeling is that the best solution lies somewhere in the middle. Both solutions reflect the troubles one gets into by pursuing research on a semi-permanent basis without direct relation either to training or to the pursuit of economic objectives. The difficulties of the American system may arise from the tendency to build up large institutions specifically as research institutions and staffed as such but in the guise of bodies attached to universities. In the United Kingdom, we have almost the same situation but we call them government institutions.

Which kind of institutions, then, should one support? My personal view is that scientific work can only be pursued over a long period with any hope of success if *either* you work with very specific but preferably changing economic objectives, *or* you do research as part of an educational training function, in which the people concerned are never engaged on it for more

59

3*

than two or three years at a time. Disaster awaits the university that sets itself up as a series of big research institutions apart from its training function. Also, disaster awaits the government establishment that sets itself up in isolation and continues indefinitely without some real and immediate economic goal. I think that particularly from the standpoint of development, this is a very important matter to get straight. Industry and the process of development are going to set the pattern, and this could be very serious later on.

COST-BENEFIT ANALYSIS IN RESEARCH

C. D. FOSTER

Planning Unit, Ministry of Transport, London

I T is the economist's lot to feel trivial and offensive when asked for his views on such large questions as those we are discussing at this symposium. One fears and expects one's professional contribution to be pusillanimous. There was no economist at *the*—the original—Symposium, only businessmen. And they did not come to dine with their abacus to work out how much the feast cost. Nor did they come with price lists in their hands, interrupting the conversation to observe that some of its splendours had been bought at too high a price ; or that the State would have got more value for its money if Socrates had kept to his trade. Such people were to have the last word but rightly they were shut out of that *élite* as people of no intellectual importance—at worst enemies of truth, at best people who upheld some other values to which they would subordinate the truth. And let us not mince matters. The economist is brought into this discussion to join in devising policies which will *subordinate* the pursuit of knowledge, the pursuit of truth, to some other values.

There is an *external* and also an *internal* reason why this subordination is demanded. The *external* reason is that much research cannot survive without government money. Conversely, most governments realize that scientific knowledge can contribute to the State's well-being and their own policies. But they are not prepared to spend money on it wholly in the pursuit of truth.

The *internal* reason is that until quite recently most people supposed there was probably a finite limit to the acquisition of knowledge. Science was vanquishing ignorance until none of importance would be left. But now for reasons both practical and philosophical we no longer believe that there need ever be an end to the extension of knowledge. In spite of the very great increase in the number of scientists there is still only a finite number, facing infinite research possibilities. Neither is there much evidence for a self-equilibrating tendency. The movement of resources into a concentration in one area of science does not itself set up any opposite and counteracting forces to achieve an optimal allocation by any rational

61

criterion. If my own knowledge of the field of economic research has any relevance as an analogy, there is a tendency for resources, especially first-class minds, to concentrate in certain clumps. Someone able is a pioneer, someone has a lucky break. An area of inquiry becomes intellectually interesting. The best of the new generation tend to follow the best of the old. "How often a man of considerable ability continues all his working life in the narrow view in which some dead and gone professor started him long after it has lost interest and all the paying ore has been extracted" (Sir George Thomson, quoted in Carter and Williams, 1957). Only a brash or unworldly first-class man stumbles into a neglected area—away from the supervision and the testimony of the very best. This should not lead to the worst distribution of resources, but there is no need to suppose it anything near optimal, even from the point of view of pure research.

The subject of cost-benefit analysis has commanded growing interest in recent years. In 1966 the annual meeting of the American Economic Association devoted a session to it, and since the early fifties a large literature has been written on economic problems of research in general which is cognate to the questions put to this symposium. Therefore I regard myself very much as a rapporteur. In the first section I shall explain the notion of cost benefit for those to whom it may be unfamiliar. The second section is a very brief review of major applications of economics to the appraisal of research. The third considers the question of why it is more difficult for economists to be useful in assessing priorities in pure science than in research development. The last section makes a few suggestions on methods of feeding information back from research development to applied and pure research so as to make it more possible to evaluate the economic returns from pure science. In all this I have taken it as axiomatic that we are more interested in the economics of scientific research than of technology.

I

One of the major roles of the economist, which has even been defined as *the* role (Robbins, 1962), is to give advice on "the allocation of scarce resources between competing uses".* The economist's business is to try to work out beforehand the prospective yields on alternative uses of

---

*This was denied by Paul Samuelson in his great work *The Foundations of Economic Analysis* (1947), on the grounds that whole areas of economic work had nothing to do with choice but were concerned with explanation and prediction. Without denying that, the development of the analysis of choice has brought back into the orbit of allocation economics all sorts of techniques first developed for prediction.

resources, and to rank them accordingly in an order of priority. Indeed the old idea of an economy which was working perfectly was one in which every resource was used where it would yield the highest return, given the economy's pattern of demand. Then one would secure the highest return from the economy's resources in general.

But in practice, of course, we sub-optimize. Investment decisions are conducted piecemeal, normally on the basis of limited comparisons of alternative possibilities. Cost-benefit analysis is the rather meaningless name given to such investment analysis when the prospective *financial* return to the investor, whether private firm, citizen, government or even science foundation, is judged not to be the appropriate criterion. Sometimes the financial return, or as it is often called the "private" return, is regarded as insufficient because of what are called external economies and dis-economies. These are financial benefits and costs accruing to others than the decision maker (the firm, citizen, and so on whose private interest is involved). Investment in scientific research is an example of investment where such external factors are usually important, because its results, its findings, are not easily kept as private property and are usually widely disseminated, so that many can take financial advantage. This is even true of industrial research, where firms find that rivals are often quick to analyse new products and to take advantage of the research embodied in them. Hence the return to society, the "social" return from scientific research, is likely to be greater than the private return to those who have financed it. This is an idea to which I shall return.

However, there are "returns" which are not financial in the same sense at all. Other values may be required to weight the returns from projects and therefore their ranking. A science foundation might try ranking alternative projects by the number of scientists it expected them to need; and then might set about trying to maximize the return on its manpower budget on the basis of the best estimates it could make of the relative worth of the projects and their probability of success. Further still from what is usually thought of as an economic appraisal, it might devise a points system, based on some index of relative desirability, and rank projects by that, neglecting cost altogether.*

Often the criterion actually used to allocate resources is not objective and well defined. It is unclear because its operation cannot be, or is not,

---

*R. N. McKean hs a very good discussion of the relation between economic criteria and other simpler indices in his *Efficiency in Government through Systems Analysis* (1958). Most economists have been interested in reweighting the ordinary economic criteria to take account of value judgments on redistribution of income (see Marglin and Maass, 1962).

expressed axiomatically. For example, the United States' space programme, as reported by Margolis and Barro (1965), has made great strides in analysing what it spends its money on. It has apparently got as far as reclassifying its budget so that each head is related to a single main objective, such as security, economic benefits, or the advancement of scientific knowledge. This is an enormous advance over ordinary budgeting, since every expenditure is related to some objective. But they recognize that this is an oversimplification, since many expenditures serve more than a single purpose, and it will only be possible in the end to rank expenditure within each head if the relevant objective can be weighted in some ranking function.

In that situation, one is limited to cost effectiveness, which has proved a very useful tool. Given the overriding objective, what are the cheapest ways of achieving it? In some cases one may be able to go further by converting the objective into an index, so that, for example, one can consider the least-cost solution as it varies according to the number of military targets to be destroyed (for a clearly worked out example of this, see Marschak and Mickey, 1954). Though this introduces more possibilities of comparison, the relation between the index on the one hand, and the cost on the other, is still arbitrary. Thus it is a method of comparing returns on a ratio basis but it cannot tell one whether a return is positive, in the sense of promising a surplus of benefits or of costs. Neither can it tell one whether it is worth spending an extra £x to destroy another y targets.

To achieve this last step, all elements in the ranking, or decision, function must be commensurate. One method in the case cited would be if someone were prepared to put a money value on destroying 1 . . . n targets. But though it is usual to make decision functions commensurate by turning all elements into money values, there is no necessity about this. Any unit will do. The first point is that an economist should be prepared to work with any "objective" decision function that can be ranked. The second point is that the selection of such a function as a criterion is not the economist's job. There is no uniquely "right" ranking function. The choice is not, in the philosophical sense, a "scientific" or "positive" act at all. It is the embodiment of one or more "value judgments" so that a ranking function is yielded. The values that a man or institution may have are legion. The choice of them is a "normative", evaluative, political or ethical decision, that is logically the choice of whoever has the responsibility for the decision. The economist may help him to clear his mind and present the criterion in operational form.

II

Cost-benefit analysis has been used widely to save money and to help assess priorities in relation to development research. The studies are of three main types. Two of these can be divided again into micro-economic and macro-economic. Micro-economic studies are those which try to tackle individual cases. Macro-economic studies try to establish propositions for the economy at large.

The first type tries to work out the *social* return of development expenditure, here defined as the ordinary financial return to the decision maker, plus and minus the financial benefits and costs that are expected to accrue to other people—the external economies and dis-economies. The classic study is by Zvi Griliches (1958). He went back over past data to work out such a social return from research into the development of strains of hybrid corn. This was clearly a case where research done by institutions had effects which spilled over to benefit farmers far and wide. As a result, their financial position improved by much more than what they had paid for the improved seed-corn. Griliches made an estimate of this external benefit and expressed it as a rate of return on the original research expenditure.

So much for the micro-economic level. The macro-economic parallels are studies which try to work out the social return from society's total research expenditure. What proportion of its gross national product should be spent on research? This is a question which has been posed to this symposium. It would take an infinite number of case studies of the Griliches type to build up a brick by brick answer to this question (and as we shall see, there would be other formidable difficulties). But both Nelson (1959) and Arrow (1962) have tried to answer a weaker question: "should society spend more on scientific research?" The arguments have been very well expressed by both authors. Both depend on *a priori* reasoning. They argue that the social return from research must be presumed to be higher than the financial or private return. This is because of the slippery nature of knowledge. A scientist making a contribution normally publishes it. Thus it becomes widely available. If it has any commercial bearing, then anybody can take advantage of it. Even industrial research finds it difficult to keep secrets effectively. It is often said that the right to a patent is only a limited protection, since other firms can so often analyse the patented product and produce something which is somewhat similar, but different enough to evade the patent laws. (Industry has more chance of keeping secrets which relate to the processes by which things are made, but even here people moving from firm to firm may be seed carriers.)

What is more, it is argued that there would be a positive economic loss if bodies doing scientific research tried to recapture all the profit from their work. The argument is the same as that developed for making free the use of a bridge. It is that once a bridge is built, the marginal cost of maintaining it is probably very low. If the bridgebuilder tries to recoup his costs by a toll, this merely has the effect of keeping some people from crossing who cannot afford the toll and so lose "benefit". This is uneconomic, because it is a cardinal principle of economists that byegone costs are byegones. They are concerned only with charges that are relevant to securing the best allocation of resources. That is, they must relate to the operating or current costs of using those resources—the marginal costs, as we call them. But we have assumed that the bridge has no such marginal costs; and neither, it is argued, has science. Once the original investment has been made, the only costs are the costs of dissemination, and to charge anything more reduces the benefits to society without any parallel reduction in the costs of producing the knowledge.

But private firms are by and large in business for profit. Though they may undertake some research for prestige, there will be a tendency for them to do less research than would yield the highest return for society as a whole. Hence the presumption that more research needs to be done than would happen spontaneously if everyone and every firm pursued only his private interests. There are two weaknesses in this argument. The lesser is that this presumes that research always produces external economies. Some scientific research at least may produce no economic returns whatever, even indirectly. (And if one were to be difficult, one could say that some defence research is aimed at reducing economic potential in other nations if not in one's own.) The great objection is that in a nation where the government is financing research, one simply does not know whether it is financing enough to close the gap, so that in total, private plus government research may, or may not, be enough to achieve the highest rate of economic growth for the economy. (One must remember here that the desideratum is that the rate of return on investment in research should be the same at the margin as the return on other investment. If one goes on devoting resources to research beyond that point, then the growth rate must suffer, since other uses of those resources would have achieved a higher return.)

Another type of study uses a production-function approach, as it is called. The attempt here is to use statistical methods to work out for a firm or industry the contribution to its output which can be imputed to certain factors, notably "capital" and "labour". This normally leaves a residual value which cannot be attributed to an input from any measured factor. There are many studies of this kind (for example, Ferguson, 1965; Kendrick and Sato, 1963). But more unusual is one where an attempt is made to demonstrate a relation between the rate of growth of "productivity" and expenditure on research and development. This was done successfully for a sample of firms by Minasian (1962).* (It is worth pointing out that other inquiries have failed to detect any such relationship.)

A similar approach has been used at the macro-economic level. Here the more usual practice has been to attribute the residual so-called increase in "productivity" to education, but there have been attempts, notably by Denison (1962; but see Bowman's reasoned critique, 1964), to use a function which permits imputation of a value to the contribution to the advance of knowledge. He suggested that the contribution of the various key factors to increased "growth" from 1929 to 1957 in the United States is: 34 per cent from more people employed, 23 per cent from investment in capital, 20 per cent from the advance of knowledge and 8 per cent from scale economies over time. A crucial problem here is to find satisfactory measures of the inputs. The very grave difficulties of doing this for research have been discussed by Kuznets and Sanders (1962). What is the proper measure of scientific input: man-hours, expenditure . . .?

However, the conclusion one is trying to draw from this is that if in the past "science" has been responsible for so much of economic growth, then the (average) rate of return on "science", costed in money terms, is higher than that on some other factors, say, "capital" or "labour". Therefore the presumption is that at the margin it would pay the economy to invest more heavily in "science" in absolute terms and more heavily in "science" relative to other factors which have shown a lower return on the same basis.

This kind of argument is not particularly secure. There is the great difficulty of defining and costing the input "science" so as to be able to measure its merit productively. But more generally, we are still dealing with heavily averaged factors. Capital is not homogeneous. The rate of return on some kinds of capital investment may be low and on others high.

Similarly, there is bound to be great variation in the economic productivity of "science". One can argue *a priori* that the fact that the *average* rate of return in science has been shown to be higher than the *average* rate of return on "capital" does not rule out the possibility that the relation of returns at the margin could not be reversed. Therefore such a

---

*There has also been work the other way round to predict a firm's expenditure on research and development; for example, Mansfield (1964).

calculation in itself does not support the proposition that investment in "science" should be increased relative to other investment. Even if examination of time-series data and independent evidence gives some confidence that the proposition should not be reversed, the fitting of such a production function does not help one decide *where* new investment in science should be made, given that the economic returns on different kinds of science are certainly different. The fitting of even more complex production functions that will distinguish the returns to different kinds of science is fraught with difficulty—both statistical difficulties and difficulties of being sure enough of the data. But it is one way ahead.

A third type of exercise is reported by Marshall and Meckling (1962) and by Klein (1962). This was a Rand exercise to investigate the costs of research and development projects. It is notorious that such projects turn out on average to be much more costly than first estimated and to take much longer. The writers believed that they had established a steep curve of learning, suggesting that there was a rapid increase in the ability to predict costs after the start of a project. If true, this would have a profound effect on techniques of cost control, and thus on costs. But it was challenged by a commentator who contended that most of the unpredictability could have been avoided by reasonable foresight even before the project began— a proposition that has quite other implications for cost control. Nevertheless the relevance of cost-effectiveness analysis of this sort for checking expenditure on research and development can hardly be doubted, and much work has been done on it since.

Here, of course, there is no macro-economic analogue.

III

But what of the economics of pure science? The two major questions we have been asked are: (1) How much money should go to science as a whole? (2) How should it be distributed between the branches of science? Even if we add a third question—(3) how can we evaluate the prospective returns from a scientific research project?—the role of the economist is meagre. Economics has much less to contribute to the rationalization of pure science than to that of research development.

There are, I believe, two principal reasons. The first is a difficulty about criteria. If development is for industry, then the criterion is usually private profit. If it is military, it may be less clear, but it is usually related to the immediate strategic objectives. But the nearer one moves to pure science, the less agreement there is likely to be over the objective of research and the more likely it is that (1) there will be a number of objectives, often held by different people, which it will be difficult to make commensurate, and (2) that some or all of these objectives will not be easily capable of expression as a well-defined decision function. Hence, the much greater difficulty that the economist has in working on pure science. The answer, of course, is sufficient clarity among policy makers over objectives to make economic analysis operational, if that is possible.

But as things stand, there is one reason why it is impossible to answer the question of how much money should be spent on science, namely that most people would agree that many values should govern the answer: the pursuit of knowledge for its own sake, science as education, as well as any economic contribution. The same is true of the division of money between sciences; and also of the prospective returns from a scientific project, since this, too, may have many objectives.

But even if one were to have a well-defined objective, say an economic one, there is another major difficulty. It has become common for economists (Scherer, 1965; Klein and Meckling, 1958) to relate the conventional distinction between pure science, applied research and development to a continuum of diminishing uncertainty. This has a certain intuitive plausibility. One says of the purest scientists that they need the greatest "originality". They it is who sail on "uncharted seas" and take "leaps into the unknown". Although they, too, more often than not, will be discovering pieces to fit into an existing jig-saw, it is always possible that they will revolutionize their fields. In general terms, it is difficult to predict whether any particular piece of work will be successful; or what, if successful, it will establish. By assumption, the world of the applied scientist is less clouded by uncertainty. By assumption he is taking something already known or hypothesized in some circumstances and applying it to others. Research development takes the whole matter a stage further and usually means taking some applied research and making it operational or even "marketable". (Is it too coarse to say that the key notion underlying "development" is wholly an economic one—"can such and such an idea be made operational—say, be manufactured—at a cost and of a quality to be marketed, or, if the end is not the market, then, in some other sense, to be tolerable"?)

The greater the uncertainty, the less useful economics is. This can be shown by considering what economics—or cost-benefit analysis—means in this context. In order to advise, an economist makes certain hypothetical conditional predictions: if P then X; if Q then Y; if R then Z . . . where P, Q and R are certain policies or decisions which it is presumed the decision maker is able to effect. A decision to build an atomic power station (P), or a conventional one (Q) or a hydroelectric one (R) would be examples of such decisions. So would decisions to devote resources to various research projects. X, Y, Z represent future states of affairs that it is predicted will result from P, Q, R. From the point of view of the economist, each future state X . . . is composed of two kinds of event: (1) the events which he is advancing as relevant to the decision between P, Q, R . . . and (2) the rest which, though nonetheless predicted, he is advancing as events to which the decision maker is indifferent when deciding between P, Q, R . . . It is the first kind of event which is here relevant to the economist's art: the ranking of P, Q, R in an order of priority. It is these that must be capable of reflection in an "objective" criterion, "ranking" or "decision" function where the rank,

$$D = D\,(b_1, b_2, b_3 \ldots)\,P,\ Q,\ R.$$

(The "b"s are the relevant events and D represents some policy by which their "values" are made commensurate.)

There are three necessary elements in this process. The first is the prediction of the events themselves. This is the "scientific" element. Let us suppose the prediction is that quantity x will be sold at price p; or that such-and-such a research project will eventuate in landing on the moon. Secondly there is the process of assigning a value to that event, which is more obvious in the first example than in the second. (What is more, we *normally* judge that "value" is a constant function of the money made.) The third element is the process of combining the "valuable" events into a single value for the function. (This again seems easier in a commercial situation, where all the "valuable" events appear to have a money value and so are immediately commensurate, than if, say, P implied *both* landing on the moon *and* an advance in computer technology.) Both these last two elements are, as we have seen, not "scientific" judgments.

It is also clear that the "future state of affairs" that an economist is interested in may be larger or smaller than that which interests the scientist. The scientist often abstracts from all sorts of preliminaries and side-effects to consider the final outcome of a research project. It is that which usually gives it "value" for him, whether encapsulated in a scientific paper or some "developed" artefact. The economist is bound to consider all the events from the initial decision P through to the last event caused by P. That is his "X". This is logical, because any or all of these can add to the cost or benefit of X and so alter its ranking. On the other hand, as has been pointed out, he is interested in only those events to which he judges "value" to be attached. In trying to decide whether a given railway line should be modernized by being electrified or converted to diesel fuel, he is not interested in the different technologies *per se*, but only in so far as they affect the "values" of the alternatives.

To return to the main point of the role of uncertainty in defeating cost-benefit analysis, it is clear that the scientist and economist have opposite interests. From a purely formal view the economist finds it easiest to work when there is least uncertainty about the future events he is interested in. Uncertainty works in the normal way to reduce the validity of his estimation of future net benefits; but the effect of uncertainty is often compounded by the doubt it throws on the ranking of P, Q, R. (Incidentally, it is scarcely ever sufficient for an economist to deal with uncertainty by defining some "certainty" equivalent such as $\dfrac{Z_0 \leqslant Z \geqslant Z^0}{2}$, where the proposition is that it is equally probable that Z lies at any point between Z_0 and Z^0. For what is critical is the probability that the real value will affect the ranking. Hence the need to conduct what is called "sensitivity" analysis by parametric variation, to establish these probabilities.)

The scientist, on the other hand, more often than not is not interested in predicting the outcome of his research. The purer it is, the more impatient the scientist is likely to be at any such probing. Indeed Sir Karl Popper (1957) has argued "that if there is such a thing as growing human knowledge then we cannot anticipate today what we shall only know tomorrow . . . no scientific predicter can possibly predict, by scientific methods, its own future results". Thus, the scientist often asks to be backed on his merits and to be allowed to experiment his way forward.

However, I hope we have already indicated the way round the problem.

Logically, one can only not predict the unpredictable. But in foreseeing research one can work by analogy so far as there are elements in what one is doing which are known—that are further along the continuum towards applied research and development. Moreover, there are elements in the purest research project which are capable of some prediction of performance.

We do not behave as if successful research were a random event. Rather, one hears "pick your man and back him". Our system of education is designed to pick the best people to do, and later lead, research. Many would feel that intuition and wisdom are sufficient guides to the choice of people to do projects.

Further systematization is possible and work has been done to try to establish the characteristics and combinations of research workers who are likely to succeed. However, to my knowledge, most of this work has been biased towards development (but see Intriligator and Smith, 1966) or has been part of the study of the sociology of science and is clearly unrelated to efficient research in the cost-benefit analysis sense. The kind of questions that are relevant here probably presuppose a division of manpower into certain skills, such as (1) research leader, (2) first-class research worker, (3) other qualified Ph.D's, (4) research assistants. And we would want to measure these in man-hours or years. Then we could try to quantify answers to questions such as:

(1) Is there any evidence of economies of scale in the use of manpower?
(i) Evidence that *similar* projects tend to be completed more quickly, in the sense of using fewer man-hours in total, if more resources are employed simultaneously?

(ii) That *similar* sets of projects tend to occupy fewer man-hours, depending on the balance within the team of people with different skills?

(iii) That *similar* projects tend to be completed in fewer man-hours if more than one team is independently at work on the same thing—counting the man-hours spent by members of all the teams as a cost? (The logic of this has been examined by Nelson, 1961.)

(iv) That *similar* projects tend to be completed in fewer man-hours if *like* projects are being run simultaneously in the same institutions (or perhaps institutions *per se* have a stimulating effect?).

(v) If *like* projects are being handled sequentially by the same teams so that they become accustomed to the same work, are they completed more quickly, or conversely, would some variation in the work-pattern be more productive?

(2) Turning from manpower to other resources, it would be useful to look for patterns in the use of resources.
(i) What does research of certain kinds typically cost? What is the frequency distribution of cost?

(ii) Can one say anything from experience about the effects of the substitution of manpower—of the various skills—and other resources?

(iii) As with manpower, is there any evidence of economies or dis-economies of scale in the use of these resources?

(iv) Is there any evidence that cost-control procedures have brought down cost without reducing the success rate?

One would have to be especially careful how one treated failures—

some of these are also usually *costs* of success.* The relevant question is: with hindsight, should we have been able to predict in advance that a project would not succeed?

By asking questions of this sort retrospectively one should be able to learn a great deal about the research process. (If one cannot, then research is much more like a purely random event than one hoped.) If such back-checking enables one to differentiate between types of project, and even between sciences, one can begin to apply cost-benefit analysis. One can begin to cost various projects on that basis and *rank* them. Normally it would not be right to price scientific manpower according to its earning power. Highly qualified scientific manpower is usually more valuable than that. There are two ways of trying to deal with this problem realistically. If for the moment we consider that all "successes" are equally important, then one could try to maximize the number of "successes", subject to con-straints on the number of scientists (of the different skills) available.† Or if this suggests a simultaneous approach to the problem that is impossible, one can do a few test calculations to try to determine what is the "real" or "shadow" price of a scientist of a given skill, and then use this shadow price in the calculations instead of the money price.

But it is not easy to go on from there to link this with economic criteria, should one want to do so, to calculate the social return. All the techniques developed in Section II seem to fall down. The approach used by Griliches fails because normally it is very difficult to establish a precise link between a particular piece of basic research and a final commodity sold in the market. Even if one can, to impute a productivity in value terms to that research ordinarily defies measurement. Further, the effect of basic research may be widely diffused. The Nelson and Arrow type of argument for more basic research is not easy to use, in so far as one does not expect profit-maximiz-ing firms to do much pure research, whereas non-profit-making bodies do.

The production-function approach is virtually impossible, because measurement of pure scientific inputs and outputs is very difficult, and because in any case they are small relative to research and development—which brings us back to the other procedure of trying various methods to make research projects more efficient and cheaper by cost effectiveness, which we have briefly discussed.

---

*The difficulties associated with defining and measuring other people's futures as costs of somebody's success are considered by Kuznets (1962). They are very important since the neglect of these may overstate the return for research many times.

†The budget constraint problem has been discussed widely, for example, Steiner (1959).

IV

Thus, though economics has had a recent and rather successful surge in application to research development, it is much less easy to see how it can be made useful for the resolution of national science policy as a whole. Even if we can clarify the appropriate criterion, there will always be uncertainties. Such analyses of the costs of various research techniques as may be useful do not really touch the problem with which national science policies are most vexed. But perhaps some rationalization can be achieved by the application of what may be called *indicative planning*. For example, it is often felt that in some sense some countries, especially the underdeveloped ones, devote too many of their resources to certain sciences—for example, nuclear physics—which (1) are scientifically fashionable because intellectually stimulating, (2) very often do not contribute obviously to economic growth, but (3) seem to be militarily useful, and are thus irrelevant to nations who do not want that kind of striking power. Further, such kinds of science often happen, by coincidence, to require very great resources which, in practice, is often thought to mean a "brain drain" of scientists from countries able to provide them more easily.

Alternative policies would be: (1) to divert scientists into branches of pure science which it is thought (a) would be of greater economic benefit to the country in question, and (b) would thus be more likely to keep first-class scientific manpower at work productively; (2) to divert the same kind of manpower into applied research and technology, also assumed to be more productive. A difficulty about the second course is that it may be difficult to persuade would-be pure scientists to become applied scientists.

The economic analysis of this problem is not likely, in my opinion, to succeed by economic research at the macro-economic level—or indeed through any of the techniques that I have discussed so far. What is needed is evidence that pure science is useful for economic growth and that some of the less populated sciences in a given country should have more resources devoted to them. Even from the standpoint of economic growth, there may be many lines of argument employed. For example, one often hears that a strong tradition of pure sciences is needed in the universities if scientific education in general is to be good. Pure science fertilizes applied and development research.

But to consider the direct relationship, if any, between science and economic growth, I believe that what many industries and countries need is a good reporting system and a good economic forecasting system, specially designed as an aid to research. To try to explain what I mean, let me take the field in which I have most immediate interest: transport research. We are at present engaged, in the British Ministry of Transport, in building various economic models which we hope will have predictive power for the future. But they will be conditional predictions, in the sense that one knows that what will actually happen will be sensitive to many policy variables. We believe also that the future will, and should, be altered by research.

When, for example, one tries to forecast the proportion of traffic that will in future be carried by road and rail, one is examining existing data here and overseas with two purposes in mind. The first is to have the best idea one can of the conditions which affect the modal split, as it is called, between road and rail for various traffics. But, secondly, in doing so one is looking for certain critical conditions which, if they were changed, would alter the modal split appreciably, presumably for less total cost, or more generally for a preferred split in terms of the cost and quality of service. To take another field in which we are interested, if one could cut tunnelling costs by half, an enormous difference would be made to the programme of transport investment that one would want to implement in cities, and also to the future size, dispersal and general development of many cities.

The procedure that one would want to go through next, of course, is to see whether economic answers to these many questions is a matter of development and applied research, or whether in some cases more basic scientific research is likely to be needed. One would then want to develop a national science policy which will provide that the required resources will be where they are needed. Such manpower forecasts should help to indicate the relative claims of different branches of science.

The same kind of appraisal of research could also be relevant to a nation. Many authors have argued that less-developed countries are under a particular technological disadvantage when they try to industrialize, especially when they try to industrialize for export. When they follow the principle of comparative advantage and try to develop those activities, say with a high labour intensity, where they should be able to produce more cheaply than more developed countries, they find that if they do very well in invading foreign markets, foreign firms often put their scientists and technologists to work to find a cheaper synthetic or other substitute. Greater scientific resources may therefore always keep the more developed countries ahead in the economic race. It is very important that the scientific resources that a less-developed country has should be used in a planned manner, following an economic appreciation of the areas where the concentration of these resources may make possible a breakthrough of a kind to establish an export industry in which that country is likely to have a comparative advantage for some time. Unfortunately, such planning is itself usually easier in a more developed country, with its greater tradition of innovation, science and economic model-building. It would, for example, be easier in Britain.

One finds, if one allows any long-term model of an economy to "run on" for a large number of years, that it begins to give some implausible values. Industries may, because of the growth paths assumed, become so large that one cannot conceive how they will dispose of the goods produced, unless there is a vast increase in exports. Other industries will require implausibly large amounts of specific inputs which may be difficult, or increasingly expensive, to obtain domestically, or by import. These are prospective bottlenecks to which research may be directed. In the past it has been usual to delay giving attention to them until the situation has been almost upon us. Because it is much more difficult to predict the pattern of demand many years hence, there is some justification for this.* (This of course is where the less-developed country has the advantage, as it is probably more satisfactory for it to look to demand experience in more developed countries and use that as a rough approximation for the future.) Nevertheless, it is the case that there are many industries in many countries which do not adapt either themselves or their sources of raw materials until years after the warning signals have been clear to all who can see. Often it may be too late. Again, it is by probing what answers are possible, through development and applied research, that one may get some idea of where more basic research is needed.

SUMMARY

Section I gave a brief characterization of cost-benefit analysis. It is usually described as the act or art of calculating a rate of return on investment when the purely financial rate of return is thought to be a wrong or misleading criterion. Sometimes there are said to be external economies or dis-economies—that is, receipts of payments accruing to people other than the person or firm making the investment. Sometimes quite other criteria are needed which are all of a form which would rank alternative investments according to some function which subtracts negative values—costs—from positive values—benefits.

---

*But Schmookler (1966) has argued that it is a perception of what is likely to be demanded, as well as what demands can be created, which is the primary force stimulating technological change, not reductions in costs.

Section II gave a brief account of some economic techniques which have been used to evaluate investment in development research. Five methods were discussed: (1) The working out of a return in a specific case where there were substantial external economies; (2) *A priori* arguments suggesting under-investment in research because the social return is greater than the financial return; (3) The fitting of production functions to industrial and firm data to suggest the profitability of research in those units; (4) The fitting of a production function to national data which allows one to give a value to the "advance of knowledge"; and (5) The development of techniques to reduce the cost of any research programme.

Section III argued that it was more difficult to apply all but the last of these techniques, the further removed the application along the spectrum from research development towards pure science. This was because criteria tended to become more confused and less agreed, and also because of the greater uncertainty of the outcome in pure science. On the other hand, the use of cost effectiveness can be rewarding.

Section IV argued that perhaps the best way of attempting to answer the major questions posed at this symposium is to try to forecast research needs, working backwards from a general forecast of an economy and industry to identify important bottlenecks at which research would be needed to break through.

REFERENCES

Arrow, K. J. (1962). Economic welfare and the allocation of resources for invention. In *Rate and Direction of Inventive Activity: Economic and Social Factors*, pp. 609–625, ed. Nelson, R. R. Princeton: Princeton University Press.

Bowman, M. J. (1964). Schultze, Denison and the contribution of "Eds" to national income growth. *Journal of Political Economy*, **72**, 450–464.

Carter, C. F., and Williams, B. R. (1957). *Industry and Technical Progress: Factors Governing the Speed of Application of Science*, p. 54. London: Oxford University Press.

Denison, E. F. (1962). *The Success of Economic Growth in the United States and the Alternative Before Us*. Supplementary Paper No. 13. New York: Committee for Economic Development.

Ferguson, C. E. (1965). Time series. Production functions and technological progress in American industry. *Journal of Political Economy*, **73**, 135–147.

Griliches, Z. (1958). Research costs and social returns: hybrid corn and related innovations. *Journal of Political Economy*, **66**, 419–431.

Intriligator, M. D., and Smith, B. L. B. (1966). *American Economic Review, Papers and Proceedings*, p. 494 *et seq.*

Kendrick, J. W., and Sato, R. (1963). *American Economic Review*, **53**, 974–1003.

Klein, B. (1962). In *Rate and Direction of Inventive Activity: Economic and Social Factors*, pp. 477–497, ed Nelson, R. R. Princeton: Princeton University Press.

Klein, B., and Meckling, W. (1958). Application of operations research to development decisions. *Operations Research*, May/June, 352–363.

Kuznets, S., and Sanders, B. S. (1962). In *Rate and Direction of Inventive Activity: Economic and Social Factors*, pp. 19–43, 53–85, ed. Nelson, R. R. Princeton: Princeton University Press.

Mansfield, E. (1964). Industrial research and development expenditure. *Journal of Political Economy*, **72**, 319–340.

Marglin, S., and Maass, A. (1962). *Design of Water Resource Systems*. Cambridge, Mass.: Harvard University Press.

Margolis, M. A., and Barro, S. M. (1965). In *Program Budgeting*, pp. 120–145, ed. Novick, D. Cambridge, Mass.: Harvard University Press.

Marschak, J., and Mickey, M. R. (1954). Optimal weapons systems. *Naval Research Logistics Quarterly*, June, 116–140.

Marshall, A. W., and Meckling, W. H. (1962). In *Rate and Direction of Inventive Activity: Economic and Social Factors*, pp. 467–497, ed. Nelson, R. R. Princeton: Princeton University Press.

McKean, R. N. (1958). *Efficiency in Government through Systems Analysis*. New York: Wiley.

Minasian, J. R. (1962). Economics of research and development. In *Rate and Direction of Inventive Activity: Economic and Social Factors*, pp. 93–141, ed. Nelson, R. R. Princeton: Princeton University Press.

Nelson, R. R. (1959). The simple economics of basic scientific research. *Journal of Political Economy*, **67**, 297–306.

Nelson, R. R. (1961). Economics of parallel research and development efforts. *Review of Economics and Statistics*, **43**, 351–364.

Popper, K. R. (1957). *The Poverty of Historicism*. London: Routledge and Kegan Paul.

Robbins, L. (1932). *Nature and Significance of Economic Science*, p. 16 *et seq*. London: Macmillan.

Samuelson, P. (1947). *The Foundations of Economic Analysis*, p. 22. Cambridge, Mass.: Harvard University Press.

Scherer, M. F. (1965). Government research and development programs. In *Measuring Benefits of Government Expenditure*, pp. 14–15, ed. Dorfmann, R. New York: Brookings Institution.

Schmookler, J. (1966). *Invention and Economic Growth*. Cambridge, Mass.: Harvard University Press.

Steiner, P. O. (1959). Choosing among alternative public investments. *American Economic Review*, **49**, 893–916.

DISCUSSION

Carey: In the American budget process, we are finding that cost-benefit analysis is a very helpful tool in coping with problems of choice at the *development* end of the research spectrum, that it has some usefulness at the centre, where we are dealing with *applied* research, and that it is not much use when one reaches *basic* research. Decisions on the allocation of resources for basic science are "level of effort" decisions for the most part. We do not, however, include within "level of effort" decision making the one-of-a-kind, high-cost investment choices in basic science—for example, the question of the 200 Gev accelerator. We isolate such decisions for much closer critical analysis, and each is decided explicitly on the basis of such considerations as the presence of a critical mass of scientific "know-how" and readiness, the asserted need to protect a "lead" in the field, and so forth. But the main point I am making is that notwithstanding the well-advertised sophistication in the development of cost-benefit analysis, basic research investment is still largely worked out intuitively by the "level of effort" method.

Ackoff: May I describe an application of one of the methods that Mr. Foster mentioned in the research conflict, when he discussed utility evaluation. A major government laboratory in the United States is organized into 15 functional departments and had an annual budget for major capital equipment of about three million dollars. The head of each department was asked to identify major equipment needed—items such as electron microscopes, centrifuges and so on. The cost of the list of items received was about nine million dollars. The problem was how best to cut down to what money was available.

It was done as follows. Using a utility-measurement method (described in chapter 6 of Churchman, C. W., Ackoff, R. L., and Arnoff, E. L. [1957]. *Introduction to Operations Research.* New York: Wiley), each department head was put through a procedure in which he assigned a weight to each department, based on his opinion of its relative importance to the organization as a whole. (When these assessments were published, they did more to produce goodwill in the organization than anything that had ever happened, because the weightings of the department heads turned out to be incredibly consistent.) The 15 weights were averaged and a general weight was thus obtained for each department. A list was then made of 192 items of equipment, and each department head was asked to indicate which items would be of use to him, whether he had requested them or not; the average number of items listed was 35 per department. Then, again using a utility measurement, each department head put weights on only those items which he had listed as useful to him. The sum of the weighted weights was obtained for each item. This was divided by its cost, which gave the amount of weight that could be obtained per dollar. These were ranked in order of diminishing return, and selection was made from the top down until the amount available was used up. Thus the total weighted value received was maximized. The whole process took about three days, whereas the selection of new equipment by the former method, political pressure by department heads, took about three months. The selection of items had to be made one way or the other. The procedure described produced generally acceptable results without loss of goodwill, judged by the fact that very few modifications were subsequently made to the list of items selected for purchase.

Weinberg: Is there any evidence that political pressure would have been a poorer way of making the allocation?

Ackoff: There is one major piece of evidence. The director of the laboratory estimated that previously it had taken approximately six months after items were selected for purchase for the department heads to communicate effectively again. This was no longer the case! Furthermore, this procedure did not use the judgment of anyone other than those who had formerly been involved, but it did so systematically and fairly, eliminating political pressure and intrigue.

Weinberg: One might reflect on the temper of a laboratory where the making of allocations caused such a disturbance. There are other ways of doing this satisfactorily, without going through a mathematical procedure.

Foster: Let us list the other possible methods. There is dictatorship—the decision of priorities by one man or a cabal. There is committee decision, which gives great scope to bargaining ability and to the use of "political" and tactical pressures. Are these really better than Professor Ackoff's method, which, as he has said, takes less time and usually generates less heat than the second, while being more democratic than the first? Nor are those scientists who are best at political pressure *necessarily* those to be encouraged. Is there not a lot to be said for asking people to clarify their priorities?

Bondi: There may be a lot to be said for this, but before I can believe that some method is good or the best, I want clear histories of cases that are bad and worst. One should get a great deal of illumination of right decision making from a clear knowledge of wrong decision making.

Ackoff: That seems to say that you will tolerate any amount of inefficiency so long as you cannot measure it.

Bondi: No. I am saying that I do not know what is efficiency or inefficiency unless I have some measure. In your case, I could not judge other than by the criteria you use, which are really secondary criteria—how long the process takes, how soon people are on speaking terms again, and so on. They are important, but secondary, criteria. I would have to fall back on those, unless I had a good primary means of evaluating your (or any other) method, and this must involve frank confessions of wrong decisions made in the past.

Adams: It seems to me that Professor Ackoff's system of allocation may be no better than the solution by committees. For instance, a first-rate scientist wanting some peculiar equipment which neither his department nor the others wanted would have the same difficulty in convincing others that his good was synonymous with the common good. Also, in time departments would surely tend to support others simply in order to be supported by others?

Ackoff: This can be analysed as a game theoretical problem. It can be shown that the best strategy in the procedure described is to judge as accurately as possible one's own values. There is no way to do any better for oneself than by being truthful. To improve his "chances", a departmental head must get the rating of his department up; he has to persuade other people that the activity he heads is important.

Freeman: Were all the departments agreed on the goal of the laboratory? And what was the value of the largest single item of equipment?

Ackoff: This was a highly mission-orientated laboratory. The largest single item cost several hundred thousand dollars.

Rexed: One of the biggest Research Councils in Sweden has for several years used a very similar method for grading applications for research funds. The applications are divided into groups of rather similar subjects, and for each group referees are chosen from outside the Council, who are asked to allot priorities to all the applications, according to some ten criteria: originality, feasibility, and so on. These values are then put together and a ranking list is derived for each group. These ranking lists are given back to the Council which decides what weight each group should have relative to the others—because there is the additional possibility that one group, say psychiatry, is felt by the Council to deserve a higher weight than another group, say anatomy, because the Council would rather favour psychiatry than anatomy. Once these primary evaluations within and between groups are made, it is easy to pick the best projects within the set limits of resources. The whole operation goes smoothly and there are very few objections to the final decisions and very little change, although if necessary, cases are taken up for individual discussion in the full Council. The system makes it possible to perform this difficult job in a reasonably objective fashion. I would think that, as long as our abilities to judge correctly between individual projects are as small as they are, we should study methods like this one carefully. An important point is that one must have a fairly homogeneous field, but that qualification can be met.

Pannenborg: I do not want to comment on Professor Ackoff's procedure as a *method* of solution, but the *problem* is a sub-optimization which does not appeal to me at all. There is something fundamentally wrong with a laboratory where the demand for instrumentation is three times greater than the available funds. Either there are too many people for the total sum of money, or the atmosphere in the laboratory is one of empire-building in hardware, and either way something else has to change.

Ackoff: This is to say that there is something wrong with a person or organization that aspires to more than he or it expects. I would argue that there is something wrong only if this is not the case. Why should aspirations be constrained by one's budget?

Pannenborg: This assumes that the number of people is fixed, and that everyone increases his demands because he knows they will be cut down; but this is not a true optimization. In free boundary conditions, you should supply the responsible people in the key positions with everything they need, and if there is a limited total sum of money, then work with fewer people of a higher quality.

Rexed: This consideration is important in a situation where there is a limited amount of money and there are more people than could reasonably be supported with this amount. Then the solution should follow Dr. Pannenborg's lines, and one should support the best people to the full, if they are in the areas that one wants them to be, and weed out the weak ones.

Foster: The method of giving weightings can be adapted to this situation. One can use it to determine who will be sacked! What is at issue is, again, who is to decide this—a dictator, a committee, or a voluntary procedure such as Professor Ackoff's?

Ackoff: I do not understand the logic of Dr. Pannenborg's argument. If I asked a group of poverty-stricken people what they would like for the next year and they exceeded their budget by a factor of three, I would not conclude that they were empire-building.

Pannenborg: Either they can use the equipment, and then one should give it to them, or they are asking for more than they need.

Ackoff: The budget was imposed from outside the organization, not from inside. The organization competed for scarce funds with other laboratories. It did not expect to get all it needed, let alone all it wanted.

Pannenborg: That is why I say that this is a sub-optimization, because you have initial boundary conditions which avoid the proper optimum.

Todd: Professor Ackoff's method happened to be tried by an organization with a limited budget, which is not an uncommon circumstance. The method should be regarded as of general interest, as a way of distributing a given sum of money in one area.

Bondi: It seems, however, a method likely to work well only in a highly mission-orientated group, where every department agrees that in some sense the others are necessary. If it were tried in a university, each department would cut out all the others!

Ackoff: We have also tried the method in a university, and that does not happen, although what you have predicted is exactly what the heads of departments in the university predicted would happen. People are always amazed to discover how reasonable other people are. One should be careful in proceeding on an assumption of avarice or irrationality on the part of research workers or administrators. It is not justified by the facts.

Adams: I would expect the reverse of Professor Bondi's situation. It often happens that people support others in order to be supported by them. I would expect that after a few years, people would get to know how the system operates and proceed to abuse it for their own good. They would support each other's choices by pre-arrangement rather than by dis-passionate judgment.

Ackoff: This is a considerable worry, but we can show that in a situation where activities are interdependent, by forming a coalition one can do nothing but hurt oneself. That was true in this university because of special conditions, because the activities were interdependent. If they were not, then the conditions would not be satisfied, coalitions could be effective, and the system would not work.

Bondi: Therefore, the system could break down in a university?

Ackoff: Yes, it could.

OPERATIONAL RESEARCH AND NATIONAL SCIENCE POLICY

RUSSELL L. ACKOFF

Management Science Center, University of Pennsylvania, Philadelphia

A T a meeting of this type it is quite natural to look at science as a socio-economic institution. As an institution, science is a subsystem of a more inclusive nation-system. Because of our effort to focus on science it is easy to fall into the trap of thinking of it as a relatively detached subsystem, rather than as one which is closely coupled to the other subsystems that make up a nation. In addition to the danger of looking at science as a closed rather than as an open system, there is another danger which arises from viewing it as a black-box whose internal operations are of no interest. From this latter point of view all one needs to consider is the relationship between inputs and outputs.

I believe that it is essential for us to look at science both from the outside in and from the inside out. It may well be that a minor modification in another subsystem can do more to affect the productivity of a nation's scientific effort than anything that can be done to or within science. It may also be that internal adjustments in the way science operates may have more effect on its output than manipulations of the inputs to it.

The "input–output" orientation which tends to dominate much of current planning efforts is devoted to finding out how inputs and outputs have been associated in the past. Such associations are generally sought by means of regression analysis. However, no matter how much statistical sophistication is employed in such analyses, they cannot provide more than descriptions of past relationships. If one adds to such descriptions the assumption that the system which transforms inputs to outputs will remain stable in the future, they can then be used as a basis for prediction, by extrapolation. Such descriptions and predictions explain nothing; hence, whatever else they may yield, they cannot yield understanding. Regression-based predictions of the effect of changes of input-policy on outputs run a considerable risk because of the assumption of stability that is involved in them. Research and planning directed toward improving the output-to-input ratio of an activity like science should be directed, at least in part, toward finding changes in the system's structure which will significantly improve the past input-to-output ratios. Regression equations, no matter how much they are embedded in and obscured by complex econometric manipulations, provide us with no basis for designing proposed structural changes, and they do not even provide a basis for evaluating proposed structural changes once they are formulated.

It is necessary, therefore, to develop an understanding of the functional relationships within the subsystem of science, and between science and other social subsystems. Such understanding must come from an analysis of structure and functioning rather than from extensive and intensive description. In brief, social planning requires theory as well as facts; without theory, it is like sex without a partner.

It is apparent that the yield of a unit of money spent in science depends to a large extent on the effectiveness with which its output is used. For example, one would not expect any specific scientific discovery or technological development to have the same economic and cultural impact on England and India. This aspect of scientific productivity is perhaps best seen by changing our normal perspective, from which we see too little spent on science and technology, to one that proceeds from the assumption that the basic problem in national science planning is not to increase scientific output but to increase the rate of its exploitation and assimilation by the culture. Perhaps some nations should share the point of view of the old farmer who dismissed the government's agricultural expert, who was trying to impose new farming methods on him, with, "Go away, son, and stop bothering me. I'm already not doing as well as I know how."

The problem, put in less prosaic terms, is one of balancing the components of the nation-system so that the outputs of each subsystem are exploited for the social good as effectively as possible. Detection of current imbalances is essential if we are to estimate the extent of our inventory of unused or under-used knowledge, and the rate at which new knowledge can be absorbed.

I know of one company in the United States, for example, whose Research and Development Division produced seven times as many saleable products as the company had capital to exploit. Most of its research and development output had to be put out to others on a royalty basis that was not very profitable. There is such a thing as too large an investment in science, because the investment made in unused output reduces the ability of society to use what it has put out. The concept of science and society which is employed in planning must allow for this possibility.

Therefore, it seems important for planning purposes that we have at least a minimal conception of the operation of the total nation-system of which science and technology are a part, and that we develop some quantitative understanding of how it operates. I should like to propose such a conception and to indicate how its translation into a quantitative form might be accomplished.

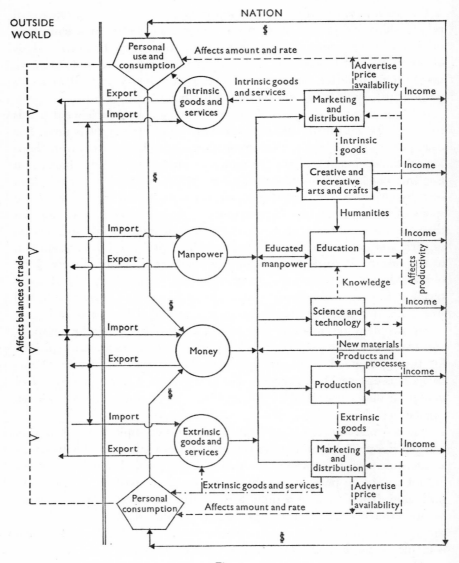

Fig. 1

The conceptual model is shown in Fig. 1. In this model resources are of three types: manpower, money, and extrinsic goods and services; that is, goods and services which are useful as instruments for obtaining other things that are valued. These resources flow into six types of activity: education, science and technology, production, marketing and distribution of extrinsic goods and services, creative and recreative arts and crafts, and the marketing and distribution of their output. The output of the creative and recreative arts and crafts is intrinsic goods and services; that is, things and activities which are ends in themselves. These include recreational as well as cultural activities; athletic games as well as operas, television as well as theatre, and parks as well as paintings. The operation of a museum, theatre or ball-park involves the marketing and distribution of intrinsic goods and services.

Each of the six activities to which resources are allocated produces income. Income is used for personal consumption, for institutional consumption or for export. Each of the resources may be either imported, or exported, or both. An uneven balance of trade of goods and services will produce either a net inflow or a net outflow of money.

Extrinsic goods and services flow from production to marketing and distribution; thence either to personal consumption, institutional consumption, or export. The flow of intrinsic goods and services is analogous.

Education affects the productivity of each other type of activity. It also affects the desire for, and awareness of, both intrinsic and extrinsic goods and services. I use education in a very general sense: as communication which informs, instructs or motivates people. Therefore, it includes much more than formal educational processes; for example, it includes much of the activity of parents, press, radio and television.

Education changes the quality of manpower and converts initially unusable manpower into a type which is socially useful. Hence, it feeds back to the pool of manpower.

Science and technology correspond approximately to research and development. The output of science is knowledge which is, in turn, an input to the educational process. The outputs of technology are new products and processes which can be used to perform more effectively any of the activities, including research and development. Technology also develops new products and services for consumption, or improves those already available.

Intrinsic and extrinsic consumption produces the satisfaction that people derive from living within the nation. This in turn affects their levels of aspiration which, when aggregated, affect national goals and objectives. These goals and objectives clearly affect the way that public and private resources are allocated to the various social subsystems.

This model does not "cover everything". It is not intended to. On the contrary, it is intended to be as simple as possible, and yet be useful as a basis for developing the type of quantitative model of a nation that is required for effective science planning. The objective of planning research should be to determine how far we can go with how little. (Einstein went quite far with just e, m and c.) Complexity is not a property of phenomena nearly as much as it is a reflection of our state of ignorance. Any process that we do not understand is more complex than any that we do.

How can we go about converting a conceptual model such as I have described into a mathematical model which explains and provides quantitative predictions of the effects of possible interventions in the processes represented? As I have already indicated, I do not believe that this can be done by regression analyses. We must proceed by the only method we have yet discovered for systematically acquiring quantitative understanding of any phenomenon: *experimentation*.

In the democratic societies with which I am familiar, there is almost an innate abhorrence of social and economic experimentation. We think it demeans the subjects and threatens with the possibility of excessive public control of private lives. Yet, curiously enough, no other type of society manipulates and varies the form and content of its control over its members as much as a democratic one. Democratic nations constantly change taxes, tariffs, interest rates, zoning rules, laws, regulations, transportation and communication systems, metrics and even the clock. The major aspects of experimentation—manipulation and control—are already widely practised in such societies. They even attempt to measure the effects of changes in public policy on national performance. But here is the rub: they usually do not let the design of the evaluative procedure affect the way the public is controlled or manipulated. The evaluators are called in *after the fact*, when it is too late to do an adequate job of evaluation and when the possibilities of gaining understanding are almost completely destroyed. For example, in industry we have found that no amount of retrospective analysis of advertising and sales can yield as much understanding of their relationship as can even a very simple experiment in a few market-places.

In the United States we have just missed a marvellous opportunity to perform useful experimentations in connexion with our so-called "Poverty Programme". Instead of designing these programmes as experiments to inform us how to reduce or remove poverty, we assumed we knew the answers. Only when the failure of such programmes was obvious was any effort made to determine what their effect had been. By then it was too late. Instead of changing our methodology we have only changed our programmes. There is little consolation in knowing that we won't make the same errors twice.

Science and other subsystems of our nation-system must become the subject of experimental study. Put another way, the science of science must become an experimental science.

Regression analysis can be useful as a filter, to select combinations of variables, relationships between which should be sought by experimental methods. For example, if there were no regressive relationship between the percentage of income spent on research and development in an industry and its rate of growth, experimentation would not be indicated in this area. If there were, one could then proceed to design experiments to measure the effect which increased expenditures on research and development have on such growth. Similarly, if we could find no relationship by regression analysis between expenditure on research and development per faculty in a university and the quality of the education which it provides, there would be no reason to investigate further. In both these cases it is very likely that a relationship can be found. Assuming this to be the case, at least with respect to universities, one might proceed to design an experiment as follows.

I consider only the simplest type of experiment to indicate the sort of thing I mean. Suppose we consider two types of department: physics and psychology. Let us select four universities each of which has both types of department. Two of these could be randomly selected for supplementary support for research in physics, and the other two would receive supplementary support for research in psychology. Achievement tests could be given to students in both departments in all four universities before the grants were made, and periodically over the life of the grant, say, five years. Initial differences in quality of students could be taken into account in the analysis of the results. By extending the experiment to involve different sizes of research grants, thus involving more universities and more subjects, it would be possible to determine the educational yield of varying amounts spent on research, by subject-matter. The design could be constructed so that no university feels slighted. Nothing would be done to prevent departments involved from seeking additional sources of research support during the experimental period.

Experiments could be conducted to compare the productivity of different kinds of research establishment, and to evaluate various mixes of fundamental and applied research. One could go on in this vein indefinitely. The point is that most developed countries are already spending a great deal in the support of science and technology, but they are *not* doing so in such a way as to obtain a better basis for future policy making than they have at present. If experimental designs are used as a basis for the allocation of national resources to science and technology, feedback can lead to adaptation, and gradually improving policy making can be expected while basic understanding of science, if not the nation, is being accumulated.

The most successful application of operations research to an industrial company of which I am aware has followed just this pattern. The major problems of this company were originally in the area of marketing. At first, very small and simple experiments were designed which involved minimal disruption of normal company practices. The results were immediately useful and productive. Confidence in the method developed slowly and, as it did, more and more marketing policies were implemented so as to permit their experimental evaluation. Today, every change in marketing policy is experimentally evaluated, even where the models extracted from previous work are used to select the policy to be employed. Each month, the marketing policies that are applied to each of about 200 markets are fed into a model of that area, yielding a prediction of its sales. At the end of the month, actual sales are compared with the prediction. If the deviation is larger than would be expected from chance alone, a study is launched to determine the reason for the deviation. When the reason is found, adjustments in the model of the market are made if necessary. Research is continued until the reasons are found. In this way the market models are constantly being improved, thus producing not only better predictions, but also a better basis for selecting policy in each area.

It has taken almost eight years to reach this stage in the company. The returns have far exceeded the cost. In a recent public address, the general manager of the company attributed to its planning savings of $45,000,000 in operating costs last year. This was about 10 per cent of its gross sales. In the same period, the company had the largest increase of sales and profits in its history, and larger than any company in its industry has ever had.

Other companies, and certainly national governments, have as much intelligence as has the company to which I refer. But the company has one thing that few other companies and fewer governments have when it comes to policy making: *guts*. There is no riskless way of making progress, not even in science. Therefore, although the skills required to develop the knowledge needed to do better policy making in national science policy are available, it is not at all clear that the courage to use these skills is. Until it is, discussions such as these can be little more than academic.

BIBLIOGRAPHY

The reader is referred to the following publications, and also to the references contained therein:

Churchman, C. W., and Ackoff, R. L. (1955). Operational accounting and operations research. *The Journal of Accountancy*, **99** : **2**, 53–59.

Churchman, C. W., Ackoff, R. L., and Arnoff, E. L. (1957). *Introduction to Operations Research*. New York: Wiley.

Churchman, C. W. (1961). *Prediction and Optimal Decision*. Englewood Cliffs, N. J.: Prentice-Hall.

Ackoff, R. L. (1966). Specialized versus generalized models in research budgeting. In *Research Program Effectiveness*, pp. 171–185, ed. Yovits, M. C., *et al*. New York: Gordon and Breach.

Ackoff, R. L. (1966). The meaning of strategic planning. *The McKinsey Quarterly*, Summer issue, 48–61.

DISCUSSION

Adams: I find Professor Ackoff's advocacy of experiments very attractive, although I consider that simulations made with a rough computable model would be less upsetting to the community than live experiments. However, supposing that one does an experiment of this kind, the problem I foresee is that—by analogy with, say, plant-breeding experiments, where there is a great number of factors that can influence the final result—one must carry out control experiments simultaneously. Have control experiments been carried out in parallel with the experiments made so far, so that one can be sure that the final effects are related to the right causes?

Ackoff: This is the principal problem in the design of experiments. Fortunately, R. A. Fisher provided a way out: statistical experimental design and the analysis of covariance. For example, suppose one wants to study the effect of advertising on sales. Advertising certainly has a small influence, compared with the combination of all the other factors which affect sales—availability, price, competitive behaviour, and so on. One has to develop a way of forecasting sales which takes into account the uniqueness of the particular unit to be examined. The better that forecast is, the better off you are. This can frequently be based on regression analysis. Then, one measures the deviation of the performance from the prediction. This makes it possible, with experiments in twenty more or less metropolitan areas, to detect changes in sales, due to changes in advertising, of as little as two per cent, 95 per cent of the time.

4*

Adams: I can see that your method will work well if the initial investment is close to the final product and to its sales, but will it work as far back as an investment in research and development, where many factors may mask the effect of the original investment?

Ackoff: Not yet. But we are designing such an experiment now.

Adams: I wonder if you have been able to alter any of the many assumptions made in the operations of large organizations and to measure the effect of such alterations?

Ackoff: Yes, we have. In fact, only experimentation allows one to do that. Because experiments are done under controlled conditions and can be restricted to a fairly small part of the system, managers and administrators who would never allow one to test assumptions on the system as a whole, will sometimes allow one to test their assumptions on a small part of the system.

Rahman: An attempt was made in India to find out the items of equipment that various Indian laboratories would like to import, in four fields— namely defence-orientated work, items relevant to export activity, those relevant to substitution of imports, and those needed for attacking the food problem. We obtained a large list of the equipment that each laboratory wanted, and found that when they indicated the order of priority in any of these four fields, the status aspect of the equipment had greatest weight.

Secondly, with regard to the experimental method, we have found in India that when a recommendation is made by scientists on the basis of a study of the existing situation, the final decision may totally ignore such a study or analysis of the situation. For instance, we made a study for the Fourth Five-Year Plan of the Council of Scientific and Industrial Research and reached a certain figure for the requirement for industrial research in the country. At the end, the Planning Commission—totally ignoring the work of its Working Group, which had recommended a sum of 1,640 million rupees—recommended for the Fourth Five-Year Plan of the Council 460 million rupees, on a rather *ad hoc* basis. This result affected the scientific community adversely, because they felt that the exercise was quite irrelevant and unnecessary and that all that matters is that one has the right approach to the people who decide, in order to get the allocation one wants. So I would agree very much with Professor Ackoff that science has to be considered in terms of a total social system and the budget of a country if one is to understand the situation.

Shimshoni: Whether you use regression analysis or another kind of analysis, the dependent variable seems to be what one is interested in. What kind of work has been done, and with what results, on assessing output in quantifiable terms in cases where one wants to measure outputs which have no simple or "coefficient" relation to such available data as sales and profits? With the great number of laboratories in the world, there is perhaps a chance of making a cross-sectional analysis, if one could find a way of measuring their output.

Ackoff: The nearest thing to measurement of the non-monetary output of research and development of which I am aware is measurement of the output of educational programmes by the use of achievement test scores. Few are satisfied with this measure, yet most feel that it has some relevance. The effort has focused attention on improving these tests so that they better measure the kind of achievement that is felt to be relevant. Achievement tests could be used in fields other than education; such tests have been used to determine how much knowledge scientists have in fields other than their own. Such measures are by no means perfect, but neither are the initial measures normally used in industry. However, we have to start by making our measures explicit, however imperfect they are, so that they can be criticized; with public discussion, there is some hope for improvement; as long as evaluation consists of some kind of unconscious mental gyration, there is no way of systematically improving it.

Foster: Many people have studied how one might measure scientific output; for example, much work has been done on the output of papers, by means of citation analysis (see Price, D. J. de S. [1965]. Networks of scientific papers. *Science*, **149**, 510–515). Of course, there is the obvious difficulty of differences in quality between papers. At the other end of the spectrum, much work has been done on whether there is a statistical relationship between input into research, in terms of expenditure, and the profitability of a firm, but this is complex and difficult to show.

Ackoff: This is why I made the remarks I did about regression analysis. We have found that in some cases expenditures on research and development regress better on *past* sales than future sales do on these expenditures. This is not surprising, if one knows how budgets are prepared. This example shows the danger of relying on regression analysis to establish causal connexions.

Weinberg: During the course of the meeting so far, we have travelled through ninety degrees. The line of thinking represented by Professor Ackoff and Mr. Foster—which I find perfectly fascinating and extraordinary —is orthogonal to the point of view I expressed in my paper. If I can use Professor Ackoff's "guts" analogy, the philosopher looks on this as a visceral problem—a question of values—whereas Professor Ackoff and

Mr. Foster regard science policy as a cerebral issue. This is as sharp a difference as it is possible to have, and it is reassuring that this difference should have come out so clearly, because I think that our discussion should centre on these two different assessments of the problem.

As I look at Professor Ackoff's diagram (p. 86), I see very many "gut" kind of assumptions implied in it. In the first place, there is a single box called "science and technology". Does this mean that "science and technology" are visualized as a *whole*? Some of us, including Dr. Adams, I think, reject this notion of science and technology as an entity. Again, how does a flow diagram of this sort help Mr. Carey in the Bureau of the Budget to decide whether to give the seven thousand million dollars for sending a man to Mars? Thus in general, much as I am impressed by the ingenuity of systems analysis in reducing the allocation problem to a matter of cerebration, I think that the "gut" issue of *value* remains untouched by such cerebral pyrotechnics. Let me say that I realize that this elephant is vast and complicated and that we are all blindly groping over different parts of the creature. Those of us who have been running the circus establishments perhaps incline to handling what we think is the "guts" of the elephant, but we shall try to retain open minds on your method of approach!

Ackoff: We are too easily discouraged by the apparent complexity of the science system and the social system of which it is a part. One can take any "box" in my chart and expand it into a flow diagram more complicated than mine. In so doing, we might be ignoring an important lesson to be derived from the history of science: the less we understand something, the more variables we require to explain it. Consequently, it is useful to start as simply as possible and to see how far we can go with how little, rather than to start by seeing how little we can accomplish with how much. This is a matter of research style. It reminds me of advice given in medical schools: if you are confronted with a patient who has one of two possible diseases, one incurable and about which you cannot do anything, and the other one that you can treat, do not hesitate—treat it. It seems to me that the position that Professor Weinberg is taking is that the disease is incurable, so let us forget about it. I am suggesting that there is an alternative.

Weinberg: We have ample precedents in the past of doing fairly successful social engineering without making your type of analysis. Consider the Land Grant Colleges, which worked magnificently and are probably more responsible than any other single factor for the great success of American agriculture. We did not have flow diagrams, but we got the Land Grant Colleges.

Ackoff: One could find at least equal evidence of failure in the absence of analysis.

Adams: If it is at all possible, I am in favour of using models. However, in my paper I tried to emphasize that science is more part of the whole activity of a society than an activity in its own right. In this respect I think I differ a little from Professor Ackoff, who appears to regard education and industrial production, for example, as activities separate from science and technology. Surely all these are part of society and science is part of them.

Ackoff: There is no point of difference. You may be right about the model, but I do not know that it is deficient before using it. In research one works through a whole series of models. The final one seldom has any resemblance to the original. Your suggestion may provide the direction in which the model should be modified. One might also decompose education into primary, secondary and higher levels; such things must be considered as one goes along. However, I would argue that the first model should be the simplest conceivable one and one should see how far one can go with it.

Adams: I agree with that completely.

Shimshoni: Professor Weinberg mentioned the Land Grant Colleges. This idea had tremendous impact, but it was probably the "county agent" system and the political sophistication used in persuading farmers to accept the results of the Land Grant Colleges that seem to have had the largest effect.

It might be useful to look at the question of the use of models, analysis and quantification in deciding on research in the following way. There are probably three kinds of people, or three kinds of roles, concerned. First, there are those who have to make decisions quickly. They range from politicians, who often have to decide on the spur of the moment, to administrators, who may have a little longer. The second role is that of those who are analysing research—for example, by developing and trying models. The third role is assumed by those who are creative in a technical sense—the scientists or engineers or those directly involved in supervising their work.

There will be much feedback from this third group to those analysing the process of research. Also, those directly involved in the technical creative process have not always the time, any more than the politicians or administrators, to wait for the results of such an analysis.

The approaches of the practitioner of science and the analyst of science are naturally different—but are not antagonistic. There is room for both. Indeed, a systems analysis will often indicate the exact places where additional research is needed.

Bernal: I am very impressed by Professor Ackoff's paper; he has introduced a new dimension into the discussion. What Professor Ackoff referred to as "guts", I prefer to think of as "horse sense". His work is highly sophisticated operational analysis on a mathematical level, but he comes round to the point of view which could be reached more simply by "horse sense". I do not know whether "horse sense" includes the "guts", but obviously they belong to the same animal and both are needed.

Ackoff: On this distinction between science and what Professor Bernal calls "horse sense", others would call "common sense" and I refer to as "guts", I have always been struck by how uncommon common sense is. Also, it has the very curious property of being more correct retrospectively than prospectively. It seems to me that one of the principal criteria to be applied to successful science is that its results are almost always obvious retrospectively; unfortunately, they seldom are prospectively. Common sense provides a kind of ultimate validation *after* science has completed its work; it seldom anticipates what science is going to discover. I would agree that science and common sense have to interact. The dichotomy is unfortunate. To use it is like assuming that the head and tail of a coin can be separated because we can look at them or talk about them separately. The difference between a great scientist and a poor scientist may lie more in his art and common sense than in the methodology he uses.

BRIEFING THE DECISION MAKER: A SIMULATION APPROACH

Krauch: I would like to mention some experimental work being done by West Churchman and others at the University of California at Berkeley (Churchman, C. West, Kohler, B., and Krauch, H. [1967]. *Experiments on inquiring systems*. Report of the Social Sciences Group, Space Sciences Laboratory, University of California). It is a simulation of three modes of preparing decisions, designed to find the optimal way of briefing the decision maker (a politician, a manager, or the public).

This programme started two years ago. At that time one of our larger sponsoring institutions in Germany wanted to make a decision whether to spend money on research on automation. There were two opposing proposals. Both agreed that research must be done, but they proposed completely differing ways. The foundation was thoroughly undecided and called in a number of experts. At the same time, we set up a laboratory simulation of the relevant power structure. We simulated German industry, different types of university professors, a union leader, and representatives of the foundation. We wrote a scenario embodying the two proposals. We arranged a group of judges to observe the game.

This simulation was run three times in differing modes. First, we instructed the role-players to create an ordinary rational debate. The second mode was a little more sophisticated, more psychodynamic; it was an ordinary polite debate. In the third case, we instructed the role-players to fight and to try to smash the underlying assumptions of their opponents. The results were quite striking. The judges said that only the third approach really enlightened them and enabled them to make a decision.

From a practical point of view, it was interesting to learn from this experiment that in reality nothing would happen. About a year later, negotiations started, and it turned out that automation is not a very pressing problem in Germany; industry and the unions drew back and did nothing. This was identical with the outcome of the experiment. Secondly, the experiment showed that industry would be afraid to lose qualified manpower in electronics. The third finding was that German university professors have a strong interest in getting small sums of money for research distributed to their chairs, but not in starting a new major effort, with a new centralized institute.

About a year ago a larger programme was started which has been running now for several months in the laboratory of the School of Business Administration in Berkeley. Here our decision-making problem is the allocation of government funds for research and development in the United States, and our subjects are students of the Business School; in addition, we broadcast these presentations over a local radio station and asked the public to participate, of whom 320 joined in.

Again, the dialectical or Hegelian type of logical structure was judged to be most effective in instructing and in revealing the underlying assumptions, as can be seen from Table I.

Table I

JUDGMENTS BY 320 PARTICIPANTS IN THE EXPERIMENT "RESEARCH AND BROADCAST" CARRIED OUT AT BERKELEY, CALIFORNIA, IN FEBRUARY 1967

Programme I was a monologue by an expert, programme II was an ordinary "polite" debate, and programme III was a dialectical presentation. Programmes II and III were balanced out in information content, length and sequence. Participants who listened to more than one programme gave the judgments shown.

	Programme I (Percentage)	Programme II (Percentage)	Programme III (Percentage)
The most informative programme was	27·6	36·4	36·0
The most interesting programme was	15·5	38·1	46·4
The clearest interpretation of the information was given in	23·8	36·7	39·5
The programme that best revealed the underlying assumptions was	20·7	27·9	51·4

In our laboratory experiments, all subjects are first tested for social and educational background, knowledge of the issue and general political awareness. We then put them in a small room in front of a teletype unit, where they listen to one of the programmes. One group listens to the ordinary, rational debate; the next to a polite debate; and the last group listens to the hot, dialectical type of debate. All presentations use the same data-base of research and development statistics and similar information. The difference between the ordinary debate and the dialectical debate is as follows. Speaker A in the ordinary debate selects a piece of the data-base and makes his optimal case out of it. The other speaker, B, without referring too much to this, picks another piece of the data-base and makes his optimal case out of it, and so they proceed. In the dialectical debate, A picks out the first piece of the data-base and makes his optimal case, then B picks the *same piece* of the data-base and argues in exactly the opposite way, making the best point for his position. In addition to that, he tries to destroy the underlying ideology of the opponent. And so they proceed by building thesis and antithesis, destroying and building up a synthesis. The testing is not yet finished but the first results suggest that there is again a significant difference between the modes of presentation.

This and other kinds of simulations can be used to anticipate future situations and to improve the decision-making process.

DECISION MAKING IN RESEARCH POLICY
AT THE INDUSTRIAL LEVEL

A. E. PANNENBORG

Philips Research Laboratories, Eindhoven, The Netherlands

B EFORE we embark on the discussion of what research to do—the arguments that must influence the answers to this question making up the main part of this paper—it is important to examine why an industrial enterprise engages in research at all. But before doing this one should, if not define, at least outline, what is meant by research in industry.

An industrial firm cannot hope to continue to survive if it does not pay attention to the renewed, improved design of its products, or to the continuous modernization of its production methods, or to both aspects. This activity, directly related to the products and their manufacture, is generally called "development". The people engaged in it should have the engineer's creative urge to see things made.

Experience has taught modern man that basic changes and improvements often stem from newly discovered basic knowledge and insight. Nowadays it is recognized, even by the general public, that progress in technology leans heavily on the results of scientific discovery. Research in industry can contribute to technological progress through increased understanding; through the adaptation for use in engineering of results obtained in pure science; and through supplying new scientific results, when these are not readily forthcoming from other sources. Research is thus one of the possible tools with which an industrial enterprise tries to realize its aims. As I am not an economist or sociologist, I cannot pretend to be able to define these aims in detail, but continuity of employment for the workers and of profits for the shareholders—in other words, the continued existence of the enterprise as a whole—would certainly figure largely in the description of aims. This continuity will be determined by the position of the enterprise relative to its competitors—that is to say, ultimately by the kind, quality and price of its products. In the face of competition, an industrial enterprise will therefore strive to improve the variety and quality of its products and to lower their manufacturing price. This intention, weighed against the observed and expected rate of change of technology in the particular branch of industry, determines the decision of the management whether or not to embark on research.

Because of the complexity of modern science, research is expensive. If the size of the firm does not allow it to carry out its own research to sufficient depth, partnership with a number of firms in a research association is one possible solution. Another method, which avoids the permanent financial burden of a research laboratory, is to sponsor work in a non-profit-making research organization. However, the well-known difficulties of the process of transferring research results into development undoubtedly are considerably increased when applied research is carried out on behalf of a particular industry but not under its own direct management. The "not-invented-here" mentality is already difficult enough to suppress in the relationships between different departments within one firm!

The degree of organizational separation between research and development depends strongly on the type of industry. For example, in the process industries and in the automobile and aircraft industries, no clear-cut dividing line can be drawn, and this usually results in one laboratory organization dealing with the whole spectrum from research to design, whereas in the electrical and pharmaceutical industries, the distinction is desirable and warranted. The type of internal organizational structure influences the use a particular firm can make of outside research sponsored by it.

I shall now restrict myself to large industrial firms carrying out research, and examine the considerations which lead up to decisions about the research programme. It is logical that those scientific disciplines basic to the products or manufacturing methods of the firm in question should be represented in its research, embodied in scientists of sufficient standing to be recognized in the scientific world outside industry. The required standing can be maintained only if these scientists are able to work actively in their field. If there is a small group of scientists working in a particular subject area, it is advantageous to have both very basic and somewhat applied work going on at the same time.

Although in development work in industry all projects should be specified beforehand, in industrial research, a certain freedom for the individual scientist is essential, particularly for the mature, senior research worker. Here it is the task of the director of the laboratory to protect his staff against the ever-present demands of product-division managers.

In general, one of the most difficult aspects of research policy in industry is obtaining the correct balance between work done in order to safeguard an established product position for the future, and work directed towards the opening of new avenues. One might call this the strategy of choosing between the defensive approach and the offensive. In establishing the balance, it is essential to have the courage *not* to work, at least temporarily, in some areas. This means that it is important to observe carefully the rate of progress and the possible onset of saturation in the various relevant fields of basic or applied science, in order to stop work in time and to free research capacity for work in more promising areas.

It is difficult to describe in general terms what is meant here by "promising". One very clear instance is given by the indication of a major breakthrough in insight, in concept or in technology by one of the research workers or research groups within the organization. The swift exploitation of the consequences, with sufficient manpower, is desirable. One should take care not to assess as necessarily promising for one's own firm those scientific innovations that receive a maximum of publicity and consequently become fashionable in the scientific world, but where, with increasing frequency, it is being found that the industrial consequences cannot match the quality of the discovery.

Many problems of determining research policy can be reduced to the common problem of correct timing. We all know examples of first-class research results that had no real consequences in science and technology, because they were produced at too early a moment, in the context of the scientific community or society in general. Equally, it is hardly necessary to point out that an industrial firm is liable to die if it does not recognize in time the advent of a revolutionary change in one of the technologies that are vital to it. The real art of research management in industry is to achieve the correct balance between competence in the recognized important fields, and more speculative ventures, either into new territory or in anticipation of major changes. The choice has to be made within the limitations imposed by a finite potential of men and money.

This immediately raises the question of the most economical size of the research organization within a given company. Unlike the situation in development, however, the efficiency of research cannot be determined in a quantitative manner. This rules out an objective answer to the question of size. A factual comparison of competing firms is a yardstick frequently used, but one with evident inherent limitations.

Another consideration for industrial research policy is the subject of patents, so foreign to pure science and so essential to industrial research. Though contributions in the form of better processes or products, possibilities of major diversification, and a constant stream of expert advice to development groups, are the most important tasks in life for an industrial research department, it should also provide its firm with a patent position by which money can be derived from licences, and—more significantly—which allows freedom of manoeuvre in negotiations with other firms. This applies especially to the large industrial concern, which would be strangled in a jungle of patents if there were no way out in the form of cross-license agreements of general scope with its equally large competitors.

From my experience, a negotiating position in such a situation is assisted more by unassailable patent property in one small sector than by a large number of isolated patents spread over a wide subject area. This has an important consequence for industrial research policy: one should direct part of the research capacity of the concern to subject areas where "research competition" is weak or absent. If new and patentable results are obtained, one should continue the work, even for many years, disregarding the possible absence of a short-term application of its results.

A discussion of research policy would not be complete without reference to the role of the government as a sponsor of research. This role of government became a necessary and generally accepted one during the second world war for purposes of military research. After the war, government-paid research also became usual in nuclear energy and space technology. The tremendous scale of government-sponsored research in the United States and the leading position of its industry have induced Western European governments to draw conclusions about cause and effect, but there is no direct parallel, because in the United States most government money invested in research is given out to private industry, whereas in Western Europe the larger part is spent in government-run laboratories. The conclusion drawn is apparently that governments have a responsibility to support purely civilian research projects in private industry, in order to close the technological gap between Western Europe and the United States. But as long as this is done on a national basis it will lead only to the duplication of the British, French and German research programmes. As long as every European country considers it vital to be engaged in research in all the "prestige" areas of science and technology, the resulting fragmentation of the European research effort will give Europe no chance to break even in industrial output with the younger industrial powers in the world.

CONCLUSIONS

Research is carried out by industry as an additional (and sometimes essential) means to attaining its objectives, such as continuity of employment, profits for the shareholders and expansion of sales. In between research and production is the activity customarily called "development". Though there exist a great many definitions of industrial research as opposed to development—all open to controversy—one relevant observation points out the use of the scientific method (analysis) as essential to research, in contrast to the predominant use of engineering methods (synthesis) in development. The major tasks of the research laboratory in a private enterprise might be:

(1) Improvements in existing product lines, either by extrapolation from existing knowledge and experience or by new solutions of the original aim.

(2) Diversification.

(3) The creation of a patent position sufficient for the firm to be able to negotiate successfully with its competitors.

Research policy will be influenced by factors external to industry, such as the observed or expected high rate of progress in a particular branch of science or technology, but more often by typical industrial boundary conditions, such as the competitive position of the firm or the size of its profit margin.

One of the most dangerous habits in making research policy is to follow fashion in science. The chances of an important contribution or breakthrough by a particular research team are small in fields where armies of research workers all over the world are already engaged. Industrial research policy is often most aggressive in those firms not having a dominant market position.

DISCUSSION

Todd: It emerges from Dr. Pannenborg's paper that one can extend the problems of the industrial company to those of an entire industrialized country, because a country can be considered as a vast industrial complex which has to be looked at in the same way. His point about the habit of following the fashion in research, in particular the efforts now being made in several European countries to stimulate the economy by increasing government intervention, is also an important one. There is a strong tendency to concentrate on almost exactly the same areas of research.

Ackoff: Dr. Pannenborg said that research in a company cannot be evaluated; I think it has been evaluated. I know of at least four cases in which growth models of specific companies have been constructed and optimal allocations for research and development have been obtained. (See Dean, B. V., and Sengupta, S. S. [1962]. Research budgeting and project selection.

I.R.E. Transactions on Engineering Management, December, 158–169;
Ackoff, R. L. [1966]. Specialized versus generalized models in research
budgeting. In *Research Program Effectiveness*, pp. 171–185, ed. Yovits, M. C.,
et al. New York: Gordon and Breach.)

Pannenborg: Within a research laboratory engaged on scientific and
technological projects over a fairly wide front, it is essential to leave enough
freedom for "spontaneous mutations" in thought. In a laboratory organization which is entirely related to one large project, and where the transition between research and development is not a sharp one, one probably
can analyse the research organization on a cost or efficiency basis, but in
"Little Science", where the results of a piece of work are very often used
in completely unexpected directions, one cannot calculate the efficiency
and the quantitative usefulness of research.

Ackoff: But you have contradicted yourself! You have just predicted that
research will always produce an unpredicted result, and that fact alone can
be used in constructing a model. One cannot predict specifically *where* the
benefits will come, but one can predict that there will be benefits, and
what their frequency and magnitude will be. This is all that is required for
rational budgeting.

Pannenborg: I disagree that there is a comparison which can be expressed
quantitatively and meaningfully. Certain aspects of the whole research
operation make it impossible in principle—for example, the consultancy
role. Consultancy resulting in the prevention of abortive operations in the
product divisions can never be assessed, in principle, for its contribution to
the profits of the company.

Ackoff: There is a large area called "the economics of lost opportunities"
which directs itself to this problem. (See, for example, Churchman, C. W.,
and Ackoff, R. L. [1955]. Operational accounting and operations research.
The Journal of Accounting, **99**:2, 53–59.)

Dalyell: May I revert to the point raised by Mr. Freeman (p. 41), regarding the mechanism of shrinkage? I understand that Dr. Pannenborg finds
less of a problem in his enterprise in identifying when the saturation point
has been reached than Professor Weinberg finds in relation to a government enterprise, and I would like guidance on this. How should decisions
be made as to when the time has come for a mechanism of shrinkage? For
instance, by what mechanism would one decide that a government laboratory ought to be given a different "sense of mission", to use Professor
Weinberg's phrase?

Weinberg: I have rather a personal view on this. I agree with Dr. Pannenborg that every institution has an innate desire to survive, and this is per-

haps its strongest motivation. It is therefore difficult to ask it to commit suicide, or even to change its way of life. But one thing that could be most useful in the operation of government institutions would be to encourage management to identify as much as possible with the larger unit within which the institution works. This means that the directors of large government institutions should be as closely involved as possible in the actual establishment of a science policy, so that they not only bring to its formulation their own viewpoints and experience, but also temper their concern for the survival of their institutions with the larger needs of the society, as they sense them from their contacts at the higher level. The cabinet system of government was invented to handle this difficulty; the people responsible for the lower levels are brought into the higher levels, and thus when a decision is taken at a higher level the government has already brought along with them the people who will carry out the decision.

Pannenborg: The problem of reducing work in an area is two-fold. There is the recognition of the moment when to reduce work on certain lines, and the execution of the decision once it has been taken. Execution is fundamentally easier in industry than in government, because in industry it is usual to transfer scientists to more applied jobs—in development laboratories, sales departments, technical documentation—so that a reduction of staff in a certain area is made easier by the fact that the same area will often be continued for ten or twenty years in the manufacturing operations. The problem of dismissing personnel is therefore much less.

Adams: It may not be too difficult, as Professor Weinberg and Dr. Pannenborg have said, to determine when research should be decreased in government and industrial science, but in university science this problem is now taking a different form. Instead of a subject becoming played out, as has been suggested by Mr. Freeman, it is often difficult to take the next logical step because it costs too much. For example, the United States, Europe and the Soviet Union are now facing important decisions about the next stage in high-energy physics, which involves building accelerating machines in the energy range 200–1,000 Gev. There is no doubt that this research field is exciting and important and there is no shortage of brilliant physicists engaged in it. The difficulty is to justify the expense involved. We may find many fields of research cut off in their prime in the future simply because money is not forthcoming in sufficient quantity to continue them.

Carey: We have been discussing quantitative decisions; can Dr. Pannenborg say something about his approach to qualitative decisions—the judgments and measures by which one tells whether research in process is of high, average or marginal quality? Much of decision making is focused on questions of increments, while the *base* tends to be taken for granted, so that one is building on a "bedrock" which no-one penetrates systematically. Where does one begin to investigate it, and—to continue the analogy —when one has probed this bedrock, how does one judge what one has extracted? In the American system, when we talk blithely about financing 17 thousand million dollars' worth annually of something called research and development, the arguments focus upon the rate of acceleration and the amounts of additional investment and for *what*, whereas there are in reality considerable possibilities for substitution without increasing the total investment. We have found it very hard to develop an apparatus to produce these valuations. For one thing, few people want to do it, because few people want to become judges. Has this occurred to you in your system, and how do you deal with it?

Pannenborg: The size of an industrial unit of research is usually such that the responsible people at the top can form an opinion of the personal quality of the research workers, and this is probably quite different from your approach. You are working on a much larger scale, with such large quantities of money and so many people, that it would be difficult to make this qualitative judgment directly. In our laboratory we have a management group of 12 and a total complement of 2,200, and in the majority of cases we reach a unanimous opinion on the quality of a particular scientist. It has been said that—varying with the subject area but certainly on the more basic side of research—it is better to bet on the man than on the subject. Here, therefore, one will see a very pertinent decision-influencing aspect. In more applied work, it is usually more a question of a team of people, and one can consider the sales success—that is, the success with which research workers transfer their resources to their colleagues in development. From my own experience, these decisions are so strongly influenced by the people directly concerned that the subject of their research is almost secondary.

Carey: In other words, this becomes a question of peer judgments.

Saint-Geours: Dr. Pannenborg spoke of the objectives of the firm and said that one of the main problems is determining what is promising, but he did not mention the word "market". He appeared to assume that decisions flow from advances in research and technology to the product, but is it not true that often decisions flow from the product to the research? What is the part played by the commercial department in determining the research objectives of a firm?

Pannenborg: The answer differs for different branches of industry. I mentioned only in passing that in a very large organization it is vital for the research department not to be an "ivory tower". Everyone in a responsible position in research has the continuous task of maintaining interaction with the product divisions. In a firm producing professional equipment, interaction with the marketing experts, who are usually engineers themselves, is decisive. In firms making mass-produced consumer goods, research people try to keep salesmen far away, because the salesmen and even manufacturers of consumer goods tend to be so conservative and unimaginative that they would kill all research. Furthermore, mass-produced goods can more easily be judged by the public in general.

In this question of what is promising it is vital to consider not only markets, but also the objective technological and scientific standards, coupled with the patent position. I know several instances, not only in our own laboratory, where great perseverance has paid in the long run, because it pays to be alone on a line of investigation. In industry, if you are really alone, it usually means that you are more advanced; though the application is not seen so soon, you can usually build up a patent position which will be unbeatable when the application is finally achieved. We have sometimes carried through a project in the face of great doubts, and I think that this is the task of research in industry—to be independent and to persevere against resistance for perhaps decades. This holds for the industry of a country as a whole, too, and means that it may develop a specialization which is unbeatable in the world.

Saint-Geours: It depends on the branch, of course. In the pharmaceutical industry, for example, the needs of the market play an important role in determining decisions.

Szalai: Research is an activity where even with the best people, the "spin-off" is often much more important than the immediate results. For instance, I do not know how scientifically useful putting a man on the moon is, but the miniaturization and sub-miniaturization that has come out of the project is very relevant. There is also the *invisible* "spin-off" which can become visible. In smaller countries the question often arises of whether to do some not very basic research or to buy a licence. In Hungary, in one period we bought very few licences to manufacture, and it proved very expensive, because of the cost of research needed to re-invent in another form what has already been invented elsewhere. Then we began buying licences, but this proved to be expensive in another way. If people work on a problem—whether they solve it cheaply or expensively or do not solve it at all—they acquire a certain problem-solving ability. By buying a licence you buy the product of research, but you cannot buy this invisible "spin-off" of problem-solving "know-how", and when the same people have to solve another problem, this knowledge is lacking. We have this situation in many small countries.

Todd: Of course, you might buy licences and put the people to work on something else. Is that not basically the way in which the Japanese got started?

Szalai: Yes; but my point is that if you buy licences you will have a great problem in maintaining an adequate level of "know-how".

Bernal: We have talked a lot about motivated research, but we have not talked about other aspects, particularly how the discoveries in fundamental science are applied. A discovery of a new principle might have many applications in various industries, but there seems to be no mechanism for seeing that this happens. Ideas are put forward in scientific publications and there is no way in which it is seen to that industry takes up their application. It requires quite a different kind of work from that of following up a scientific problem.

Ackoff: Professor Bernal has raised an important point about the dissemination of the output of fundamental science into the culture. This is a problem to which some institutional efforts have recently been directed in the United States. Several government agencies have been created for disseminating to the public at large, and to industry in particular, information attained through fundamental research supported by the government. The National Aeronautics and Space Administration has set up regional centres for the dissemination of some of its fundamental research output to industry.

GENERAL DISCUSSION

Rexed: If one looks at the allocation of resources to science from the point of view of decisions made by governments, one comes to a viewpoint rather similar to that of Dr. Adams in the discussion of Professor Ackoff's paper (p. 95). It is not really useful to think about the money available for science as one large pot of gold and to try to find priorities to allocate it. It is useful, rather, to try to sort out various scientific activities, especially applied and developmental activities, in connexion with the fundamental functional areas of social importance to which they are related. For instance, defence research is naturally related to military security, and one can allow the part of government which deals with the one to decide about spending on the other. In the same way, responsibility for research on transport systems can be given to the ministry dealing with communications generally. They can then view the possibilities in transport research and development as part of the long-term planning of that area.

Again, as a beginning, we should apply the principle that no research and development should be done unless a systems analysis shows that research will give a greater possibility for improvement than any other change in the total system—maybe rationalization, maybe a new road—could provide. Only if a comparative analysis of all the possible ways to correct the situation shows that research is the most valuable one, in the short and long term, should one engage on it. But I feel that no department except that having executive responsibility in the field can decide.

When research has been divided up among various functional areas, such as health, transport and energy production, there will be a residue of research which cannot be so allocated, and this will be the research that is usually combined with education. Even here, one can begin to ask what the minimum requirement of research is, even if one cannot state the optimum requirement.

In this way, one reaches a definition of the research and developmental work needed for a country. The final science and development budget will then be an addition of all these sums, rather than a division of some initial sum of money.

To take Professor Weinberg's example, he said that the decision to spend millions of dollars to send a man to the moon, which he called the most important scientific decision made since the war in the United States, was taken with almost no debate by the scientific community. But perhaps it was not necessary, because the decision was not primarily a scientific one. The only thing needed to be known from the scientists was whether the project was scientifically and technically feasible. The rest was a purely political decision. If for political reasons of prestige and military reasons you have enough arguments to put a man on the moon, and to bear the cost, you should do it. The scientific community had little to add in one or other direction in this decision. This means that this part of the budget was rather irrelevant to other parts, because that money could not be exchanged for something else. For instance, even if one part of the community had objected to the moon project and said that the same sum should be given to sociology—clearly, there was no chance of this! You need a different kind of reasoning for obtaining money to stimulate sociology.

In conclusion, I feel that one can take functionally related areas and in principle apply the thinking of Professor Ackoff and Mr. Foster to them. I hope that some countries, perhaps Sweden, will start to do this.

Todd: You say that one should not think of a "pot of gold" to be divided up among various competing claims. However, there *is* a limit to the amount of money that a government is prepared to spend on science. If it were decided on political grounds to put a man on the moon, then because of the state of the national budget, in Britain at least, one would find that requests for large sums for other purposes would be refused because of the amount of "science and technology" already being done through the moon project. There may not be a pot of gold to divide up among science, but without some coherent way of conveying to government the relative virtues of the various ways in which money could be spent on science, we shall get nowhere at all.

Rexed: That is true. There is also a certain limited manpower resource, in a small country at least, and if a large part of it is devoted to one problem there is less for anything else. On the other hand, if a country really feels the need to do something, it has ways of *increasing* its resources, and it is one of the skills of the politicians to get hold of those resources in order to achieve the political goals. In other words, I do not want to suggest that resources are unlimited—of course they are not—but it is a more flexible situation than a simple division of something finite. First, one must force the politicians to fix the social goals to be attained—this is very close to Professor Weinberg's point—and then one must reason from these fixed social goals how to solve the problem, whether by reform or by research. Incidentally, this is very much the kind of reasoning that Professor Bernal used in his classic book *The Social Functions of Science*. It is an interesting case of the importance of philosophers in this field of analysis.

Todd: I do not attempt to deny the need to set social goals; but as things stand, if these things are not said explicitly, we shall find ourselves in the position that one would be in if there really were a finite sum to be divided.

Dalyell: Professor Rexed says that politicians should be forced to select their goals. If this is a central argument, I wonder how he thinks this can be done in a small country? I can understand that in large countries like the Soviet Union or the United States, major goals can be fixed, and perhaps this is a good argument for forming a European technological community. However, in terms of a relatively small country, one must be more explicit about what one is asking of the politicians.

Rexed: I meant only that in many developed countries today politicians seem often to be relegated to a secondary level of importance. They are very much in the hands of the technologists—using the word in the broadest sense to include sociologists, economists, engineers and medical men. These people with special skills produce a number of alternatives and according to their own choices, they press certain of these alternatives on the politician, who has to choose rather quickly among these and often for rather short-term reasons. This is perhaps only a tendency so far, but there is a real risk that political life will degenerate into something like this. Very rarely do you see a politician who can transform his party politics into a humanitarian vision. Of course, one does not look upon politicians as specialists; they are the representatives of all citizens and therefore should try to discover the basic needs of the population that they represent. In any community, large or small, there are social goals that seem of primary importance to every citizen. This is something that the present situation asks of the politician and if the present trend continues, one wonders what will happen to political parties in the future.

Braun: If we took a few broad national goals and tried to rate them as the governments of our countries would, we should find quite different orders of priority for each country. We might take goals such as nutritional levels, community health, national security, housing standards, transport facilities, economic growth and national prestige. From these priorities will evolve the "market research", or assessment of national needs, for science. Before shooting off scientists to do scientific work, one should first see where to aim! The present system is that one takes a slice from the total budget, converts it into scientific bullets, shoots into the air and hopes to hit a few birds. Sometimes one hits, but the shooting becomes so expensive that it cannot easily be stopped. If space programmes, for example, were stopped, the respective economies would be affected; hence it seems that one cannot afford to stop.

Our task is therefore first to get a clearer picture of national goals; then to use the national goals as guidance in the assessment of needs for scientific endeavour; and then to reconcile these needs with each other and arrive at some priority rating. One could then try to relate these goals or these scientific objectives to the qualified manpower, the technological facilities, the capital of a country, and the time it has available, as well as its special favourable conditions. There are many small countries which could contribute to research by exploiting their natural and climatic conditions—Peru has been able to do high-altitude research, for example. Even very poor countries have some special condition on which research can be done, without having to imitate the great powers. But national goals should be the first consideration.

Carey: One can economize, even internationally, in reaching these goals. Every country would give high priority to research on food or health or transport or economic growth, yet some countries are far more advanced in their technological and scientific development and are producing results on such a scale that they ought to be transferable. The international dialogue should concern itself with this. Also, what can be afforded will vary from nation to nation. Dr. Braun refers to the consequences of abandoning, let us say, the programme for putting a man on the moon. That would not necessarily induce an economic setback, if there were a substitutable effort. In the advanced countries we have no shortage of these alternatives, and we have an urge to embark on all of them—urban technology, water research, oceanography, weather modification, and so on. I have no doubt whatever that our aerospace capability and investment could be re-programmed readily and fully towards alternative goals. What bothers me very much is the thought that each country takes a nationalistic view of science and technology, and supposes that it must create its own capability and start from scratch to solve all problems.

Whitehead: An attempt has recently been made to predict, as an experiment, the growth of research and development expenditure in Canada for the next ten years or so (see p. 173). It was extrapolated from past growth trends to take into account the relative social and economic needs for research in the various scientific disciplines. It even synthesized projects of various sizes and considered the continuity of growth of research in individual departments, even in individual establishments.

Assumptions with regard to specific future programmes were purely hypothetical, but the model thus created served two very useful purposes. It showed that the limits within which future growth might occur were not as wide as might be anticipated, because there are many constraints upon it. It also showed the kind of decisions which would be needed in the creation of some sort of national plan for research and development. It served to illustrate what could be done, given real plans and real projects.

Carey: In the United States, politicians are certainly not reticent about promoting new ventures in science and technology. I can think of a number of Senators and members of the House of Representatives who, single-handed, have succeeded in persuading the executive to invest in projects— in experimental technology; in high-speed rail transportation, to cope with the problem of massive concentrations of people; in noise as a social nuisance; in harvesting the sea; in weather modification; in population control; in creating a social science foundation with government funds. There is a passionate interest by many politicians in Congress, who are exerting pressure and who serve as an action-forcing influence on decision making and on public investment. Whether this is a phenomenon of a country that does not know what to do with all its wealth, I do not know.

SCIENCE POLICY IN MIXED ECONOMIES

FRANCE'S SCIENTIFIC POLICY

J. Saint-Geours

Ministry of Finance, Paris

T HE urgent necessity in recent years to speed up and reorganize the research effort in France has led both government and administration to try to state the options of scientific policy before having been able to think sufficiently about the problems created by the determination of such choices. Moreover, such "theoretical thinking"—by which I mean thinking not grounded in the experience proceeding from action— probably would have proved to be of little help. To introduce into practice a completely new concept, disputed by some people, required action of a rather high degree of complexity or, more precisely, it had to harmonize elements which were highly heterogeneous, on account of both their intrinsic nature and the position of those holding the power of de- cision—that is, to harmonize research for military purposes, fundamental research, industrial research, and so on.

INSTITUTIONS CONCERNED IN SCIENCE POLICY

To understand how the choices are actually made and how the main trends of France's scientific policy are defined, it may be useful to offer some information about French institutional complexity.

The bodies involved are numerous and their procedures very various. At the ministerial level, seven or eight departments supervise research centres; however, the main responsibility is shared by four departments. Within the limits of the total appropriations defined in a long-term programme, the Ministry of Defence has wide freedom of action for its research policy, given the military missions decided upon at the top level. This research may be done in centres belonging to the Ministry, in public agencies, or through agreements with private industries.

The Ministry of National Education is responsible for the main part of fundamental research. Historically, research activity is not separated from educational activity. As an establishment of higher education, the university includes numerous laboratories. On the other hand, the Centre National de la Recherche Scientifique, an agency quite close to the universities, has more than a hundred laboratories and gives diversified support to scientific research. As a high percentage of research finance originates from public funds, the Ministry of Economy and Finance is directly concerned with this, not only on account of the State's annual budget, but also because it plays a part in the definition of the middle-term programme, generally when the (five-year) Plan for scientific research is prepared. Thus the volume of aid to fundamental research and to the development of research in industry is determined for five years.

The Ministry of Research is also concerned with general policy concerning research, particularly as the Commissariat à l'Energie Atomique and the Centre National d'Études Spatiales are linked to it.

At the ministerial level it is thus clear that responsibilities are shared according to the traditional functions of the ministries, and that harmonizing goals and the means for achieving them naturally is not easy. It seemed necessary, therefore, to create administrative authorities with both general and co-ordinating functions. The first is a standing administrative body whose duty is to propose the general guide-lines of research (excluding military research): this is the Délégation Generale à la Recherche Scientifique et Technique, responsible to the Ministry of Research. Its general function is carried out in two ways: on the one hand, it is concerned with decisions on the financing of 24 "combined activities"* and aid to industrial development; on the other hand, it works as the secretariat of the three principal co-ordinating and programme-establishing agencies.

These agencies intervene at clearly distinct levels of scientific policy. The Plan's Research Commission, consisting of civil servants, scientists, manufacturers and trades union leaders, has two functions: it prepares the elements of a middle-term scientific policy, and defines equipment programmes for civil public scientific research and the financing of the combined activities for which the Research Development Fund is responsible; it makes a synthesis of the research needs of various sectors of the national economy, above all the military, nuclear and space programmes. The Commission is specially active during the time when the Plan is formulated.

In contrast, the Consultative Committee works continuously. It is concerned with formulating suggestions or advice for the government

---

Actions concertées—in which research workers and users of research results are brought together in certain fields.

about any problem concerning scientific and technical research: programmes, organization, and so on.

Lastly, the Inter-ministerial Committee for Research, the supreme body as far as orientation and decision are concerned, links together the relevant ministers, the Commissaire Général du Plan, the Delegate General for Research, and the President of the Consultative Committee, under the presidency of the Prime Minister. It must be added that, in fact, some particularly important decisions are taken by the Head of State in a restricted Council.

Such a large institutional system is intended to assist the exchange of information, to co-ordinate the efforts undertaken, and to make the general and particular choices in the field of national science policy.

GUIDING PRINCIPLES OF SCIENCE POLICY

What is the general principle guiding these choices? French science policy tries to reconcile the freedom of research workers and manufacturers and the government's will. The nature of the economic and political system, in which creative thought, initiative and decision making are fairly decentralized, accounts for such freedom. It is justified by the fruitfulness of many independent, competing efforts. The intervention of the government is nonetheless justifiable, since it is in charge of the nation's independence and economic development, and is the only authority which can raise the resources required.

It is not easy to delimit the freedom of private activities that are not bound to obey the imperatives of a national policy. The context within which this freedom is exercised is, roughly speaking, the university laboratories and private firms. By setting forth their requirements, by contributing to the working out of the Fifth Plan, and by their very existence, these institutions have a direct impact on science policy. Accordingly, science policy often proves to be much less a choice favouring one type of research work against another, than the reconciliation, within given financial limits, of competing scientific or industrial interests. Scientists and manufacturers—the former more than the latter—enjoy great freedom when it comes to the use of the means put at their disposal. Accounts are seldom rendered, or they lack precision. Also, a great part of industrial research is in the competitive field: it is free, autonomous and secret.

Nevertheless, the determination by the (five-year) Plan of the overall amount of public resources allocated to different types of research project —the so-called "research envelope" (*enveloppe recherche*)—provides an opportunity for defining the main guiding lines and for assessing current efforts. A first significant determining factor is the influence of existing research teams. A second is the fact that certain research projects have a strategic character—that is, that the advances and the results obtained can be used for various purposes. Though this criterion is not formulated explicitly, we can observe that, as a rule, preference is given to research projects related to expanding economic branches. Defence interests also have a great impact. Finally, the wish to improve fundamental knowledge about man and matter plays a prominent part in determining allocations.

I think personally that it is hardly possible to give a more systematic formulation and to show a stricter rationality when making these choices. Government decisions will be more strongly grounded and will have greater impact, the more costly is the apparatus to be supported. Of course, the shortage of financial resources eliminates highly expensive research projects in favour of the less costly ones which may be especially interesting. But we can observe also that when big schemes occupy a substantial place this may be to the detriment of more profitable research.

In the field of civil fundamental research, the branches considered in the Fifth Plan as the most useful to the advancement of knowledge are the following:

The exploration of the world: inert and living matter, astronomy, the atmosphere, the oceans, the earth's crust and core:

Technical development to meet the increasing requirements of quality and adaptation to severe conditions of employment;

Improvement of the conditions of human life: health, education, environment;

Techniques for collecting, transmitting and processing data; automation and control techniques.

Applied mathematics, physics and chemistry receive 50 per cent of the resources allocated nationally. Earth sciences, oceanography and agronomic research together receive 22 per cent. The biological, medical and human sciences also receive 22 per cent.

Within these fields, 80 per cent of the appropriations is allocated to the establishments proper; and 20 per cent, in view of the 24 "combined activities", goes to support, under contract, continuing research programmes at institutions that are already equipped. The programme of each activity is drawn up by a scientific committee composed of independent representatives.

However, we should emphasize strongly the prominent place taken by large public programmes with a political significance, apart from the "research envelope" described already. On the whole, the resources needed by these programmes appear to be much higher. Among such programmes we must distinguish between what belongs to fundamental research proper and what pertains to the field of industrial production—prototypes, standardized non-profit-making production, and profit-making production. All this is extremely hard to determine. When research expenses can be isolated we observe that the proportion corresponding to research—strictly speaking—is *comparatively* small (as in space research), and in certain cases (as in aeronautic research), *very* small.

The four branches demanding the highest appropriations are atomic energy, defence, aeronautics and space research. Until recently, they were supported mainly for political reasons of national security, of autonomy and of prestige, and not in order to promote the advance of researches which could be useful from other points of view. In the past few years, however, greater attention has been paid to the following three points: the impact of such large programmes on the general economic balance; the direct economic profitability of such programmes, including estimated future profitability; and the significance of these programmes for the advancement of knowledge and technology. It is hoped thus to establish a relationship between these efforts and the development of industry. Efforts are now being made to quantify this.

In 1966, the government became interested in supporting industrial research more directly than by the expensive by-way of these big public programmes: it now takes part in financing the development of the results of such research. Those firms which carry out an operation considered as promising but uncertain, may obtain assistance, in the form of subsidies refundable if the operation is successful, of up to 50 per cent of the development outlay. Although the initiative is usually with the industrial units, such a procedure is used to a certain extent to direct the achievements of industry. In this respect, some preferential areas on which to concentrate resources have been listed by the Minister of Research, the Minister of Industry, and the Minister of Economy and Finance, based upon industrial policy as defined in the Fifth Plan—for example, electronics, the application of automation to machine tools, polymers, land transportation, and so on.

PROBLEMS OF NATIONAL SCIENCE POLICY

The experience of the past few years, although short, raises questions about the justification, the coherence and the efficiency of national research policy. Should answers be found to these questions, the choices required by this policy would be easier to make.

The importance of the sums involved raises the question of the efficiency of research. To clarify notions which are often a source of confusion, we should differentiate between the commercial productivity of a particular piece of research, the more general economic productivity of a certain amount of the research carried out in a given branch (chemistry, for example), and the usefulness of research for the healthy growth of the economy.

Whatever the field, it is clear that the cost of research is often very difficult to establish: for example, the amortization of equipment does not always make sense where fundamental research is concerned, nor is the salary of research workers a useful index. Further, the cost of research is difficult to apportion to a particular result. Did such-and-such research aim at this result? What is the proportion of diffused improvement of knowledge and of specific effort in the achievement of this result? How can unfruitful research be taken into account?

The results of research cannot easily be assessed. Many of them do not depend on evaluation by the market mechanism (health, national defence, and so on). Besides direct economic profitability there can be more widespread advantages which take place in a long-range economic process, for instance the fact of not being totally dependent on foreign countries in leading sectors. Moreover, a given discovery may in itself represent only a stage in the development of a useful product, without any value *per se* and without profitability for some long time.

In spite of difficulties, it is nevertheless necessary, and possible, to improve the assessment of costs, as well as the analysis of direct and indirect results. So far as methodology is concerned, theoretical or practical studies have been undertaken to establish a relationship between costs and results. For example, one line of research, which has hardly started, aims at relating research input, evaluated in terms of research workers, to industrial output. Individual studies concerning a few enterprises or disciplines are trying to relate research, innovation and profit. These efforts at clarification are only just beginning and neither the concepts nor results are yet clearly defined.

Efforts are being made to improve the efficiency of research administration. Too often, research—especially of the most expensive type—has been undertaken without a serious estimate of costs, or a programme, or any appreciation of the results expected. The adoption of evaluative techniques, time-tables and flexible procedures aiming at assessing the results obtained and at redirecting the research if necessary, is being aimed at, either through better organization of research administration, especially in fundamental fields, or by economic studies of big public programmes with a high research content.

These endeavours, although not very demanding so far as exact knowledge is concerned, illustrate the concern for reinforcing the relationship between research effort and economic policy. In this respect, it is important to see the true nature of the problem. France, as a medium-sized country (by the economic standards of the twentieth century) has available only limited resources for the great adventures of modern research. Also, she is far from having the productive capacity of the American economy. In industrial development and research, the keynote can only be a concentration of effort, consistent with the necessary diversity of a nation that wishes to retain a broadly based economy and pluralistic ambitions.

Without doubt, Professor Raymond Aron would say that it is not proper to identify industrial development with growth, especially as we do not know exactly what economic growth is. I cannot enter into a discussion on this point here. I admit that growth is defined as the increase in the quantity of goods and services wanted by men, which either may or may not be evaluated by a market mechanism. I put forward the view that on the one side, growth depends largely on the research and innovation effort, and, on the other, that France must make a choice among the possibilities offered in order to maintain her chances of sharing in the progress of both industry and research, in a comparatively autonomous way.

Consequently, without jeopardizing the indispensable liberty of fundamental research, a minimal amount of clarity and order must be introduced. Since research makes use of expensive equipment and numerous research workers—and therefore commands an appreciable fraction of these national resources—its economic utility must be considered in order to direct our choice towards one field rather than another. Discussion between scientists and economists should allow for harmonizing the freedom of research, the improvement in basic knowledge and economic boundary conditions.

On the other hand, we must endeavour to cope with the risks of isolation in fundamental research. As a matter of fact, the latter may be considerably stimulated through the practical and fruitful applications it may generate. From this point of view, public authorities in France are trying to improve the necessary continuity between fundamental research, applied research, and development in industry and agriculture. Three steps have been taken in this direction: firstly, universities and industry have been brought closer together through the creation of liaison officers or joint institutions, and the possibilities of concluding agreements and exchanging workers. Much remains to be done, however. Secondly, there is the "combined activity" procedure which links research workers and users of research results in certain precisely defined fields—electronics, for instance. Lastly, there is the creation of the Agence Nationale de Valorisation de la Recherche (ANVAR), an establishment charged with facilitating the application of discoveries.

Beyond concerns relating to national defence and autonomy, the problem is to know how far the big public programmes with a comparatively high research content are useful to the economy. We have seen the problems of methods raised by this question. Somehow or other, the atomic, aeronautic and space programmes have to be aligned with the general aims of the French economy. Attempts are being made to ascertain the driving effect they may have in leading sectors.

The major research programmes supported by the French Government for reasons of general policy are to be viewed against the background of the inadequacy of the research effort made by industry. Government action is centred on the existing national programmes, but so is the research effort of the whole country in three areas, namely atomic energy, aeronautics and electronics. We cannot claim that research in these areas, in spite of the substantial sums invested, has gone beyond the minimal level necessary for efficiency. It might therefore be advisable to resort to a more stringent type of selection. Moreover, other less glamorous but economically more useful areas may have a shortage of resources and research workers.

For such reasons, we are at present trying to determine the branches of industry in which the research effort is inadequate, in order to remedy the situation either by granting facilities of a general type, or through specific financial assistance in the form of contracts or of governmental contributions to research development. Two difficulties, however, must first be overcome before we can succeed in restoring a balance. On the one hand, accurate criteria must be found in order to decide whether research work or research development is really inadequate. What kind of indexes should we seek? Would a good measure be the resources devoted to research work and research development compared with turnover, this percentage then being compared with that of competing industries in other countries? One can easily see that this type of measurement is much too aggregate and that the machinery of the research department in an industrial firm is likely to provide information as significant as the financial index of the effort undertaken. On the other hand, each country has its own characteristics, its scientific and industrial history, often with extreme differences between the levels reached by the various branches of its industry; consequently, comparison from country to country may not be very significant. The study, branch by branch, of the balance of patents and licences and of its evolution may be more revealing. But statistics showing the number of patents and licences conceals a complex reality. It would be necessary to know accurately the innovations corresponding to these patents.

The other difficulty is a more serious one: to ascertain whether the research efforts undertaken in the various branches of industry are adequate or not, one is obliged to refer to industrial development standards. In this connexion, it is obvious that there exists an intimate relationship between the industry's research policy and the nation's industrial goals, if these have been defined.

The government, together with the administration, and in conjunction with the industrialists, is therefore induced to formulate, at least in a summary way, a strategy of French industrial development in terms of its qualifications, its chances of expansion in the various branches, national ambitions, and the part it seeks to play in the international division of labour. In so doing, France may be turning its back on the liberal doctrine of *laissez faire* but without giving up the use of the basic market mechanisms. The difficulty is not only to determine the criteria of choice, but also to combine governmental actions and the changes in pattern accepted by the industrialists with the spontaneous trends of the market.

In any case, for a country like France, it seems to me that formulating a policy of industrial research necessarily requires methodological advances in the determination of criteria of choice in the field of industrial policy.

Thus, although we are going ahead in the matter of scientific policy as well as in that of expenditure, we are still far from having solved the main problems of conception and implementation raised by such a policy. In this respect, I have been able to speak more of difficulties than of solutions. We must not delude ourselves with vain dreams. A realistic approach compels us to confess that such is indeed the present position of the science of science so far as the definition of a national science policy is concerned.

OBSERVATIONS ON NATIONAL SCIENCE POLICY IN SWEDEN

BROR REXED

Science Advisory Council, Stockholm

EVERY developed country has a research policy. To a greater or lesser extent, this may be a conscious matter and may be dominated by central bodies connected with the government. One aspect of research policy is the general attitude to the conditions and needs of research; at best, this "philosophy of research" will be common to both scientists and administrators within the country's research structure, as an active factor behind the decisions of research workers and research authorities. It is important that there is continual and intensive debate to keep this research philosophy alive, to deepen it and to extend it. Other aspects of a country's research policy are expressed in the directives and lines of action of various bodies controlling research. In many countries, there is also the important sector of research policy that is formed inside industries, when these plan and carry out what are often large programmes of research as an aid to production. Finally, the government, by general statements, programmes and practical measures, helps to form the national research policy.

It is only to be expected that no country can present its research policy in a form which is comprehensive and completely and rationally analysed. Too many factors are involved. But a more or less articulate research policy is to be found in the actions of the authorities and private interests in various fields of research, and the total picture of research policy can be observed and analysed. In many countries this is an important task for the "research on research" which is now developing, and the results of which may steer future development.

Discussion of research policy can illuminate its problems from several sides. One obvious approach concerns the trends and possibilities in various branches of science. It is a question of deciding what can be achieved by research and directing resources accordingly. An alternative approach is to relate the conceivable results of research to various social requirements in education, medical care, defence, social welfare or industry. Then there is the fact that all kinds of research may yield directly useful results. It may be maintained that, in the last analysis, it is these that we are endeavouring to obtain, and therefore research projects and organizations should be judged in the light of their final results. A further point of view is concerned primarily with the organization of research and the various institutions, official bodies and authorities that have to make decisions about the needs of research and the manner in which personnel and laboratory resources are used. This is the natural point of view for political decision makers.

These various approaches to problems of research policy have their different advantages and disadvantages, their strong and weak points. A complete picture can hardly be obtained from any single point of view, but instead requires that they are combined with, and supplement, each other. Here, I would like first to consider some problems and viewpoints concerning the organization of research. This is a natural approach for someone who has been engaged for several years in various fields of research organization. I shall continue the discussion with reference to the present organization in Sweden. This is, of course, a limitation, because each country has arrived at an organization of research which reflects its historical development in politics and administration, and which in some respects depends on particular national circumstances. On the other hand, it is evident that the organizational structure of research in all countries exhibits certain common features. Some institutions and functions must exist if a country is to carry on research at all. Consequently, problems of research organization which are similar for many countries may be discussed through the problems of a specific country.

The organization of research in Sweden may be described as a system with three different levels. On the first level are the places where research is done—that is, institutions and laboratories with their own research leadership. There are various kinds of research activity at these places. There is basic research within the universities and institutes, where entirely free research is mainly represented. Government laboratories for agriculture, public health, communications and defence deal with applied research in the fields concerned. Other institutions are devoted to the requirements of industry and commerce, either in research institutes, with combined government and private support for the study of, for instance, production methods in a particular branch of industry, or in private industrial laboratories that deal with the development of products for a particular market.

The second level comprises the administrative bodies and authorities who plan the direct research in the various categories of research laboratories and decide the extent of their work. The University Chancellor's Office is at this level, with comprehensive planning functions for research at universities and other institutions of higher education. The planning sections of this Office are five faculty councils that cover the most important areas of basic research (the humanities, social sciences, medicine, natural sciences and technology). All applications for grants—for additional personnel, among other things—and suggestions concerning organizational changes at universities and other institutions of higher education are submitted to the government through the Chancellor's Office. The faculty councils have some 40 members, of which about two-thirds are engaged in research.

Also at this second level are several research councils, whose purpose is to supply the best possible financial support to the most active and skilful research workers in their particular field, both inside and outside the university organization. Moreover, these councils follow current research and take the initiative to ensure that it conforms to national requirements. Through its members, each council must therefore maintain a broad knowledge of the national and international situation within the branch of science concerned, as a basis for an efficient allocation of priorities and initiatives. The research councils have some hundred members, of whom three-quarters are engaged in research. Councils exist for both basic and applied research. The councils most concerned with basic research are those for the humanities, social science and the natural sciences. Both basic and applied research are supported through, for instance, the council for medical research, the council for research in agriculture and forestry, and the council for technological research. The councils for traffic safety, building research and consumer research are almost entirely for applied research. Recently, a research council was initiated for environmental research (dealing with air and water pollution and natural conservation). The academies may also be included at this level: they are primarily forums for discussion of scientific trends and general assessments of research. Among them are the Academy of Sciences, the Academy of Engineering Science, and the Academies of Literature, History and Antiquities.

The second level also includes the boards of various national laboratories and technological institutes, which are concerned with research projects and the resources for applied research in their respective fields. Government support for applied research is given through independent foundations such as the Iron Ore Foundation, the Norrland Foundation and the Institute for the Utilization of the Results of Research. These foundations are not completely responsible for development in their respective fields; they aid development by contributions at strategic points in fields that are otherwise the special interest of branches of industry. They grant money for the technical development of products, and endeavour to encourage new types of production by assisting innovations and patents. The grants are given to private firms, and often involve a division of the cost of a project by a contract between the foundation and the firm. The government also contributes to the development of industrial production by large orders covering the costs of research and development of equipment for government departments (for example, System 37 Viggen, an aircraft for the Air Force). At the same level as these public bodies are the company boards in the private sector; within their fields they decide the volume of applied research and development needed to maintain a place in the market and to expand production.

The third level is the most central, and includes the government bodies concerned with research policy. In the public sector, the final responsibility for the administration and allocation of grants rests on various departments or ministries, with the minister as the final decision maker in each case. In Sweden, the various bodies in the organization of research at the second and third levels are associated with many government departments. Actually, only the Department for the Civil Service and the Foreign Office have nothing to do with research. Most research bodies are under the Ministry of Education, the Department of Industry, the Ministry of Agriculture (which includes forestry) and the Ministry of Defence. Collaboration in international research is also under the appropriate ministry. Budget resources for research expenditure on the part of the various ministries are decided by consultation with the Ministry of Finance.

An advisory body to the government is the Science Advisory Council, set up in 1963. This Council acts as a permanent committee within the Prime Minister's office. The Prime Minister is the chairman of the Council, and of the smaller working party which deals with current matters and makes preparations for Council meetings. The Council has 30 members, who are engaged in research or the administration of research in both the public and private sectors. The meetings of the Council are also attended regularly by the Ministers of Finance, Education, Defence, Trade and Agriculture. The working party consists of five members of the Council and two civil servants who are responsible for research matters in the Ministries of Education and of Trade. The Council secretariat is under the leadership of a secretary who is a member of the Council and its working party, and who, in the absence of the Prime Minister, leads the working party.

Thus the Science Advisory Council includes not only active scientists, but also "consumers of research" from both the public and private sectors. In accordance with its directives, the Council is a forum set up by the government for discussion of the long-term development and direction of the country's research. It deals with questions of research in all fields, from the humanities to technical applications. The Council is an advisory body without routine commitments and without administrative control over other research bodies. Nor does it have any duties directly connected with the annual budget. It is principally concerned with long-term planning of research investments and the organization of research. The Council and its working party estimate the total of investments required for research, both in money and personnel, and recommend how resources should be divided between various executive research bodies. Thus, it helps to shape the national research policy on the broadest possible basis. It also discusses Swedish participation in international research projects. The fact that it includes representatives of research interests in private enterprises indicates its importance as a contact body in questions of the allocation of research between the government and the private sector.

What principles are embodied in the organization of research in Sweden, and what are the problems associated with its structure? A problem at government level is how the government's treatment of research matters should be organized, and how decisions and actions in research matters should be co-ordinated within the government. Two methods present themselves, and different countries have followed either one or other of them. One way is to have a minister for research—a Minister of Science—who represents research in the government. An advantage often claimed for this method is that scientific research is then directly represented in the government by a person who can use his knowledge and influence to clarify the importance of research. Against the idea of a special minister of science, it may be pointed out that from the point of view of other ministerial departments research questions are an important part of a department's planning, and are so intimately connected with the other measures and decisions of the department that they should not be treated separately. For instance, defence research cannot be taken out of the hands of the Ministry of Defence, nor industrial research out of the hands of the Ministry of Trade or the Department of Industry. Many countries, therefore, have chosen instead to have an advisory and co-ordinating body at government level, and have usually included this in the Prime Minister's secretariat, often under his leadership. This arrangement reflects the idea that the task is one of co-ordination and collaboration between various ministries. It is also possible for the ministers concerned, and their assistants, to obtain advice on matters of research from this government research body. A body for the co-ordination of research can state its conclusions on budgetary questions in a form appropriate to the manner in which such questions are dealt with in the various ministries. The arrangement thus allows a co-ordination of research matters even with regard to the budget, and has the advantage that these matters can still be dealt with in the ministries to which they naturally belong. This is the alternative that Sweden has chosen.

The organization of research in Sweden is highly decentralized. Important questions are decided upon with full responsibility by bodies at the second level—the University Chancellor's Office, the research councils, boards of laboratories, and so on. The latter are responsible for planning and surveillance in their separate fields, and on the whole they distribute funds without detailed instructions from the government. But important decisions are also made at the first level. The questions that the ministries have to deal with are questions of principle or organization, or are concerned with weighing matters for the budget.

This decentralized organization is divided into many parts at the first and second levels. It could be called multiform, in contrast to a highly concentrated organization for directing research. It is particularly at the second level, with its large number of research councils, laboratory boards and boards of foundations, that this multiform arrangement is apparent. The fragmentation and heterogeneity of this system, leading to weaknesses in research leadership and difficulties of co-ordination, has been held to be a disadvantage. The advantage is that active research workers in the directing bodies at the second level can be given considerable responsibility and independence. Such a many-sided research organization allows persons who are well-informed and active in research to participate, and leads to a more efficient direction of research. The fragmentation of research leadership is counteracted in the Swedish system by the central government advisory body, the Science Advisory Council, which can consider research from the national point of view and give advice to ministries about any of the administrative bodies at the second level of the organization.

An advantage of the Swedish organization of research is that active scientists take part in decisions and planning at all levels. The planning of research and the giving of advice on it undoubtedly call for a high degree of expert knowledge, particularly with regard to measures that affect the development of research in the long term. But this brings us to the question of how far active scientists should contribute to the administrative procedure which must precede the formation of a government's research policy. The method adopted in Sweden, as in several other countries, is that active scientists take part in committees at all levels of the research organization even up to government level. The final preparation of material on any matter is carried out by civil servants in the administrative bodies concerned, and the final decisions are made by politicians of ministerial rank. This would appear to be a correct and essential principle. It should be possible for scientists' opinions to be presented objectively and with authority at all levels up to that of the responsible ministers, but the scientists cannot be responsible for the final decisions. For the large questions of organization and priorities in research, those who make the decisions must take account of circumstances which lie outside the field in which scientists are experts. Scientists should be "on tap but not on top", in other words.

What is the Swedish expenditure on research and development? With due reservations, because our statistics of public and private investment in this sector are still far from perfect, I shall give some figures. I shall concentrate on the years 1964 and 1965, since we have investigated the expenditure of private firms in industry during this period, using the recommendations of the Organisation for Economic Co-operation and Development.

First, the public expenditure in research and development rose from 407 million Swedish crowns in the budget year 1963/1964 to 475 million in 1964/1965 (see Table I). I have tried to sort out different fields here, always including both basic and applied research. It can be seen that if the

Table I

SWEDISH PUBLIC EXPENDITURE ON RESEARCH AND DEVELOPMENT IN CERTAIN SCIENTIFIC AREAS

In million Swedish crowns

	1963/1964	1964/1965
Natural sciences	67	76
Technology	177	211
Medicine (including pharmaceutics)	62	73
Agriculture (including forestry)	34	39
Social science	37	41
Humanities	30	36
Total	407	475

humanities, social science or agriculture are given the index 1, then medicine or natural science have the index 2, and technology has the index 5.

Secondly, Swedish industry increased its expenditure for research and development from 700 million crowns in 1963 to 730 millions in 1964, a modest increase of 4 per cent (see Table II). It may be noted that almost all of this is development work. The manpower used is shown in Table III. The number of man-years rose from 14,300 in 1963 to 15,350 in 1964, an increase of 7 per cent. But the increase was concentrated on qualified personnel, increasing by 12 per cent, whereas other personnel decreased by 1 per cent. This must be a sign of better utilization and rationalization. Furthermore, it must be noted that government contracts for development work amount to something between 100 and 200 million crowns in each of these years. These sums are included in the industrial expenditure.

Table II

RESEARCH AND DEVELOPMENT COSTS OF SWEDISH INDUSTRY

In million Swedish crowns

	1963	1964
Running costs		
Fundamental research	3	2
Applied research	73	83
Development work	552	563
Capital costs	72	82
Total	700	730

Table III

MANPOWER USED IN RESEARCH AND DEVELOPMENT IN SWEDISH INDUSTRY

Figures in man-years

	1963	1964
Qualified personnel	8,900	10,000 (+12%)
Other personnel	5,400	5,350 (− 1%)
Total	14,300	15,350 (+ 7%)

Finally, what does this mean relative to the gross national product? The national expenditure on research and development was 1,130 million crowns in the budget year 1963/1964 and 1,277 million in 1964/1965, an increase of some 13 per cent (Table IV). The sums mentioned are 1·3 per cent and 1·4 per cent respectively of the gross national product for those years, which in this sort of comparison places us in the group of countries that includes France, West Germany and Holland.

Table IV

SWEDISH NATIONAL RESEARCH AND DEVELOPMENT COSTS RELATIVE TO THE
GROSS NATIONAL PRODUCT

In million Swedish crowns

	1963/1964	1964/1965
Public expenditure	415	497
Percentage of gross national product	0·49	0·53
Private industry	715	780
Percentage of gross national product	0·85	0·84
Sum total	1,130	1,277
Gross national product	84,000	93,000
Research and development as percentage of gross national product	1·3	1·4

A number of problems of allocation occur within the framework of a national research organization. In many cases these may be regarded as questions of optimization: it is a matter of weighing aid to various activities and types of research and development against one another. Let us consider some of these problems.

The first concerns a comparison of Sweden's research production with international research activity. Sweden probably produces not more than 1 per cent of the world total of scientific results. This means that in both basic and applied research, in both the public and private sectors, we must attempt to strike a just balance between the amount and kind of our own research and the results we can obtain from abroad. Through the contacts of individual scientists we must be closely connected with research laboratories in other countries. It is also necessary to have an active and efficient apparatus for information and documentation. New techniques are being built up to enable the relevant data for a particular research worker to be extracted from information stored in a computer memory. Systems of this kind are already available for medical research, for chemistry and physics, for atomic energy and space research. It is probable that within 5 to 10 years there will be computer memories with such a capacity that the entire literature in a group of sciences could be stored in full. It is a major task for current research policy to see that a well-balanced and comprehensive system for information and documentation is built up.

Another balance that has been discussed a good deal is that between basic and applied research. All basic research presumably will have useful consequences eventually. But no country can perform all the basic research which its applied research and development needs. This, of course, is particularly true of small countries, and to a high degree in the increasingly numerous fields of Big Science. So there is really no upper limit to the amount of research a country can undertake, because in such an international field each country can increase its proportion of the total research in accordance with the resources it is prepared to devote to this purpose. The problem is to judge the minimum amount of basic research that is required if a country's productive activity is not to deteriorate. Over and above this minimum, further resources can then be expended to satisfy various interests.

In deciding the minimum volume of basic research necessary, there are three aspects to be considered. The first is that such research is of great importance in the scientific training of research manpower. Those trained in research are needed for the extension of research, both that backed by the government and that in industry, and in leading positions in education, the hospital service, and administration. It is, therefore, necessary to provide the universities and other places of higher education with resources that allow those engaged in research to keep at the front.

Another part of basic research is necessary because it belongs to fields that are currently in the forefront of development and are a foundation for important applications in expanding sectors of society. Some of these fields belong to Big Science—to research projects that are each some hundred times more expensive than other research. If resources are to be made available within the limited means of our country, it is clear that there must be a high degree of specialization and concentration. All universities and institutes cannot be treated alike, and a painful phase of change and reconstruction is ahead of us.

The third consideration for basic research is the needs of industry and trade. Private firms in Sweden are not so large that they can pay for all the basic research they need as a groundwork for their applications, yet they have to compete with large concerns abroad that are in a position to carry on extensive basic research. In Sweden, the division of effort must be such that government-financed research answers for almost the whole of industry's basic requirements. In making research policy, one of the tasks is to analyse in detail what different branches of industry require in the way of basic research.

As regards the need for applied research, of both more general and more special types, in many sectors of national life, public bodies are responsible for this work. Defence research and the development of power are obvious examples, as are also the hospital and health services. But education, the social services, the national economy and general administration are beginning to appear as sectors of marked scientific development. Communications and natural resources are other examples of areas where private enterprises or organizations cannot be said to be responsible for research or even able to carry it out. A further difficulty with these areas of research is that the social usefulness of their results cannot easily be measured. That is to say, there is no clear relation between the cost of the research and its utility.

In order to attack such a problem as the optimum balance of research and rationalization measures, the responsibility for research in functionally interconnected fields of application should be united under a single government department. The planning section of this department should be extended with a research section, to give the department immediate access to scientific and technical expertise, to assist its planning work. Defence research is an example of concentration of this kind that has already occurred. Natural resources, communications and commerce are other departmental activities that should be extended to include research planning. Such an arrangement would allow the ministries concerned to estimate the effect of a research effort, and thus judge what resources may be needed for research as compared with other types of development and extension in the relevant fields of activity.

Another problem of assessment in research policy concerns the division of expenditure between the public and private sectors. Different countries vary a lot in this respect. In small countries it is usual for basic research to be paid for entirely by public bodies. Collective requirements for applied research of the kinds just mentioned must also be paid for out of public funds. But even in cases where applied research is of direct importance for private enterprise there may be need for government support, despite the fact that the purpose of the applied research is more or less directly to increase the yield of the industries in question. It may be that the branch of industry is so divided into small units that firms cannot themselves carry the research expenditure that proper economic development requires. This is the case, for instance, with forestry and building research. In other cases, it may be a question of research that is of importance for a whole branch of industry but has little competitive value for the individual firms. This applies to the development of general methods of analysis and process control, to standardization, and to some problems in the development of materials. Where such questions dominate it may be useful to have government-supported institutes for industrial research, such as those for the cellulose industry, textiles, and cement and concrete. It may also be valuable to organize institutes for industrial research across the boundaries between branches—for example, for research on corrosion, catalysis or operational analysis. Representatives of private industry in Sweden recommend a combined effort backed by the government and private interests in a number of such research fields. Although this can hardly be the principal direction of effort for national applied research, quantitatively speaking, there are certainly useful lines of development deserving further support.

In many countries there has been general public support of industrial technology through orders that include work on applied research and development. The most striking example in this respect is the United States, where the high proportion of research investment from the government is due to the enormous orders for applied research and development in connexion with nuclear weapons and the federal space programme. It is evident that this implies a strong stimulus for certain types of industry, and even leads to the raising of civilian production as a by-product, through the development of materials, electronics and machine tools, for example. Even in Sweden, there are instances of such effects of military development; a motor car factory, and a considerable part of the electronics industry, originated through this type of government support.

Whether or not it is appropriate to stimulate the development of industries by government orders depends on whether there is a public or collective need that is satisfied by the industrial research capacity thus created. For a small country such as Sweden, this is not the case to any great extent in the fields that are typical of this in the United States, because we do not intend to develop atomic weapons and have no military reasons of national prestige that are strong enough to bring about a large programme of space research. If contracts for technologically interesting research are to be of any importance in Sweden, it must be in fields where increasing demands on technology make a venture of this kind worth while. Possible examples are the communications system, the medical and hospital services, education and teaching methods, and the continued development of power production. A current problem of research policy is to investigate whether, and how far, the government should support the development of new technology that is of direct significance for the exporting industries, either by broad research in materials or in electronics, for instance, or by placing large orders in industrial sectors where there is rapid technological development.

In Sweden the greater part of the research and development expenditure in industry is borne by industry itself—500-600 million Swedish crowns (100-120 million dollars) annually. An important question concerns the methods by which this industrial investment can be supported and stimulated by the government. Private enterprise always suggests first a decrease in the taxes on profits, which would give firms a better chance of carrying out various kinds of investment, among them investment for research. A variation of the same idea is special tax reductions for research. However, measures of this kind have their disadvantages. For a firm, research expenditure is a part of the production costs, and must be included in the price of the product. It is therefore necessary to make an estimate of the advantages of producing a new technique as compared to the purchase of patents and licences. If subsidies were to make research too cheap, this might lead to an economically undesirable trend in the firm's effort.

Special research funds within private enterprises appear to be of greater interest. At the present time, leaders of industry are strong advocates of this alternative. By setting aside money in such a fund during a period of years they would be able to accumulate resources for large research investments that may be necessary in the future. Such research funds would become taxable income on being released for research and development work. From the government point of view such an arrangement would mainly lead to a displacement of taxes between different years. From a firm's point of view it would provide a possibility for concentrating research, in the interests of efficiency. It seems that this idea of allowing firms to form research funds is worth closer investigation.

From general economic considerations, many countries have found strong arguments for local direct support of a research or development project, and have even put this into practice. The government funds called EFOR and INFOR (Foundation for the Exploitation of Research Results and the Institute for the Utilization of Research Results) exist for this purpose. The idea is that there are fields where the application of research takes so long, or where projects are so expensive, that development work implies too great a risk or gives too little return to a private enterprise, and is therefore left undone. From the national point of view, however, it may be worth while helping a particular development by subsidies, which can later be repaid by firms wishing to utilize the results, either by their buying licences or by reimbursing the research costs. Interesting and valuable results have been attained with such funds in the United Kingdom. In Sweden, we are also experimenting with this form of support for product development, but as yet our experience is too small to permit any final conclusions. But it can at least be said that private industry has shown surprisingly little interest in this kind of government aid. It may be that the possibilities are not properly realized. The question of how much support should be given to industrial production through these channels is therefore not yet ripe for a decision in Sweden.

This brief review of some problems of research policy in a small country shows that it is not possible to consider research as a closed and connected system of activities. Instead, we must attempt to put research and its applications into a functional context, and in different spheres there are very different factors determining the scope, type and direction of a national effort. To judge these different needs it is necessary to have many separate organs of research policy. In Sweden, we have endeavoured to create an organization from the level of government down to the places where research is carried out which satisfies these requirements, and where scientists and administrators can collaborate at all levels to solve problems in a manner that combines scientific analysis and social integration.

DISCUSSION

Weinberg: It seems that the University Chancellor's Office performs a function in respect to research in universities in Sweden that is not too different from that of, say, the National Science Foundation in the United States.

Rexed: The University Chancellor's Office has control of the permanent structure of the universities, because unlike the United Kingdom, in Sweden we have direct government control of universities. They have very few private means. To a certain extent the University Chancellor's Office gives money to universities for research projects, but most of the money for research comes through the research councils.

Weinberg: The support of research in the universities is then organized rather differently from the way it is done in France, for example, where I understand that research in the university is strictly part of education.

Rexed: We have much the same system as France, though the organization differs. The budget for the permanent structure in Sweden comes from the Ministry of Education and the flexible additional sums come through the research councils; France has the same mechanism, with support for research coming from the Centre National de la Recherche Scientifique.

Todd: It is not too different from the British system, which is also a dual system. The University Grants Committee gives a general grant to each university which is used in part for research, and particular projects receive financial support through a separate channel, namely the research councils.

Weinberg: My personal feeling is in favour of more sharply identifying university research with the educational function of universities. This has the merit of being simple in principle, but has obvious demerits also.

Bernal: From Professor Rexed's paper, it appears that British material standards for the equipment of laboratories seem to be much lower than the Swedish standards, and to be much more comparable to the French standards.

SCIENCE POLICY MAKING
IN THE UNITED STATES

William D. Carey

Bureau of the Budget, Washington

THE American policy-making system has developed extensively during the past two decades, largely in response to urgent dynamics in the national economy and in our external relations. There are many faces to this evolution, but few are as interesting—or perplexing—as the process through which science and public policy interact.

It is clear that science occupies a conspicuous place in national policy making. To those who value academic freedom through undirected scientific research, this arrangement poses some difficult philosophical questions, but none so insuperable as to call for disengagement. The outlook is toward strengthening, rather than dissolving, the close ties between government and science.

The tradition of a public policy toward science, in its current form, is a relatively recent invention. Indeed, the difficulties encountered by the United States Government in understanding and administering research and development programmes are chiefly the consequence of the scale and rate of growth of public investment in these areas in a comparatively brief span of years.

In 1940, the national government spent about $75 million on research and development. By 1953, it found itself spending $2 billion (thousand million) a year, and in the budget for fiscal year 1968 the figure stands at about $17 billion. Not long ago the various administrative departments and agencies were asked to project probable levels of government support for research and development to 1970, and the total figure produced by this exercise exceeded $22 billion. In the entire Federal Government budget, nothing else matches this propensity for growth.

The government's involvement in research and development constitutes two-thirds of all expenditures in the United States for this purpose. Yet, while the government provides most of the money, it actually performs only a modest portion of the research and development directly. Almost two-thirds of the Federal funds are expended through contracts with private industry. Barely 20 per cent is spent in government laboratories, while about 13 per cent is given over to grants and contracts with universities and other non-profit-making institutions. Three-quarters of all federal expenditure for research and development are attributed to defence, space and atomic energy. What is plain is that in a single decade, driven by forces not wholly altruistic, science and technology have come to have a role of extraordinary importance in United States public policy.

What makes total policy making so difficult in the government's handling of science and technology is the institutional setting within which we must work. Science-and-technology, while undeniably a governmental responsibility, is not a unitary function. It is pluralistic. We have no parliamentary minister to establish goals and measure results. We have no Department of Science and Technology, and indeed we resist one with intensity. Science and technology are not so much national missions as they are sub-missions, fused to the particular major purposes of administrative departments and agencies. They are, in short, means for the achievement of larger ends: the promotion of commerce and industry, the development of agricultural productivity, the pursuit of health, welfare and education, the maintenance of military superiority, and so on. Science and technology therefore are ladled out of many pots, in each of which something distinct has been brewed, yet are unrecognizable as a coherent and balanced synthesis to which the term "policy" can be applied.

Moreover, this pluralistic character is not limited to the status of science and technology in the Federal Government. The same traits are observable in the framework of the American scientific community. One finds diversity rather than unity in the scientific professions: a proliferation of specialisms, an independence of thought and opinion, a disinclination for consensus. Government does not communicate with anything resembling a parliament of scientific opinion, but rather with an array of spokesmen who represent their own fields of science or sometimes only themselves. If this does not spell efficiency, it nevertheless goes a long way toward spelling freedom for science in the open society to which we are committed. It is a choice, and a price, that we accept cheerfully.

The difficulties of determining policy appear in still a third dimension, which arises from the separation of powers in our national system of government. The executive arm may, despite the circumstances I have described, by heroic measures succeed in producing a fragile synthesis of research goals, but the legislative arm can substitute its own set of judgments and enforce them through the law-making and appropriations apparatus. Presidents and the Congress have met on a collision course more than once over issues involving scientific and technical judgments. The Congress, for example, will consistently vote more funds for medical research than the President deems prudent, but less than he requests for basic research or oceanography. I think it must also be pointed out that the United States arrived at the present prodigious effort in research and development not nearly so much by conscious resolve, as by responses to action-forcing stimuli, including Sputnik.

With all this, new alignments have emerged in the political culture of the United States. It used to be that scientific research avoided entanglement with political institutions as a matter of conviction. But the wartime truce between government and science demonstrated impressively that public funds, administered with benevolence, made order of magnitude advances possible, and the lesson stuck. Reluctance to take government funds switched to insistence that the government underwrite research on a growing scale. Science no longer is the poor cousin in government's family circle.

Still another institutional result of the new interface between technology and government is the industrial complex which came into being through government contracts in the defence, aerospace and atomic energy sectors. So formidable is this government–industry network, that even President Eisenhower lost his accustomed composure long enough to sound a sharp warning of the potential dangers inherent in this relationship to a free and balanced society. To be sure, this problem is not strictly the result of our research and development effort alone; it is even more a function of the demand and supply factor with relation to defence and space hardware. Yet it is the constant infusion of new standards for hardware performance made possible through research and development that induces the obsolescence which keeps the cycle going.

Such then is the environment of government-supported research and development. Indeed, it can be said with considerable truth that we, in the United States, have been exceedingly conservative in adapting our administrative institutions to meet the assault of science and technology. We cannot gloss over two quite different concerns: one, that of the scientific community, both in and outside government, that centralized research administration would give government too much control over scientific choices; the other, that of government, though never so stated, that such centralization of science and technology would distort its importance to the detriment of weaker and more needy claimants on the national conscience and its treasury. In short, it suits both the science community and public administrators to continue the old habits of departmentalization, as though nothing at all had changed in the past decade and a half.

Problems of co-ordination naturally result from the diffusion of research and development responsibilities among the executive departments and major administrative agencies. For example, 13 major organizational units in the executive branch conduct research and development in meteorology. Eight agencies are engaged in supporting oceanography. Five agencies are concerned with space research and development. Eight are involved in water research. Eleven conduct or support medical research. Across the entire field of scientific research and development we find no fewer than 35 executive departments and agencies. It is this nightmare that, coupled with the vast sums of money we are spending, has induced concern about overlapping, duplication and loss of efficiency. One hears the insistent question, "Who is in charge?"

The problem is reduced somewhat in scale by the fact that 90 per cent of all expenditures for science and technology are administered by five departments and agencies: Defense; Space; Atomic Energy; Health, Education, and Welfare; and the National Science Foundation. But these constituencies themselves are so large, and so widely engaged in research and development enterprises, that co-ordination is not a thing to be taken for granted.

Various administrative devices have been adopted to minimize the task of co-ordination and the risk of malfunctioning. An impressive array of committees has come into being which cross both departmental lines and subject-matter specialties. A Science Information Exchange has been established to serve as a common clearinghouse on projects being supported in and outside government. Centralized distribution arrangements have been contrived for fanning out the flood of technical reports which threatens to drown research scientists in an ocean of paper. The Bureau of the Budget has begun to focus responsibility in such complex and multi-lateral areas as meteorology by designating one agency as co-ordinating agent. And the Presidential budget process itself constitutes a strong influence for co-ordination in scientific as well as non-scientific areas.

But while we can point to progress in day-to-day administrative co-ordination of research and development, I find less optimism insofar as national science policy is concerned. We are beginning, at last, to realize that our government cannot continue to endow science and technology by the same unrestrained standards that sufficed in the last decade. If choices have to be made, government plainly must have some structure of priorities to guide decision making. To the extent that a synthesis of public policies toward science and technology may be said to exist, this makes the definition of priorities that much more practicable. Even without a national policy, however, the attempt must be made to reach a rational approach to scientific choice, because otherwise decision making is entirely opportunistic. One might well ask: whence should come the initiative for proposing criteria for decision making—from government which pays the bill, or from the scientists who have so much at stake? I think it is plain that the initiative should come ideally from the scientific community; but if it does not emerge soon, government will have to attempt the task for itself.

THE POLICY-MAKING NETWORK

Decisions about government-supported science are reached in a framework that, in oversimplified terms, can be called four-dimensional. It begins with the scientific community: the university-based centres of inquiry and creativity, the national laboratories which are government-financed but non-governmentally managed, the in-house government research installations, the independent research worker, or the industrial or not-for-profit contractor engaged in open-ended research or development. These are the principal watersheds whence research or development proposals typically well up and enter the policy-making channels.

The second dimension includes the executive departments and programme agencies which engage in or support external science. Because the United States Government is pluralistic in its administration of science, research and development proposals are reviewed and evaluated within departmental criteria and standards of relative merit and relevance to the immediate and long-range mission interests of the department. If one department rejects the proposal, it may manage to win acceptance from another, for good and sufficient reasons and not because of bureaucratic perversity. The possibilities of several departments unknowingly supporting identical research projects are limited by the existence of a Scientific Information Exchange which runs a live inventory of approved research projects as a central management service. It is limited also by the existence of interdepartmental research committees in various scientific disciplines, through which research strategies and priorities are shared.

Within the departments, then, the dimensions of science programmes are worked out and assembled into budgets. At that point, science enters into competition for resources with the non-scientific elements of the department's programme. What follows is the usual managerial exercise in balancing requirements and weighing choices, against which to ration available resources. If the department has a conspicuous tradition or orientation toward research, the claims of the scientific component may be irresistible. In less enlightened communities, the going will be more difficult, and it is significant that President Kennedy saw to it that every department with a potential for utilizing research was given either a policy-level Assistant Secretary or a Scientific Adviser who would supply a strong role of both advocacy and oversight in the scientific field.

This second dimension—the departmental setting—exercises the principal force in the policy-making structure. The departmental missions legitimize investment in science. The departmental appropriations are the conduits through which science is funded, research facilities are built, scientific manpower is educated and sustained, and information systems are developed for dissemination and feedback purposes. Finally, accountability to the public for the effectiveness and utility of science and technology paid for by the taxpayers is accomplished chiefly through Congressional scrutiny of departmental operations and expenditures.

It follows that we in the United States have devolved great responsibility upon the mission agencies of the government for recognizing scientific opportunities, for sustaining the nation's research capabilities, for creating new scientific initiatives, for determining where the public interest lies in matters of science and technology, for stewardship in seeing to the quality of publicly supported research, and for anticipating emerging national problems and rates of social and technological change which call for long-range research strategies.

THE PRESIDENTIAL SCIENCE STRUCTURE

The third dimension of policy making is at the Presidential level. In less than ten years we have experienced a transformation of the White House staff machinery for dealing with science and technology. Before 1957, the connexion between science and the Presidency was at best tenuous, and the decision making was largely *ad hoc* and focused upon limited but acute differences of policy which could not be settled at lower levels. In this arrangement, staff work for the President was carried out mainly in the Bureau of the Budget.

In 1957, this business-as-usual climate was rudely jarred by the Soviet Union's success with Sputnik. The relevance of science and technology to national prestige, and to public policy, became painfully apparent. What was apparent also was the fact that a decentralized network of policy making for science left the Presidency insensitive to opportunities and options, unequipped to take policy initiatives, and bereft of an objective adviser who would be bilingual in science and politics—the role of inter-locutor. President Eisenhower thereupon took a step that had long been urged on him by the nation's scientific community, and created the post of Special Assistant to the President for Science and Technology. At the same time, he reconstituted an existing defence-science advisory committee as the President's Science Advisory Committee (PSAC) and moved it into the White House orbit, where it would have direct access to the President. A year later he created still a third element, the Federal Council for Science and Technology (FCST), made up of the heads of executive de-partments with scientific or technological roles, thus providing for a policy-level network body to exert an integrating influence upon the pluralistic administrative structure of governmental research and develop-ment. To provide for consistency and oversight, he designated his Special Assistant as chairman of both PSAC and FCST, thereby forming the rudi-ments of the United States version of a minister of science and technology. With these steps, the Office of the President became energized and staffed to take stock of the government's scientific affairs and to provide inputs to the policy-making process that had, up to that time, relied upon improviza-tion and the perspectives of the Bureau of the Budget.

In 1962 a further major step was taken, under prodding by the Congress. President Kennedy acted to create the Office of Science and Technology (OST) as a standing unit in the Executive Office of the President, on a par with the Bureau of the Budget, and the staff of the Science Adviser was transferred to the new Office. The Special Assistant to the President now "wore four hats"—as Special Assistant, as Director of OST, and as Chair-man of both PSAC and FCST. And in 1966 the Congress itself acted to create in the Executive Office a Council on Marine Sciences and Engineer-ing, headed by the Vice President of the United States.

As we see it today, the Presidential science policy apparatus can be said to comprise a heptagon—a seven-sided structure leading up to the Presi-dent of the United States and consisting of:

the Special Assistant for Science and Technology;
the Office of Science and Technology (OST);
the President's Science Advisory Committee (PSAC);
the Federal Council for Science and Technology (FCST);
the Bureau of the Budget;
the National Aeronautics and Space Council (NASC);
the National Council on Marine Resources and Engineering Develop-ment.

Four of these bodies are headed by the Special Assistant, two by the Vice President of the United States and one by the Budget Director. They are not uniform in their roles and influence, nor do they act together as a corporate board of directors for science. A brief discussion of roles is in point.

(1) In his capacity as Special Assistant to the President, this officer carries special status as an intimate counsellor to the President. In one sense, he serves as a bridge from the White House to the nation's scientific community, a lightning rod for ideas that might otherwise be lost in the traffic, a sensitizer for opinions, attitudes and value judgments, and perhaps a buffer to absorb occasional outbursts of criticism and undertake conciliation. The Special Assistant can advise the President on substantive issues from a different position from that he might feel obliged to take as Chairman of either the PSAC or FCST. Moreover, the Special Assistant, as a staff officer, advises the President under the protection of executive privilege, which means that he cannot be compelled to disclose his dealings with the President to outsiders, including sceptical committees of the legislative branch. Finally, as Special Assistant he can be assigned special missions by the President, including representational duties in international science negotiations and understandings.

(2) The role of the President's Science Advisory Committee may be described by quoting a cogent statement by one of the early Special Assistants, to this effect:

"There has been misconception that my office and the Science Advisory Committee have operating responsibilities. We do not. We have no operational responsibility, for example, for the development of missiles or satellites. We have, of course, made intensive studies of . . . our missile and space programs for the President. Neither do we have any responsibility to decide policy. My function and that of the Committee is to provide answers to questions raised by the President, to undertake assignments for him of an advisory kind, to mobilize the best scientific advice in the country, and to make recommendations in regard to ways by which U.S. science and technology can be advanced . . ."

As to style: the PSAC is a diversified group of between 15 and 20 of the most notable men of science in the American community, along with an equal number of "consultants at large", as well as several government members. They meet as a body for two days each month to assess progress and issues affecting science and public policy. But over and above this, PSAC provides special panels drawn from outside its own ranks to examine in depth, and report on, specific science issues. The majority of its special reports are made public, but others may be classified. In its early years, PSAC concentrated up to 90 per cent of its efforts on problems related to security, including offensive and defensive weapons, but for the past two or three years this preoccupation has been diminishing steadily, and we would today estimate that over two-thirds of the PSAC output is concerned with non-military questions.

I must make it very clear that the President's Science Advisory Committee does not qualify as a national deliberative institution charged with public policy for science. It is there to enrich Presidential staff work rather than formulate (unasked) public strategies for science and government. These features, taken together, suggest both the utilities and the limitations of the Science Advisory Committee.

(3) In the Office of Science and Technology, the direct offspring of the original version of the Office of Special Assistant to the President, we find the core staff unit in the White House matrix for science policy making. Its role is that of a staff arm of the President, with neither decision-making nor operations functions. Nevertheless, it speaks to and for the President in carrying out its critical duties of discharging the responsibility of the President for the co-ordination of Federal science and technology functions. This Office is expected to advise and assist the President regarding:

Science and technology programmes, plans and policies of government agencies, taking into account the relationship with national security and foreign policy as well as the advancement of science and technology in the nation;

Assessment of scientific and technical developments and programmes in relation to their impact on national policies;

Review, integration and co-ordination of Federal activities in science and technology; and

Participation by the scientific and engineering communities in the strengthening of science and technology in the United States and the Western world.

These prosaic and stately outlines of OST's mission fail to suggest the real world in which the Office exists. Staffed so austerely as to invite disbelief—about 25 professional positions—the Office is constantly engaged in lively problems of science policy, science conferences, technological problems and international issues. It feeds advice to the President and to departmental policy officials on the entire range of contemporary problems —arms-control negotiations, supersonic transport decisions, nuclear testing, energy policy, rocket propulsion, information technology, weapons systems, the mix and direction of the space programme, relationships with academic institutions, high-energy accelerator physics, support for basic science, and more. In short, it performs the usual diversified role of a central staff agency at the Presidential level—advising, guiding, admonishing, stimulating, criticizing and evaluating. It also provides the staff support needed by the Special Assistant for Science and Technology, the Science Advisory Committee and the Federal Council for Science and Technology. Although there is no way to measure this tangibly, OST also injects the factors of advocacy and protection for science into the unstable environment of public policy—but it is advocacy disciplined by an awareness of the importance of objectivity and responsibility in considering the larger framework of Presidential decision making. In that setting, effective staff work must be of a very high order if it is to survive. The Office cannot become a lobby for science in the White House; yet neither can it fail to put forward a strong case for science as a national purpose, nor appear to be a third force in the interface of the scientific community and the government. In its relations with the executive departments, it must be able to make an informed input to planning and decision making, yet stop short of intruding upon the departmental authorities and seeming to impose decisions.

(4) The Federal Council for Science and Technology is a multi-agency committee of government officials, established by executive order of the President. The government agencies are those with scientific or technical missions. This Council is expected to (i) provide for more effective planning and administration of the government's scientific and technological programmes, (ii) identify research needs, (iii) improve the utilization of resources and facilities, and (iv) further international co-operation in science and technology.

In a sense, the FCST is the government's intramural equivalent of the President's Science Advisory Committee. This is correct to the extent that government officials are brought into corporate contact with the President's scientific adviser. But by no stretch of the imagination does FCST engage in substantive policy analysis in the style practised by PSAC. Its field is principally managerial, focused on multilateral programming and co-ordination, and concerned with cross-cutting problems such as consistent patent standards, joint science information systems, relations with universities and long-range planning. These are important subjects, but of a different order from the main-line agenda of PSAC.

The FCST meets once a month, chaired by the President's Science Adviser. It works through 13 committees, including committees for Academic Science and Engineering, Atmospheric Sciences, High Energy

147

Physics, International Activities, Oceanography, and Scientific and Technical Information. Some of these sub-groups are chaired by a staff officer of the OST, others by departmental officers, and staff support is furnished from the member agencies.

The utilities of FCST are: (*i*) the usual gains obtained from peer-group collaboration; (*ii*) the opportunity to ventilate common problems of policy and administration in the presence of the Science Adviser and a high-level Budget Bureau official; (*iii*) as a device for bringing key officials up to date on the policy plans of the administration; and (*iv*) as a means for conveying guidance from the White House to the chief science administrators. In addition, some gains have been scored in planning multilateral programmes and in clarifying missions in such areas as oceanography and the atmospheric sciences.

(5) Two other Executive Office elements merit somewhat briefer comment. The first of these is the National Aeronautics and Space Council. Established by an act of Congress in 1958, this body is, in effect, a sub-Cabinet group headed by the Vice President, and its other members are the Secretaries of State and Defense, the Administrator of the National Aeronautics and Space Administration, and the Chairman of the Atomic Energy Commission. Its job—beyond advice to the President on space matters—is to keep an eye on all the government's aeronautical and space activities, develop comprehensive programmes, designate and fix responsibility for the direction of these activities, promote co-operation between agencies and settle differences arising among them. The Council has its own Executive Secretary and a staff very nearly as large as that of the OST.

In some ways the Space Council demonstrates what the Federal Council might have evolved into as a sub-Cabinet science co-ordinating body. Yet the Space Council has advantages not enjoyed by the larger body. It is compact. Its jurisdiction, though formidable enough, is more limited and hence more homogeneous. Finally, it is orientated towards technology and reflects the necessity for the close co-ordination of defence, space and nuclear technologies.

(6) In 1966 a new Executive Office element came into the orbit of science policy in the shape of the National Council on Marine Resources and Engineering Development. It must be said that this body appeared, not because the President felt the need to strengthen his staff resources for oceanography, but because the Congress took matters into its own hands out of a belief that the Executive had shown inadequate initiative in this area of science and engineering. Chaired by the Vice President once again,

the Marine Council is a sub-Cabinet body charged with surveying marine science activities and developing a co-ordinated programme. It is a temporary body and is scheduled to disappear in two years.

(7) One final element of the science policy structure remains to be considered. This is the Bureau of the Budget itself. A key unit of the Executive Office of the President for nearly 30 years, the Bureau's role as a planning, co-ordinating and problem-solving arm of the President is as firmly grounded as anything can be in the half-life of a political institution. The Bureau's functions run to (i) seeing that the far-flung Executive Branch is responsive to Presidential policies and priorities, (ii) reviewing expenditure proposals as to merit, costs, alternatives and timing, and preparing the annual budget, (iii) reviewing proposed legislation to determine its relationship to the policies of the President, (iv) improving the organization and management of the executive branch of the government, and (v) looking to the co-ordination of government programmes and operations. All these functions are performed as a staff instrument of the President. Rumours and accusations notwithstanding, the Bureau does not consider that it runs the executive branch of the government.

Problems of science and technology may engage the attentions of the Bureau of the Budget from a variety of entry points:

(1) As an issue of proposed legislation—the framing of amendments to the Atomic Energy Act; a bill to establish a Sea Grant College programme, a Social Sciences Foundation or a Department of Science.

(2) As an issue of choice of expenditure—whether to embark on the construction of a 200 Gev accelerator; a level-of-effort decision on financing the National Institutes of Health.

(3) As an issue of organization and management—how to structure a new agency for aeronautics and space research; which components of scattered agencies should be regrouped to form an Environmental Science Services Administration; what criteria should be followed in choosing to do research and development intramurally or by contract with industry.

(4) As an issue of financial management—appropriate principles for allocating indirect costs to research grants; guide-lines for negotiating cost-sharing in grants to academic institutions.

(5) As an issue of interdepartmental duplication or jurisdiction—the proper assignment of responsibility for setting tolerances for exposure to radiation; the division of responsibilities between the Atomic Energy Commission and the National Science Foundation for supporting the construction of university research reactors.

(6) As an issue raised by the Congress—whether the government's

research efforts are effectively planned and co-ordinated; whether grants for academic science should be made consistently to a predictable cluster of highly rated universities or be dispersed geographically.

But the chief role of the Bureau of the Budget is the rationing of budgetary resources: the allocation process which is central to the final stages of policy making. In dealing with science and technology, the Bureau's objective is to apply tests designed to give the President assurance that the government's investment is adequate, necessary, well-justified, reasonably balanced and sensibly scaled both to policy objectives and to what the budget can stand. This is not an exercise in numbers and decimals. It becomes a penetrating examination of the content and design of scientific and technical programmes, with our programme examiners putting the questions and the departmental witnesses providing what they hope are the answers, sometimes successfully, sometimes not. To perform this examination at the Presidential level requires a professional staff capable of total immersion in complex programme areas, if only for the sake of making possible intelligent communication with the programme administrators and scientists, to say nothing of formulating responsible advice to the President.

It should be understood that the allocation process does not begin by assembling science as an integrated whole and then cutting it up in wedges of different sizes. The budget for science is not poured from a mould; rather, it rises to the surface in the form of needs and opportunities related to the missions of the departmental advocates. Thus, the Bureau will have a seasoned group of examiners who are steeped in defence-related science and technology; another group focused on atomic energy programmes; a third monitoring space science and technology; others concerned with medical research, agricultural research and academic science.

One of the primary gains to Presidential staff work in the science sector of the allocation process in recent years has resulted from the establishment of the Science Adviser and the Office of Science and Technology. This has enormously enriched the Bureau's analysis of scientific and technical issues, and the two staff agencies have worked intimately in the joint evaluation of difficult questions and options. This is not to say that we always come down on the same side of an issue. We may see it from different perspectives: the Science Adviser from the aspect of advancing knowledge and nourishing science, the Budget Director from the perspective of requirements for the non-scientific priorities of the President or outright disagreement over the relative utilities of the given investment. In such a case, both assessments are laid before the President.

The Bureau of the Budget has come to learn that problems of choice in science and technology are formidable indeed. It is a sector of public policy that depends very much on judgment, partly because of inherent dynamics, and partly because of the absence of satisfactory criteria to assist the allocation process. Social returns on investment may be possible to calculate for research in air pollution or in heart disease. It becomes more difficult in high-energy nuclear physics. And it is especially unproductive when one attempts to construct a comparative marginal analysis when faced with the choice of investing in molecular biology *or* an orbiting space laboratory. Of course, the choices are seldom presented in these extreme terms, yet we may be approaching the limits of elasticity in the resources available for increasing investment in science and technology, and a framework of marginal analysis among incommensurables may indeed have to be formulated, in which case we shall have to address ourselves to the painful matter of criteria of choice. Cost-benefit calculations, in that case, will not be simply a new nuisance invented by a perverse Bureau of the Budget, but a social necessity to rationalize allocation decisions, in place of the largely opportunistic preferences which at present affect our public investments.

Science and technology must make their case in a competitive setting with all the other claimants and hope to win it on a showing of superior investment utility. Decisions on what we shall do, and when, and at what cost, should not be left to scientists alone. They are political questions, in the end. Hence, science and technology takes its chances in the bargaining process that is common ground for all problems of choice in the allocation of resources.

THE CONGRESS

In the American national system of government, policy-making is a shared responsibility of co-equal but separated political institutions—the Presidency and the Congress. In theory, the Congress makes laws and the President sees that they are carried out. But like most oversimplified statements, this is far from a description of the actual workings of the system. Presidential power and legislative power, law-making and administration, responsibility and accountability, shade into one another in a hundred ways and affect the stability of the constitutional balance.

At the heart of this arrangement lies the proposition that governmental programmes can be undertaken only by Congressional warrant, and financed only by a Congressional appropriation. There is nothing cloudy about this. A President formulates his agenda and presents a budget and a legislative programme, but it is the prerogative of the Congress to accept, revise or reject it in any particular, and there is no question of the government standing or falling on the outcome.

Thus is comes about that the government's scientific and technical affairs are built on a framework of legislation and financial authorizations. The Congress can and does exercise a large voice in science and technology, and it can and does independently exercise precisely the same array of roles that we have attributed to the President's own executive staff machinery—advising, guiding, admonishing, stimulating, criticizing and evaluating. The legislative power to make laws implies the power to investigate, to gather facts and opinions, and to exercise oversight. The legislative power over appropriations provides full access to the plans, policies and performance of the Executive, and the consequence is that the anatomy of policy making becomes a study in the pull and push of political energy between the co-equal branches.

The Congress, like the Executive, came slowly to realize the significance of the role of science and technology in public policy. Just as with the Executive, science for some years seemed to be no more than a natural and gradual extension of the conventional mission responsibilities of the executive departments and agencies, something to be handled in the normal way by the proper legislative and appropriations subcommittees. Science policy initiative in the Congress therefore tended to depend on the interest and zeal of individual committee chairmen. In the early 1960's there emerged a succession of special legislative committees of inquiry concerned with trends, effects, costs, co-ordination and planning—and concurrently, a bad state of nerves in the research community, which had not studied political science as conscientiously as it might have done.

As matters stand today, the Congress is prepared to run the Executive a good race in science policy making. It certainly does not match the Executive in the numbers and depth of professional resources, nor in access to consultants. However, there has been established a Science Policy Division in the Library of Congress to conduct studies and make reports on the request of legislative committees or private members. Both the House and Senate have set up continuing committees to range widely over science and technology.

What has not yet developed in the Congress is an integrative mechanism to draw science policy making toward a synthesis. In the Congress, science and technology are as pluralistic as we found them to be in the Executive Branch. Legislative and appropriations committees wield power, and committee chairmen do not like to give it up to new super-committees.

There is little evidence to indicate that the reports of the committees of special inquiry or oversight have had much influence on the substantive or appropriations committees, however influential they may be on the Executive.

This apparent disarray has led to some hand-wringing over the need to equip the Congress better to cope with the problems of science and public policy. But for my part, I think we have been rather too critical of Congressional style. Where the government's chief investments are concerned —the area of "Big Science"—in atomic energy, space, defence and medical research, Congress has by my standards shown itself quite equal to its responsibilities. As for "Little Science" and its struggles to survive at the margins, the Congress has perhaps been more solicitous than its critics in the Executive. I carry no brief for a major reorganization of the Congress in the interests of science by itself; there are better reasons to seek improvements in Congressional organization. Super-committees provide no panacea, and without the powers to initiate legislation or decide upon appropriation requests, there is little to be accomplished.

SCIENCE, TECHNOLOGY AND THE ECONOMY

The presumption that economic dividends will surely flow from advancing technology is now firmly fixed in the United States political economy. This calls for continually replenishing the basic scientific capital upon which technology draws. It is more than a mere article of faith: we think that the real gains from technological improvement can be measured, in terms of enlarged total incomes. The view taken by the President's Council of Economic Advisers is that technological gains and resulting higher productivity in the United States have produced explicit payoffs—higher incomes and consumption, longer life, less suffering and illness, reduced drudgery, more leisure, and an improved quality of life that cannot be measured in income statistics.

But American motives in encouraging technological advance are more complicated than the simple urge to ease life's burdens. Technological progress, with its accompanying rise in productivity, is a factor in keeping our prices stable while wages go up, enabling us to compete in world trade. Along with this, the higher profit rates from investments in new technological advances reduce the outflow of capital and even attract it from abroad. From still another viewpoint, the steady development of new products opens routes to export expansion. These are real and earthy considerations for public policy, and they are relevant to how we treat science as the watershed for technological progress. Yet the embarrassing fact is that research and discovery *per se* are neutral in their economic impact, since there must be a willing innovator to recognize opportunities and put the scientific knowledge to use in generating technological change.

So, in addition to providing a favourable climate for scientific creativity, public policy must also provide incentives to innovators; or, to put it the other way round, public policy must help to minimize disincentives or obstacles to risk-taking for technological advance. This is because the innovator faces not only market risks but expensive investment in the modernization of capital and equipment—retooling, new plant layout, advertising and the rest. If tax policies pre-empt earnings and if monetary and credit controls are too constraining, the costs of innovation may be prohibitive, and the general economy is penalized by the physical investment time-lag. In the same way, if aggregate development costs are beyond the reach of the size and resources of the company or industry, the government may decide that it should advance a share of the costs in order not to lose the benefit of the potential technological breakthrough—and this is what explains public risk-participation in ventures like supersonic transport, or the nuclear-powered commercial vessel, or the prototype fast commuter train for the Boston-Washington run.

Public policy in the United States takes a strategic approach to economic payoffs through technological change. It comes down to a strong commitment to help the economy attain and sustain high employment so that industry can count upon an expanding market with a healthy demand for new and better products and services. Being so committed, government exercises fiscal and tax policy so as to achieve high employment and stable price-wage relationships within the parameters of annual productivity increases. To be more specific, recent tax reductions have been aimed expressly at increasing demand, in order to provide larger markets. Investment is encouraged by the special investment tax credit, supported by more liberal depreciation rules which reward firms that raise their rate of investment in new plant and equipment.

In its annual report for 1964, the President's Council of Economic Advisers saw fit to raise the question of whether a fraction of the government's dominant (two-thirds) share of the national research and development effort should not hereafter be directed to civilian fields where technological development has lagged. In response, the government advanced a legislative proposal providing for assistance to industrial associations to promote the sponsorship of non-proprietary technical investigations. In addition, the government has undertaken a programme for the dissemination of new technological information to States, universities and industrial groups in order to provide clearinghouses which can bring new knowledge to firms unable to finance direct research.

Whereas government cannot command industry to raise its research investment, it can and should set an example by generous public financing of both fundamental and applied research. It should illuminate the potential in research for technological advance and economic rewards, as well as for social dividends measured by the improved quality of life. It should provide a yardstick against which industry can measure its own performance. And it should find ways to compensate for the structural defects of low-technology industries as part of its high-employment strategy. For as long as we can look ahead, the rate of technological change will depend on public incentives, rates of gross investment, the level of economic activity, and changes in the structure of production and demand.

The most perplexing question of all has to do with judgments about the future trend in research and development investment, both public and private. This is exceedingly difficult to predict on the basis of past perform-ance because of the prominence of military and space requirements, which distort the base. My view is that combined public and private investment in these activities will show modest absolute advances from current levels, but little if any gain relative to gross national product, assuming an average increase in the gross national product of 4 per cent per annum. What seems likely is a shift in the composition of the mix, with a diminishing fraction allocated to military and space programmes and a corresponding rise in research and development related to urbanization, transportation, food and agriculture, water supply and utilization, marine science and engineer-ing, and other needs of American society. In the same vein, I lean to the belief that social changes will exert a demand on technology which will stimulate the construction, textiles and transportation industries to a more substantial investment in new products, probably with special assistance from the public sector. A third factor exerting pressure on technology will be a sharp increase in population, forcing government to assist more directly in creating jobs, in order to maintain high employment, and this holds possibilities for more guided technological advance than we have seen in the past. I believe that all these forces will produce a more impera-tive public and private policy toward science and technology as prime movers of the economy, with the public sector bearing a growing propor-tion of the costs and risks.

With this, it also seems to me that national science and technology strategies will become more concrete and that government will find itself

6*

obliged to formulate goals toward which these strategies will move. This, I think, is inevitable for a developed society orientated toward high employment and unwilling to pay the alternative price of "stop and start" economics. If I am right, the great remaining question is how government, the scientific community and industry will find common ground in stipulating the substance and priorities of these goals and strategies.

CONCLUSION

Plainly, the science policy structure of the United States is both elaborate and still not fully developed. It is essentially a decentralized system, heavily reliant on network arrangements, and disinclined toward comprehensive planning. Decision making remains essentially opportunistic for both science and technology, but as market competition becomes stiffer under stable budget conditions, the need for trial frameworks for marginal analysis, coupled with criteria for choice, grows stronger. Social values in the United States toward science and technology, notwithstanding the prodigious public investment made annually, remain somewhat ambiguous, still strongly influenced by national security and cold war rationalizations, and groping slowly toward the application of both science and technology to the human condition at home and in the world.

It takes no exceptional insight to point out where the policy structure is flawed. With different working assumptions, more central initiatives might be taken, more sophisticated attempts made at balancing, more long-range perspectives worked into science investment strategies. Perhaps we shall come to this in our policy making, but not until we can no longer afford the inefficiencies and imbalances that we now accept as the cost of diversity and an open market system for science. One can be critical of the policy-making system because it seems to react more often than it initiates. But if one takes as one's point of departure the value system of the United States, one comes to the view that the function of the policy machinery is to provide an environment in which innovation is at liberty to advance ideas and opportunities, and to see that diversity is permitted to make our science the lively thing it should be in an open society. I do not see it as the function of either the Executive or the Congress to govern science. Their function is to sustain it, give it voice in the councils of public policy, and do the best they can to link its versatility to a purposeful society.

The scope of our unfinished business is considerable. We have a massive science and technology enterprise in motion, nourished by interacting motives rather than a synthesis. What remains is to focus more clearly the role of science and technology as powerful engines of change: for foreign policy, for economic growth with high employment, for international commerce, for the solution of social stresses, and for extending man's knowledge and mastery of his environment. We have come only recently to appreciate the role of fiscal policy in achieving national economic goals, to an understanding of the potential for systems approaches to complex managerial and socio-political strategies; now we must learn how to employ science policy more effectively as a social instrument, recognizing not only its potential but also its limitations and uncertainties.

The "science of science" comes tardily to bear on these and other issues of social change. But it is still not too late. Until now, decisions have been somewhat off to the side of rational analysis. As we move steadily toward the relaxation of cold war strains, we must begin to plan for the redirection of our technology-intensive industries—perhaps to improve communications, or to apply sophisticated systems solutions to urban and educational problems, or to move on a larger scale into ocean engineering and weather control. Now is the time to do the policy analysis that can examine the costs and benefits of these alternatives, and thus provide feedback, with lead times, for the politics of choice.

We have the capability for such policy analysis. What is necessary is an effective mechanism to ask the right questions and digest the responses. There are two alternatives. One is the Congress, sensitive to the consequences of social, economic and political adjustments. The other is the Presidency, which has come very far in this century as the focus for policy innovation and strategies. The emerging passion in the Presidency to employ the economics of choice is a favourable sign. Perhaps it is not too optimistic to anticipate, in the near future, a closer working reconciliation between the *economics* of choice and the *politics* of choice in making policy in the United States.

DISCUSSION

King: Mr. Carey's paper has shown how complex is the present system of science policy and how important its interactions with other elements of national policy. His description of the role of the Bureau of the Budget is important, because outside the United States the function of this body is not understood. In the United Kingdom, for example, the Treasury approach to the allocation of resources is quite different from that of the Bureau of the Budget—financial cheese-paring rather than advice on the optimal allocation of resources in relation to the attainment of goals. This approach is an inherent part of the system in the United States. From my observation, the success of the Special Assistant to the President for Science and Technology depends very much on his relationship with the Bureau of Budget and the symbiosis which has evolved between them. Another significant difference between United States and European approaches is the separation of the government's internal role in co-ordinating its own research efforts, through the Federal Council for Science and Technology, from the President's Science Advisory Committee, with its national advisory function on the application, utilization and generation of science for the attainment of national objectives and in a long-term perspective. In many countries we combine and confuse these functions in the same body, to the detriment of both, sometimes subdividing that body into too many councils which are very loosely articulated, if at all.

It is worth mentioning some further trends in the United States. In the past few years, the level of sophistication of Congress in the discussion of scientific affairs has increased enormously and is beginning to have a real influence on science policy. In Europe this movement is just beginning. For example, at a meeting in Vienna in 1964 on science and parliament, parliamentarians from nearly all the European countries complained that the great problems of science policy, including the allocation of resources to competing demands, were passing over their heads and that they were forced to make decisions blindfold. Related to this development in Congress is the emerging role of the National Academy of Sciences, particularly through the influence of Fred Seitz and George Kistiakowsky, for which the scientists themselves are evolving a collective statesmanship and ceasing to be purely a vested-interest advocacy body for high-energy physics or molecular biology or any other single aspect of science. All these developments appears to us, from outside, as highly important.

Secondly, Mr. Carey's paper illustrates that science policy, which after all is still a very new art, is coming out of its "pre-scientific" phase. Five or six years ago science policy was simply a groping attempt to articulate the functions of different agencies and approaches within governments. Previously, such activities were generated separately and tended to remain separate. After the war we began to try to evolve science policies and to develop awareness of the need for them. However, resources were soon seen to be insufficient, relative to the potential contribution of science to national well-being, and allocation became the dominant feature. Much of the difficulty in the discussion of science policy arises from the fact that we have been naïvely assuming that the basic decisions which determine the allocations of resources for science are scientific decisions made by scientists, rather than policy decisions made in relation to national goals and public-investment policy. In fact, we are arguing on two separate planes. Science must be regarded, as has been said here, as a subsystem within national systems working in harmony with other subsystems, but we regard science, and its products, both as a service and as a means of attack on all kinds of policy problems. We continually confuse these two approaches. To me, science policy does not have its primary function in allocating resources. Such allocation of detail is necessary and possible on a small scale, but difficult in a global sense. Science policy is concerned more with the *use* of resources, their nature, size and quality, than with their immediate detailed allocation.

In many activities—defence, health, education, foreign aid, energy, agriculture—many lines of scientific attack are decided as part of the general policy for these subjects and *not* as part of science policy. Likewise, the research element of each is decided partly on a basis of the promise of science in the solution of immediate problems and partly in the hope of establishing a balance within each of these sub-policies between the various social, economic and political needs. The extent of scientific effort in each of these fields, therefore, depends not only on what science might contribute, but on the priority given to the problem in relation to other national needs, and within that priority, the proportion of effort to be provided for various activities, including capital works, services, regulatory activities, training and many other needs, in addition to research *per se*. Scientific expenditure is thus in each case determined by general political decision and not as science policy itself.

It has to be remembered, of course, that in addition to these problems of articulation between the various elements of policy, a proportion of scientific effort has to remain free for the generation of new knowledge and techniques for the building up of science itself, and for the maintenance of that impulse and vitality which science provides for society as a whole.

Problems of this kind are likely to increase as science becomes more closely involved with issues of great complexity, likely to be faced more and more in the future and requiring inter-disciplinary attack. Such problems as urbanism and the world food supply cannot be dealt with by science alone; on the other hand, in many places they tend to be dealt with without science. The problem of the transfer of technology to underdeveloped countries, and the problem in Europe in competition with the United States and the Soviet Union that is probably misformulated as a technological gap, are examples of problem areas in which science and technology have a place and where a scientific approach is highly desirable, but where there are other elements—size of country, basic political problems, flows of capital, education and management competence and strategy. More and more, science will be concerned in the attack on such problems and science policy will have to make this possible.

This is a perfectly reasonable evolution, and it does not mean that science policy is less important; it becomes more important. It has to be strongly concerned with technological forecasting and the problems of the relationship between science and economic growth; with quantity and quality in the deployment of scientific and technical manpower; with the delineation of national goals from the scientific point of view; with long-term strategies for attack on interdisciplinary problems where science can provide approaches and also develop new techniques of attack.

Goldsmith: May I ask M. Saint-Geours how one aspect of the decision-making process that Mr. Carey has described for the United States operates in France? Because, after defining the various ministries and the parts they play, he mentioned in his paper that the Head of State also takes decisions. How significant is this in terms of the general complex?

Saint-Geours: In some cases, especially over the really large projects such as the nuclear accelerator, the decision is taken by the Head of State in restricted council. The procedure for decision making did not in this case stop at the Prime Minister but came to the Head of State. More and more the big choices in atomic energy, space research, electronics and nuclear accelerators are taken by the Head of State.

Goldsmith: So the French system is quite different from the system described by Mr. Carey, because it would be unlikely in the United States that the Head of State would make this kind of decision in a very restricted group?

Aron: This comparison is not quite fair, and largely political. In France, when decisions about "big" science or "big" technology are made, they are made within the framework of a relatively limited budget, and decisions on, say, whether or not to build the Concord have such an impact on the general budget of science that the man who normally takes big political decisions *has* to take such a decision. In the United States the scale of possibilities is so much greater that there is no one decision which is relatively so big. When there *was* one extraordinarily big decision, to go to the moon, it was taken by the President almost without consultation with the specialists. So I would almost reverse your remark; in some cases the President of the United States is able to take a very big decision, but it does not matter so much because the United States has so many more resources.

Bernal: I am much in agreement with Professor Weinberg's earlier suggestion for scientific critics, but Professor Ackoff introduced the idea of the economics of lost opportunities (p. 104). These abound in science, but it is no-one's business to point them out. The mistakes that are made in science policy are not small mistakes; they are very large mistakes. There has been much discussion in the United States about the advisability of the moon programme, but it has not been effective because it was laid down by the President and therefore it is assumed that it is immune from criticism. The scientific community is lacking in the courage to stand up for its principles. There is no rational justification for what is only one astrophysical problem compared to many other problems of greater scientific value. Both the United States and the Soviet Union are throwing away and wasting precious manpower, in my view.

Carey: Because the President assigns a public policy imperative for putting a man on the moon by a fixed date, there is no guarantee, in the American system, that the public will accept the imperative or that Congress will finance it. In this case the shock to American public opinion of the Soviet achievement put so much pressure on the President, as the principal decision maker, that had he made any other decision, his position would have been almost intolerable. I do not think the President foisted a goal on the people so much as he responded to a demand by the people. The debate now runs largely to the order of magnitude of the investment in the moon programme, related to time.

Had the decision been that the United States should do a more "scientific" type of space exploration, perhaps examination of the moon or the wider planetary system through instrumentation, rather than a manned voyage, there might have been less dissent and argument from the scientific community in the United States. Had the time-scale been more extended, so that in the distribution of resources less would have been concentrated on the manned lunar landing programme, or had budgetary constraint not occurred, so allowing more opportunities for increased support of science other than space research, there would have been less argument by the scientific community. These are some of the reasons for the debate. And as we come nearer to a manned landing, the real issue on which opinion should be focused now is "What do we do next; with how much, over what intervals of time, and at what opportunity-costs?" This is the type of question that the science community should now ask, and should engage the political community on.

Todd: I would just recall what Dr. King said, and the point that I also made in my opening remarks, that decision is a political matter, not a scientific matter, and if you are worried about sending a man to the moon or anything else, the fault in so far as it concerns science policy—and "science policy" is not really a good expression for what we are talking about—is that the scientific community has got itself into the position where it has not only failed to assemble facts or develop opinions on what could be done and what the results would be, but has failed to make the connexion so that such factors are taken properly into account when the political decision is made. The only thing that science policy can ever do is to establish that connexion and see that decisions are taken in the light of a knowledge of the real basis of choice. When one says—and I take issue with Professor Bernal on this—that the scientific community has not reacted against this decision enough, I would say the scientific community cannot stop such developments after the decision has been made, because that would mean that the scientific community should exercise political power; and my belief is that if this happens, the scientists would make as big a mess as the politicians.

Foster: May I follow that up. My only quarrel with Mr. Carey's paper is that he seemed to pose a dialectical process. In the United States, he seemed to say, the thesis had been followed by an antithesis. There had been a step back from the Kennedy era towards a more realistic, practical approach in which account is taken of the multiplicity of political processes and political goals. And this was a movement away from the idea of the scientist, using reason, being king, in the sense of taking the decision. I would not have thought this realization was surprising, or should dismay us. No sensible scientist can really have been expecting the elimination of politics and pressures from political decision making, or can really have hoped for a self-consistent administrative system of great complexity from which science policy erupted all in one lump and in an internally consistent manner. All that Professor Ackoff and I have been saying is that you can raise the level of argument by the use of various methodologies and techniques, and various assemblies and presentations of facts, which are all directed to evaluating alternative ways of spending money. It is raising the level of argument that we are after, not capturing the positions of political power. It does not raise the level of argument and rationality necessarily if scientists and economists replace others in the positions of political power.

Ackoff: May I take up the question of the scientist's involvement in the total social process, to which Professor Bernal referred. The scientific community in the United States is engaged in a major revolution at the moment; the immediate cause of which is the Vietnam war. Many issues are being raised concerning scientists' involvement in the social process. There is a major controversy in the United States over the role of the university in the nation's scientific effort. A number of universities, for example, have recently decided to disallow classified research on their campuses, it being taken as antithetical to their educational and scientific functions. The debate is going on. It is clear that the scientist is coming out of his ivory tower and is becoming preoccupied with the social and political aspects of his activity.

Shimshoni: Would it be fair to say that there have been several stages of political involvement? There seem to have been successive generations politically active in the scientific community—the initial great interest in nuclear weapons policy, the concern of the President's Science Advisory Committee for defence problems, and the present interest in understanding the processes and roles of science.

Carey: This is true. When I attend meetings of the President's Science Advisory Committee I am struck by the presence of a younger generation of people, especially from industry, by their independence, and by a decided shift in the subjects discussed. There is a strong urge to be drawn into social problems, much broader than governmental roles affecting national security. This is a very healthy development, but the key to it is the demand put on both the President's Science Advisory Committee and the Special Assistant to the President by the scientific community at large. And this demand is focused most intensively on the Special Assistant to the President —on how he thinks, how he defines priority questions; on what questions are asked; and how well he is prepared to formulate them. This is the generic problem of the Presidency in an extremely complex governmental, international and social situation. This is the most critical role that the Science Adviser can perform for the President, because he has to help the President to see the problems and to pick the right questions at the right time; and it is a very fragile system, because the key points are a few people, and policy making depends very heavily on their abilities to respond.

Shimshoni: Does the scientific community feel that the President's Science Advisory Committee should be a focus for such political feelings of the scientific community, such as the earlier nuclear questions?

Ackoff: I do not think that most scientists in the United States consider that the President's Science Advisory Committee represents them or speaks on their behalf. For example, the Committee is very heavily biased towards the natural sciences, as is the total national science policy.

PUBLIC GOAL-SETTING IN THE UNITED STATES

Krauch: At a Congressional hearing in January 1966 on "Federal Research and Development Programs: the Decision Making Process", it was stated that there should be a re-evaluation of whether the distribution of more than 90 per cent of the total research and development allocation of the United States to space and defence is really in accordance with national goals. Have empirical studies been made to discover whether the American public agrees with this distribution? The German distribution of government money for research and development is very different. Twelve hundred people in West Berlin were asked whether in their opinion Germany spends enough, not enough or too much on military research. In spite of the fact that Germany is not doing very much defence research, the majority of the people thought it was already too much (Krauch, H., and Schreiber, K. [1966]. Forschung und Technischer Fortschritt im Bewusstsein der "Offentlichkeit". *Soziale Welt,* **17,** 289).

In September 1966, West Churchman and his group at Berkeley started experiments to discover how the public reflects on these long-term goals. A sample was taken from the San Francisco Bay area, and I was surprised how much this part of the American public was dissatisfied with the present distribution of funds.

On the other side, the scientific establishment, and especially Professor Weinberg, have for many years been trying to increase research and development on public goals, but projects always get stuck and not much happens. To give one example, I met Professor Weinberg in Israel in 1960. Everybody was at that time impressed by the dangers created by the water problem between Jordan and Israel, and his idea was to build a big reactor for the desalination of seawater. The economic and technical aspects seem to have been satisfactory, but I think nothing happened. Another example is superspeed land transport. This is a broad goal: everyone talks about it. The Japanese have built a beautiful superspeed train and have a new project of a very fast train which they will undoubtedly build, but the corresponding American project is still on the drawing board at the Massachusetts Institute of Technology.

I suspect that the American public is highly aware of these things, and if they were involved in some kind of simulation (and things like this have been done in city-planning in the United States, so there is no reason why it should not be effective in science policy) this awareness which already exists among the public, as it does in the scientific establishment, could be brought to bear on the broader political process which as yet does not react to it.

Carey: Concerning criticism by citizens of the structure of the budget and national priorities in using funds—you are really talking about that, I think, rather than the research and development component, which is less visible —my personal judgment is that if, say, a referendum were held on the fractions of the tax revenue that should be spent on space, on defence, on the war on poverty, on the improvement of the environment, and so on, the result would be very much in accord with present distributions, *for present conditions*. If you put the question "Assuming a trillion dollar gross national product in five or six years, what would your preference be for the way society uses its investment?", one would probably find that a very different pattern of distribution was desired.

The administrative and decision-making process is, I believe, reasonably sensitive to what the country thinks. A congressman is built very close to the ground. He is not a maker of public opinion as much as he is a mirror of it, and while most of us in the United States are not happy about present allocations, we are reasonably well persuaded that the factors that induced those allocations are not ones that we can do much to change. They are externally brought about; historical factors have led to this configuration of public investment. While we want to see a change come, we are reasonably satisfied with what we are doing at present.

One of the difficulties arises from the levelling off of government investment in research and development in 1964, after a steep acceleration in the late 'fifties and early 'sixties. Investment has remained stable, in absolute terms, since 1964, whereas the gross national product has risen by over 5 per cent per year, so that investment in research and development is losing ground. At the same time, we have also been multiplying our public policies, and becoming concerned about the shape of our cities and urban life generally, about air and water pollution, energy problems, population trends; we are committed to fighting the problem of poverty. Strategies are needed for this and some can be developed through research and development. But I see no early prospect for a major augmentation of government expenditure for research, and great difficulty in making a case that we are spending insufficient amounts on science.

Dalyell: Dr. Krauch is worried about the way in which public goals are known and yet never seem to be reached. Mr. Carey has said that one of the functions of the Special Assistant, Dr. Hornig, is to act as a lightning rod for ideas "that might otherwise be lost in the traffic". Does he see this as an effective way of progress-chasing for the public goals that Dr. Krauch is worried about?

Carey: It is certainly not the most efficient way. It happens to be effective on a case-by-case basis. I did not want to suggest that it is a satisfactory substitute for a more comprehensive policy-analysis structure, which we once hoped to create in the National Science Foundation. What we came to instead was a variety of centres of advocacy in programme environments—in the Atomic Energy Commission, in the National Aeronautics and Space Administration, in the Public Health Service, and elsewhere—to be co-ordinated through a presidential-level mechanism for science policy. We are still groping for a more effective way of recognizing scientific opportunities and relating them to goals.

Weinberg: In many respects this lightning-rod function is almost the only kind of mechanism in which the new outlooks and new points of view that Dr. Krauch mentioned can come to light. I have a deep belief in the role of the technological entrepreneur or advocate. One of the great advantages of the Special Assistant is that he represents a place in government to which the technological entrepreneur can bring his ideas, and if things are right, something will happen. Dr. Krauch mentioned the desalination project in Israel, but although publicly one is not aware of progress, much has actually happened. It is not unlikely that by about 1975 large desalination plants will be built in Israel; they will certainly be built in California. In this case there is no doubt that the Science Adviser—Dr. Jerome Wiesner—was instrumental in getting the project started, together with some articulate technological entrepreneurs and advocates, notably R. P. Hammond.

In general, in formulating social goals, the difficulty seems to be not so much in deciding on goals in broad terms but in getting hard, effective technical ideas for attacking them. Once the technical means are there, there are plenty of avenues for putting the goals into practice.

Freeman: I am not sure this is true. The public has had experience of very ambitious military and space projects which have been successful, within their own limits. It has not had experience of similarly large, very ambitious welfare-orientated research and development, and here I think there is a very important function, in Professor Ackoff's sense, of "guts" in technical and political entrepreneurs. We need political entrepreneurs who are prepared to take the same kind of risks in research and development into social problems as the military and political experts are prepared to take in military research and development. It is not simply a question of technical ideas, but also of political entrepreneurs, and technical entrepreneurs linked with them, prepared to take high risks in research into social welfare.

Binning: This is also important in the other half of the problem, that of stimulating creative scientific and technological thinking. You do not command the interest of the best technical and scientific effort in a country unless it can see that the country is prepared to take risks. I am sure that this is one reason why in the United States, in France and the United Kingdom a large proportion of the best scientific effort has devoted its energies to areas that are recognized as having high priority because of the scale of the political decisions needed for effective action. This is what generates the atmosphere, not only of the acceptance by the general public of expenditure on a large scale, but of the respect and interest of the research workers who contribute to technical success.

SUBSTITUTES FOR DEFENCE SPENDING

Dalyell: Mr. Carey, you mentioned the need to substitute new projects for defence projects in technologically orientated industry. Would you like to develop this point further?

Carey: I would start by referring to a report published in July 1965 by the Committee on the Economic Impact of Defence and Disarmament.* This was a continuing cabinet-level committee established by President Johnson and charged with responsibility for "the review and co-ordination of activities in the various departments and agencies, designed to improve our understanding of the economic impact of defense expenditure and of changes, either in the composition or in the total level of such expenditure". It is not a conclusive report but it is a thoughtful one, in which we find, for example, this statement: "Over the past fifteen years, defense industry, especially the development and production of strategic weapons, has absorbed a large fraction of our national resources for research and development. As the production of strategic weapons brings us close to our needed strength, the demands of defense on our scientific and technical resources are levelling out. Release of these resources provides a growing opportunity to use them for the improvement of civilian technology and government operations and for the strengthening of basic science. Public and private groups should seize this opportunity to improve our economic wellbeing and to raise our rate of economic growth. A reassessment of Federal policies regarding science and technology has become appropriate, a reassessment which is already producing new policy initiatives".

---

* The Committee was established on December 21, 1963, by memorandum of President Lyndon B. Johnson to the Secretaries of Defense, Commerce, and Labor, the Chairman of the Atomic Energy Commission, the Administrator of the National Aeronautics and Space Administration, the Director of the U.S. Arms Control and Disarmament Agency, the Director of the Office of Emergency Planning, the Director of the Bureau of the Budget, and the Chairman of the Council of Economic Advisers.

"Much public interest has centered on the possible transfer to civilian purposes of the new techniques of systems-analysis and of operations research, the development of which has been stimulated by defense requirements."

The report goes on to suggest ways in which this might be relevant. It also identifies kinds of research and development which might take the place of defence-orientated research and development. It suggests, for example, oceanographic research and development, and weather modification, as strong candidates, and identifies problems of urban technology and suggests systems approaches to the solution of population-density problems, transportation problems and so on in urban environments. In other words, it relates changes in social behaviour in the United States to capabilities that we have created for defence purposes but which have other uses. This report was designed not to settle the question but to illuminate it, to promote discussion and to get review. I commend it to you as being suggestive of the United States Government's awareness of the need for advance thinking in this immensely difficult policy area, as well as an indication of what we might do under conditions of disarmament.

POLICY FOR AMERICAN INVESTMENT IN SCIENCE OVERSEAS

Shimshoni: The United States is probably the only country with a science policy problem concerning the funding of research carried out in other countries. Mr. Carey, by what process do you decide the extent of funds to be spent on science outside the United States? The problem is interesting from the point of view of American foreign relations. It is also quite a problem for small recipient countries. For example, about 50 per cent of the medical research in Israel is sponsored by the Department of Health, Education and Welfare in Washington. The percentage of agricultural research supported is smaller. An important question for a small country is the extent it should depend on resources which may alter according to the will of a foreign government.

Carey: There is no very clear answer here. The decisions to export research support, so to speak, are again made within the smaller universes of the departmental or mission-connected agencies, or in the case of the National Science Foundation, not quite so mission-related. There is no aggregating of overseas research for the purposes of decision in the United States; it takes its chances in the particular market situations of departments and agencies. However, a country—maybe a developed country—occasionally approaches the United States through foreign affairs channels with a proposal for a joint funding with the United States of a collaborative research undertaking. This tends to be bilateral negotiation; the impulse, however, comes from the recipient country, even if it is a developed country. These proposals are viewed in our system on a case-by-case basis, but I think we are generally disinclined toward proliferating bilateral science arrangements. Our strong preference is for open collaboration apart from government-to-government formalities, and we certainly do not believe that United States science support in a foreign country should be more than incidental and transitional.

The other fact is that we have to consider the balance of payments problem, and in the last two or three years we have been very stringent on the standards and criteria for sending money abroad, let us say, or for supporting foreign-based research. My personal view is that the order of magnitude of balance of payment effects is almost invisibly small, but, like most irrational issues, more is made of it than it deserves and so we cannot ignore it. As a result we have been very stringent in holding down our support of research overseas, probably unwisely.

GENERAL DISCUSSION

NATIONAL SCIENCE POLICY IN CANADA

Whitehead: In Canada, two new organizations, the Science Council of Canada and the Science Secretariat, have recently been established to assist the government in formulating a national science policy, and I would like briefly to describe their functions.

The Science Council of Canada, although created by Act of Parliament, is a public body and not an arm of government. The Council consists of a part-time chairman and members drawn equally from government, universities and industry. The question of whether the social as well as the natural sciences should come under its responsibility is not clear-cut. The Act setting up the Science Council does not exclude the social sciences, and could be interpreted to include them. I believe that Dr. Solandt, the Chairman of the Science Council, feels it necessary to move in some way towards the social sciences. Certainly, the Science Council's studies of the relationship between science and society will be based at least in part on techniques derived from the social sciences.

The Science Secretariat, which together with the Cabinet Secretariat, is part of the Privy Council Office, provides staff support for the Science Council (see Fig. 1). The Director of the Science Secretariat is an associate member of the Science Council. In addition, the Science Secretariat supplies information and staff for various Cabinet committees, for a committee of Cabinet Ministers known as the Privy Council Committee on Scientific and Industrial Research, and for an interdepartmental panel composed of the permanent heads of science-based departments and agencies. The Science Secretariat also works very closely with the Secretariat to the Treasury Board.

A prime function of the Science Secretariat is to provide background information to assist the Science Council in preparing its advice to the government and to assist the government in framing its overall science policy. For this purpose, it sponsors studies of various segments of scientific activity in Canada. These studies are made by teams of consultants or by professional societies under contract with the Secretariat. The funding of these studies by the Secretariat has made it possible for many of Canada's ablest scientists and engineers periodically to devote their full time to the

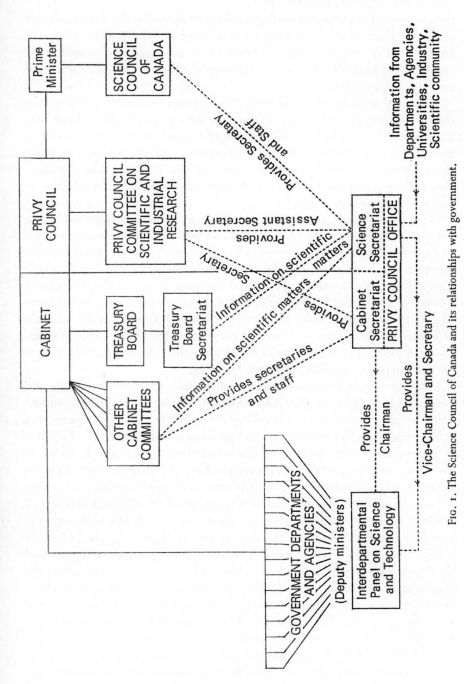

Fig. 1. The Science Council of Canada and its relationships with government.

preparation of reports that will provide guidelines for the future science policy of the country. Most of these reports will be published on the authority of the Science Council. Some of the information obtained in the studies is fed immediately into government channels to influence decisions on short-term projects.

Neither the Science Secretariat nor the Science Council has a budget for doing research, nor any authority nor executive power in allocating funds. That power lies entirely within the regular departments and agencies of government; in other words, government departments and agencies make their proposals through their Ministers to the Cabinet. The decisions about allocation of resources are made by a committee of Cabinet Ministers known as the Treasury Board.

Until 1966, the National Research Council of Canada reported to the Privy Council Committee on Scientific and Industrial Research rather than to a specific Minister, although in practice it reported to the Minister who was Chairman of the Committee. A recent change in the National Research Council Act provides that the National Research Council, like the Science Council and other agencies of government, reports to a designated Minister. The designated Minister for the National Research Council is the Minister of Industry (who at present is the Chairman of the Privy Council Committee on Scientific and Industrial Research), while the designated Minister for the Science Council is the Prime Minister.

I have been asked whether, in view of the fact that the Science Council has no funds to disburse, the Chairman's relationship with the government really helps him to do the kind of things for which this form of organization was set up—namely, to give a special position to and awareness of science at government level. Because of this whole structure, there is an ever-increasing awareness of the existence of science and the part it has to play in government policy. However, there is a strong emphasis within the Cabinet Secretariat and the Treasury Board Secretariat on the distinction between policy for science, in which they are always interested, of course, and the part that science can play in the determination of government policy, in which they generally have a more immediate interest. They recognize that the Science Secretariat is involved in both; hence the Secretariat is brought increasingly into day-to-day decisions on government policy, not necessarily related to research and development. Similarly, the Science Council is not in any sense a "research council"; its interest lies in the broad interrelationship between science, society and government.

Table I breaks down expenditure on research and development by the various departments of government in the four sectors with research and

Table I

FEDERAL GOVERNMENT SUPPORT OF SCIENTIFIC ACTIVITIES IN CANADA, 1965–1966

Expenditures (in millions of dollars)

Government departments and agencies	Federal Government	Industry	Universities	Other
Agriculture	39·2		0·1	
Atomic Energy of Canada Ltd.	49·8	5·3	0·2	
Canadian Armed Forces	17·3	26·0		
Defence Research Board	31·6	8·4	2·6	
Fisheries and Fisheries Research Board	14·3		0·6	0·3
Forestry	13·5	1·6	0·1	
Industry		24·7	2·0	
Medical Research Council	0·1		11·2	1·0
Mines and Technical Surveys	49·8	1·1	0·3	
National Research Council	40·4	3·6	21·2	1·5
Other	21·0	0·2	4·7	2·5
Total	277·0	70·9	43·0	5·3

development activities. Of the total of $396 million shown, about $294 million represents operating expenditures for research and development; the remainder consists of capital and expenditure on other scientific activities, such as surveys. In the fiscal year 1966–1967, total Federal expenditure increased from the $396 million shown in Table I to about $500 million—that is, about $25 per capita. Areas showing the most rapid rate of increase in recent years are support for university research (chiefly through the National Research Council and the Medical Research Council) and for research in industry (chiefly through the Department of Industry and the Department of National Defence). In the past two years the rate of increase of expenditure within government facilities has fallen off, however, in relation to the rate of increase of the gross national product. These changes are deliberate, in accordance with the government's belief that there was an imbalance in earlier patterns of expenditure.

I might also mention that in Canada, as in Germany, responsibility for education lies with the provinces rather than with the Federal government. The Federal government has, however, in recent years channelled funds to the provinces to assist in the cost of operating the universities. This function has recently been transferred to the Department of the Secretary of State.

The experiment on the prediction of future growth, to which I referred (p. 112), was to extend the pattern of Table I into the next 10 or 15 years in as much detail as possible, on the basis of several different sets of assumptions. It takes into account all the knowledge that we have about plans, forecasts, probable change, but adds to it hypothetical new projects. The

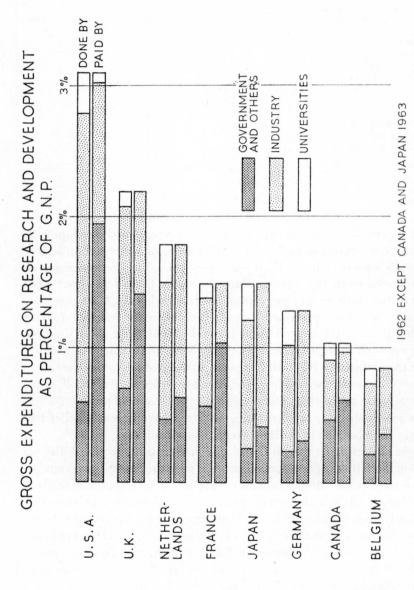

Fɪɢ.2. Comparison of gross expenditure on research and development in various countries, as a percentage of their gross national products. (Sources : Dominion Bureau of Statistics, Science Secretariat and Organisation for Economic Co-operation and Development.)

study will be placed before science policy advisers in the Science Council, as an illustration of the kind of decisions that have to be made in planning the relation of research and development to the economy in the future. There is nothing magic about the assumptions and figures we put in, but they are made as realistic as possible to form a basis for meaningful discussion.

Turning to comparative aspects of expenditure on science, it might be helpful to present summarized data on the distribution of research expenditure in various countries. Figure 2 shows research and development expenditures as percentages of the gross national product for several countries. It shows the distribution of expenditure by the three main sectors, namely universities, industry and government (work "done by"), and indicates the sources of the funds ("paid by").

Canada is roughly comparable to countries such as Belgium and the Netherlands. Nevertheless, of particular concern is the very low proportion of research done by Canadian industry—lower than any country shown, except France. This is in contrast to the United States, where industry does most of the research and development while the government still pays for most of it.

The figures for universities are the least reliable. For instance, expenditure by the British universities on research could not be shown because of the absence of reliable data. Lord Todd has told me, however, that for the universities in Britain, the position is that their material resources, other than those they receive from the government, have not increased, although their efforts have increased, so that on Fig. 2 they would come out as a diminishing amount. The figures for Federal government support of research in the Canadian universities are known accurately, but the amounts provided by the universities themselves are uncertain. For the United States, contributions by the individual State governments are omitted entirely.

Figure 3 shows growth patterns for research and development in the major sectors of scientific activity of three countries—Canada, the United States and the United Kingdom—as percentages of the total expenditures on research and development. The sudden decrease in research and development activity in Canadian industry between 1957 and 1959 was due to the cancellation of the ill-fated "Arrow" project for supersonic fighter aircraft, which was a single project big enough to make a dent in the whole pattern. The different proportions of expenditure on research and development in industry in the three countries show up very clearly. The Canadian proportion of expenditure in universities is going up at a tremen-

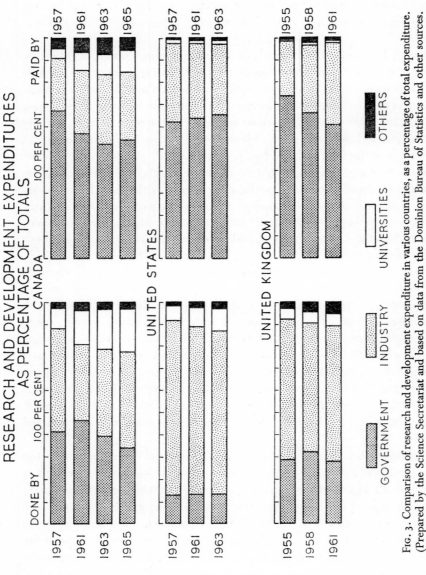

FIG. 3. Comparison of research and development expenditure in various countries, as a percentage of total expenditure. (Prepared by the Science Secretariat and based on data from the Dominion Bureau of Statistics and other sources. See [1965]. Research funds used in the nation's scientific endeavour 1963. *Reviews of Data on Science Resources*, I, no. 4, 6. [1961]. *Annual Report of the Advisory Council on Scientific Policy 1961–1962.* Cmnd. 1920, p. 13. London: Her Majesty's Stationery Office.)

dous speed. The patterns of paying for research are quite similar in the three countries, but the patterns of spending are very different. Proportionally, far less research is done by industry in Canada than in the United Kingdom or in the United States.

BASIC AND APPLIED RESEARCH

Szalai: I would like to make a point, partly in connexion with Dr. Whitehead's contribution, about orientation of research on institutions and orientation on branches of industry. This is a cardinal point. We speak of rubber research, aerospace research, textile research and so on, and even collect statistics under those headings. The National Science Foundation statistics are the only ones to attempt a double-accountancy, for field-orientated and product-orientated expenses; yet this is really essential. In the whole of national research planning and decision making, there is far-reaching ignorance about the correlation of research needs in specific branches of production with specific disciplines of scientific research. One wants, say, to develop the rubber industry and one thinks that therefore more money must be put into "rubber research"—but what is "rubber research"? It is a compound of research on chemistry, mathematics, engineering, mechanics, X-ray spectroscopy and many other things. A double-accountancy is necessary in research statistics: if something has been done for a certain product, enter it against that product, but if it has also been done for a certain scientific discipline (as is mostly the case), enter it against that discipline too.

I cannot imagine how projections over 10 or 15 years can be made without such an analysis. For instance, what was aerospace research 20 years ago? It was primarily aerodynamics. Today, aerospace research includes subjects like ceramics. We need more knowledge here. What kind of research is called "rubber research" today, what was it yesterday and what may it be next year? Branches of celestial mechanics had to be developed by the aerospace industry because never before had it been necessary to make celestial mechanics so exact as to make possible the launching of satellites. So aerospace research includes research in Newtonian mechanics. The further you go into industrial research and decision making, the more knowledge is lacking of what the composition of this type of research should be, how many engineers work in it, how many mathematicians, how many economists and so on. There is a mythical concept of industrial research—research in a "branch of industry". Some exact case-studies and basic research *on* industrial research are needed, to find out what kind of elephant it is!

Weinberg: A study has just been prepared for the Daddario Subcommittee of the Congress ([1967]. *Applied Science and Technological Progress.* A Report of the Committee on Science and Public Policy of the National Academy of Sciences to the House Committee on Science and Astronautics, May, 1967. Washington, D.C.: United States Government Printing Office). This committee sponsored the study which culminated in the report *Basic Research and National Goals.* It is interesting that in that study, concerned as it was with basic research, the institutional focus was the university. The second study is on applied research, and its institutional focus is the large multi-purpose industrial research establishment—either government-run or privately organized.

Szalai: But is it multi-purpose or multi-disciplinary? This is my point.

Weinberg: It is multi-disciplinary and in the case of, say, Bell Laboratories, single-purpose. But as time goes on, the relevance of original institutional purposes may wane. I believe that one of the central issues facing science policy throughout the world today is the redefinition and sharpening of the purpose of government institutions. If their purpose is clear, the judgment of what mix of basic research and applied research and development is necessary for the institution becomes a secondary question and relatively simple.

As my second point, may I come back to the idea that I mentioned (p. 33) slightly with my tongue in my cheek, that when one sorts out research according to its purpose, it is evident that applied research has a specific purpose and one supports it basically as an overhead on the achievement of a certain politically defined mission. One then includes a certain amount of basic research for various reasons, chiefly so that one can do the applied research better. One continues to tease out the various segments of research that can be related to national purposes, leaving finally two kinds. The first is the undirected basic research that is impossible to orientate, what I call "intrinsic basic research" and Harvey Brooks and George Kistiakowsky call "academic basic research". Secondly are the big science spectaculars like the Serpukhov accelerator or orbiting satellites, each of which has to be looked at separately.

To come back to the point I raised facetiously, but which should perhaps be taken seriously. In thinking about the role of what is called intrinsic or academic basic research, one should take that nomenclature seriously. If one agrees that intrinsic basic research is part of the educational system, and is being done to further education, then the decision to be made is how much education one wants, and the basic research necessary to carry on this education is a secondary, derived decision. Whether this is a practical matter, and whether it is possible to put the National Science Foundation into the Office of Education or *vice versa* is not at all clear—we have to be realists about tidy theoretical arrangements.

Carey: I could see the National Science Foundation under the umbrella of education. But I cannot possibly see it as a component of the Office of Education!

Rexed: I would like to see programme budgets, instead of budgets related to departments which are more or less formal institutions—in other words, I would like us to try to relate budgets to functions and to problem areas of government. The Swedish government has a strong interest in this idea, because it would make it possible to relate expenditure more closely to what the government wants to do. If that is possible, I would also like to have research expenditure related to functions and problems in the same way and considered with the programme budget. This method would help us to identify the functional areas within which, by operations analysis perhaps, one might find the place for research. In this system, one could also try to relate basic research. You could do it through education, because a certain part of the educational system exists mainly to serve a certain level of activity in a country. The exercise would have more than academic interest, because it would help to fix the attention of politicians and citizens on the importance of supporting that basic research which helps to produce people to work in these functional areas, not only in research but as leaders in its future application. Professor Weinberg has been close to this in thinking of basic research as a kind of overhead cost, but I would prefer to relate research directly, even in a long-term relationship, to activity in specific sectors of society.

Dalyell: Political entrepreneurs have a certain difficulty in justifying basic academic research, especially if costs continue to mount, as they are doing in particle physics. May I ask Professor Weinberg whether he thinks there is the potential and need for co-operation between American scientists and European scientists, particularly in relation to particle physics?

Weinberg: That is a loaded question! I am all for co-operation: the problem is to identify valid, co-operative projects that would really serve the cause of international understanding. I have a personal gimmick that I have been selling for about five years. The Soviet Union has a 70 Gev accelerator, the United States has its 200 Gev accelerator. Why does not Western Europe, instead of pushing for the 300 Gev accelerator, try to get the United States, the Soviet Union, Western Europe and possibly China for that matter, to build a 1,000 Gev accelerator? This would make eminent good sense.

179

Todd: You will find that proposal in *Hansard*, in a speech by me four years ago!

Szalai: We have been equating university research and academic research, but I do not find university research always so academic. On the contrary, because they lack funds, people doing research in universities want to compete with industrial research laboratories, trying, even with their most basic research project, to find a way to sell it to an industrial sponsor or a foundation. The simple identification of university research and academic research is not entirely true any more. But for *really* academic basic research, I know of no country that has solved the problem of financing it.

Todd: I want to return to the question of whether one wants government institutions for research at all. May I first mention a related point. Professor Rexed (p. 135) spoke of government support for putting developments of inventions into industry in Sweden, in a similar way to the National Research Development Corporation in the United Kingdom, and mentioned the initial lack of success of this kind of system. This may be because, first, not so many discoveries are made which would be useful to industry but which industry does not know about. Secondly, industry is more likely to be interested in an innovation closely allied to what it is doing already. Thirdly, I doubt whether government has any proper role in industry, apart from providing the additional capital necessary if a research project which should be undertaken in the national interest is too big to be handled within the capital structure of any one company or consortium.

Rexed: Some economists would say that the situation of private industry induces an under-optimization of research and development investment, because projects that are technologically sound and may lead to useful production are sometimes so large and have such long-term risks that they are not taken up. Secondly, every industry has a certain structure and a certain market, and this makes it unlikely to take up certain projects. For instance, if the proposed projects are at the margins of its interest or clearly outside the usual marketing apparatus, such high capital investment might be provoked, if the development succeeded, that industry is afraid to take up the project, although it would be feasible. For these and other reasons there is felt to be an under-optimization of research and development spending in industry, in that part of spending that Dr. Pannenborg called "offensive development". The defensive, passive research and development effort in industry is fairly well looked after, because it is necessary to defend areas in which the company is established. The offensive part, which is directed towards adjacent or alternative technologies, may be forgotten (cf. p. 101).

Pannenborg: If I may speak from the point of view of a large private industry in the Western world, located in one of the smaller countries [The Netherlands], we believe that governments have a task to do in research and development with regard to national needs where profitability does not provide an incentive—that is, in the military sphere and in relation to communal or public problems. If the government is tempted to intervene in more mundane areas of a potentially economic nature that have nevertheless been neglected by industry—say, because of the risks involved—then new problems are introduced, both in the sphere of management and in the day-to-day guidance of the enterprise towards its goals, and also in ensuring the transfer of research results to practical manufacture. Within private industry there is an automatic correction or negative feedback which ensures that it does not deviate too much from the final social reality of production assayed through the mechanism of the market. We at this meeting are scientists with experience in the management or analysis of scientific questions. But to be an industrialist, or an entrepreneur in interaction with a market, is just as much a specialty as the scientific specialties. In applied research the feedback loop from the industrial outlet is essential, and the environment of the government laboratory does not usually supply that. There is therefore a danger that its aims will become unrealistic.

There are special circumstances in which the government is the best body to undertake work—for example, if the basic motive is political, such as fostering national prestige and the national image; space projects are a clear example. In my own country, the government is not interested. However, the largest reserve of natural gas has been found in Holland, and a clear extrapolation would be to do long-term research on fuel cells fed by methane, but no one is doing it, because we have no heavy electrical industry which might take the initiative, and the government is not moving either. To my mind this is a clear task for the government, because this would be a further exploitation of the country's natural sources of wealth. This would then be very similar to the Canadian situation of the Ministry of Mines and Natural Resources, and rather like the desalination project in Israel, which is not so much a question for private industry as for the government. But in general, because of the difficulty of transferring research findings into practical development and manufacture, I believe that the efficiency of the process is endangered by starting research in a government laboratory and later having to go through a painful transfer into an industrial setting.

I wonder whether in Eastern Europe, with a different social structure in which the distinction between governmental and industrial management does not exist in the Western sense, this transfer process may not be easier? I believe that in certain respects it is. A professor of electro-technology from Eastern Germany with whom I was discussing the problem of material engineering for electro-technical students (which is not always easily solved, because this is a multi-disciplinary subject and chemists or physicists cannot readily be brought together into an electro-technical institute) said that he had no difficulty, because there was a transistor factory nearby and it was natural that the factory played a role in training his students. In a Western economy this could not be done so easily, because the factory would be in private hands and might not welcome students in large numbers. There are evidently special aspects to the socialist organization of society which bear on this question of transfer and interaction between government-sponsored and industrial research.

Nekola: In the socialist countries, research is financed entirely by the State. There are, of course, differences in the form of financing. In principle one can distinguish two forms, namely financing from the State Budget and from enterprise funds. Of the total sum of Kčs. 6·2 billion allocated for research and development in Czechoslovakia, 55 per cent comes from the State budget directly and about 45 per cent through the enterprise funds. It is interesting to note that in the course of the past five years the contributions from the enterprise funds have been growing faster than those from the State budget. The rate of growth of the total research and development expenditure has reached an index of 190; the rate of growth of the State budget funds has been 170 while the rate of growth of the enterprise funds has reached 220.

The form of financing does not, however, answer the substance of Dr. Pannenborg's question. I believe that the problems of the relationships in the sequence: *basic research—applied research and development—economic, technological and social practice,* are equally complex, no matter where one may be in the world, because they arise out of the complex nature of the knowledge-finding process itself. It is evident that social and economic arrangements can improve the mechanism of the relations between research and production considerably. I am of the opinion that the management of society of the type found in the socialist countries creates a good atmosphere for steady and organic interaction between science and the total social practice. There is, however, the question of how the advantages of the present management of the economy and society are used to the benefit of science and its application. The administrative and strictly directive kind of management which overestimates the role of a plan—as it used to be in Czechoslovakia, where it worked against establishing conditions for the steady and organic application of scientific results in the economy and in society—does not allow the full use of the advantages of a State-planned economy to be made. In the new system of management being introduced in Czechoslovakia at present, we are trying to set up a more favourable atmosphere for the interaction between science and industrial and economic practice. This is a rather complicated thing to do because the relations between science, the economy and practice are many-sided.

We believe that the maximal participation of scientists in the management of science, as well as in overall decision making, is the important pre-condition for the sustained organic influence of science on the development of the economy and the culture. This feature has a good tradition and is well understood in Czechoslovakia, and we are trying to implement it in relation to the new system of management. The direct participation of scientists in various governmental and State organs and the growing consciousness and conviction of society of the significant role of science in social life are aspects that are becoming very important.

In this sense, the significance of the Czechoslovak Academy of Sciences as the highest adviser of the government in the affairs of science is also being recognized. The expert reports of the Academy in all spheres of research help to extend the social and economic function of science and to spread recognition of its importance for the further growth of production, of the economy and of society as a whole.

The administrative bodies must understand the significance and potentialities of the utilization of science for the growth of society and the State, and must choose adequate forms for the State management of science. I do not believe that the maximal participation of scientific workers in this reduces the role of the State administration; on the contrary, it is increasing.

This joint decision making of scientific workers, economic experts and the State administration on problems of economic and social development may also create conditions in the cultural, individual sphere for the greater role of science in promoting economic and cultural welfare—as was envisaged by Thomas Sprat and Francis Bacon some 400 years ago.

The relations between science, production and the economy are by their nature full of conflict, which appears in socialist as well as other systems. There is still a lot to be determined and clarified here, but I am convinced that a socialist system in principle provides better conditions for the recognition and application of scientific results, because the social interest in the effective functioning and application of science is made a guiding principle and is not diluted by motives of individual profit. But the possibilities still have to be changed into facts.

Carey: May I revert to the question of sub-optimizing in industry. There appear to be developments in the "infrastructure" of industry that are relevant. The figures giving the change in the managerial direction of American industry in recent years show that over two-thirds of managerial executives in American industry are now drawn from scientists and engineers (on the assumption that a salary of 15,000 dollars or more indicates managerial work—some, of course, will be working as scientists). This is suggestive of the rapid increase in this component of managerial structure. If the trend continues or becomes even more intensive, we shall find that the top structures in American industry are densely populated with people who have an interest in learning about new results and in using this material.

Ackoff: I have seen figures which support your point. A large percentage of managers in large American corporations (particularly ones that are "technologically" based) come from engineering. Ireson reports that more than 60 per cent of graduate engineers in the United States, "either became managers of some kind within ten to fifteen years or left the engineering profession entirely to enter various kinds of business ventures . . ." These occupational and professional transitions have become a major problem in manpower planning (Ireson, W. G. [1959]. Preparation for business in engineering schools. In *The Education of American Businessmen,* p. 507, by Pierson, F. C., *et al.* New York: McGraw-Hill).

Binning: I would add that this change in the managerial structure is occurring in the United Kingdom also, although at a slower rate.

Apropos Lord Todd's comment (p. 180) about the National Research Development Corporation, when the concept of this body was first formulated, immediately after the second world war, the industrial system was generally thought of as a series of discrete processes. One did research, then did some development; one then proceeded to apply that and to work it up to a productive process; then the product was sold. This concept strikes us now as naïve, but this type of analysis was very common in the United Kingdom and the United States at that time. It was on the basis of that sort of reasoning that the National Research Development Corporation was assumed to have an independent role to play, not only to exploit private inventions which had not obtained support from industry, but also in the exploitation of ideas produced in this "sequential" process in government organizations.

Todd: Some of us did not believe this thought process at the time; however, the National Research Development Corporation was created. But I was criticizing the thought process on which it was developed rather than the organization itself.

Binning: Having established it as a permanent institution on what we would probably all now agree was the wrong analysis, it is extraordinarily difficult to change it.

Pannenborg: There is a further factor in the role of government institutes in promoting new industries and the realization of new ideas. As important as the scientific and technological questions is the climate of willingness to take risks. This applies both to people and to capital. Europe has a community which has gone much further in the way of social provision than the United States, and this promotes a wish for security in, say, the young engineer. The same holds for the whole tax structure, which influences the availability of risk capital. These factors are just as important as the managerial structure and whether research is done in a government institute or a private institute.

Saint-Geours: I would not put the problem of the sub-optimization of research in industry and the role of government for France exactly as Dr. Pannenborg did. In France the relation between basic research in the university and research in industry is not sufficient. It is part of the government's task to strengthen the link between basic research and industry. University laboratories often ignore the needs of industry, and industry more often than not ignores discoveries made in basic research in universities.

On the other hand, France is opening its economic frontiers at a moment when the evolution of science and an economic and technical revolution are proceeding very rapidly. France was formerly protected from outside, but now, and especially in the face of the dominant economy of the United States, we have to reorganize the whole structure of French industry. It would be possible to leave this to *laissez-faire*, but in the state of opinion in France this would be impossible. So the government and manufacturers must have an idea of the goals and structure of French industry over the next 10 or 20 years, however generalized. The French government, which intervenes frequently and which owns an important industrial sector, must have an industrial strategy on this point. As research, especially applied research, and the development of research are very closely linked with the growth of every branch and are one of the points of growth in each branch, there is a close link between the industrial strategy of the nation, discussed between government and manufacturers, and the research policy. It is a question of industry and government interpenetrating each other with ideas and with research on research. In France, with respect to the evolution of the whole industrial economy, industry cannot define its goals alone, apart from the government.

Pannenborg: I accept that in the present situation government has a role, through finance, to promote a country's economy. However, in the United States only 20 per cent of total research expenditure is spent in government institutions, and I consider this to be the sum that one has to pay to remain competent. The larger part, however, is spent directly in industry. In France and the United Kingdom, there is the reverse division. More than half the money for research is spent in government institutions, and a smaller fraction is spent directly in industry. Especially in the United Kingdom do you see the effect. There is a Royal Aircraft Establishment at Farnborough employing 6,000 people, but this has not saved the British aircraft industry. The proper policy would be to have fewer people in government employment and spend the amount of money saved in the industry, where you get effective transfer of ideas and a better definition of industrial goals.

Saint-Geours: I disagree with you on who should decide the goals of basic research, applied research, development of research and of the whole industry. In France, industry cannot decide alone.

Pannenborg: This is a question of getting the mechanism established. Once it is generally known that the government has large sums to spend for research and development in industry each year, industry will react and start to make proposals. In the United States there is tremendous competition to build up the company image in order to get government research contracts. This is a process of adaptation and one must give industry time to react, rather than say from the outset that 80 per cent will be spent on government institutions.

Binning: You imply that the United Kingdom spends an enormous amount on research and development in government establishments. But even in the case of aircraft and avionics, in fact we currently spend less than £50 million a year on research and development in government establishments and over £200 million directly in industry. It may be that we still spend too much in government establishments, but the majority of government research and development expenditure is in industry.

Nekola: A characteristic feature of the small developed countries is the growth of their share in basic research. There are several reasons for this, but one which may be most significant is that basic research has as a goal the creation of adaptability for accepting the results of world scientific achievements. This seems to be true of Czechoslovakia, which has an organization much like that of the Soviet Union, but it seems that the development of basic research both in manpower and in financial resources is faster. We try by means of basic research to create, not only the conditions for generating original research results and for methodical progress in particular branches of science, but for the acceptance of world scientific results and for the training of scientific workers as well. Similar problems have been brought out by Professor Rexed and Dr. Whitehead, for countries of corresponding size of population and similar economic and industrial conditions.

CRITERIA FOR RESEARCH : ROLE OF INTERNATIONAL SCIENTIFIC UNIONS

von Muralt: One has to justify the rising cost of basic academic research, and I would like to draw attention to one source of criteria for evaluating research projects that has not been discussed so far. This is the scientific community in a given area of science, which meets every three years or so in an international congress. At these meetings a general opinion about what good work is being done in which area and where is formed. In planning such congresses an international committee selects speakers for symposia and for introductory lectures. In this group a reasonably definite and fair judgment is made about quality and performance in various places of the world. Yet it has never been consulted by the agencies responsible for the distribution of money. I wonder whether such international bodies would not be willing to furnish information about the value of the research in their field. At least 15 international unions exist that organize congresses and other meetings. In the case of the International Geophysical Year, organized by the International Council of Scientific Unions (ICSU), the unions were put to work and did an excellent job! One should ask them whether they would be prepared to have certain expert groups within their structure which would be available for national organizations supporting research and needing advice on certain questions of selection.

ICSU is the roof-organization of this whole structure, and it should be asked for its collaboration.

Szalai: My knowledge of international scientific unions is that they tend to be in the hands of establishments who know very little about the newest trends in research. It took quite a fight before the International Mathematical Union could be convinced that mathematical logic and some branches of knowledge which play a great part in present-day computer science are "worthy" parts of mathematics.

Goldsmith: Professor von Muralt's suggestion is a very interesting one, although there is also a great deal to be said for the doubts expressed by Professor Szalai. But certainly the International Geophysical Year was a magnificent expression of international scientific collaboration,

7*

particularly when we remember that the representatives on the central body of ICSU are *national* scientific bodies. The International Biological Programme that is now getting under way is another example of international collaboration of this kind. One of the problems of approaching ICSU for this purpose would be the need to tread very delicately, because internal political problems are involved, but this does not minimize the suggestion. The Auger Report, produced by UNESCO in collaboration with the United Nations (Auger, P. [1963]. *Current Trends in Scientific Research.* Paris: UNESCO) was a good example of this kind of examination of what is happening in science and which are the main fields of development. It would be useful to have from time to time, on an international scale—and here ICSU, which is largely dependent on UNESCO funds, might be prepared to put up the suggestion—such broad reviews, in view of what we now know about the rate of change of growth in science. Possibly the United Nations Conference on Trade and Development might do such a review for the growth of technology.

SCIENCE POLICY IN PLANNED ECONOMIES

SCIENTIFIC POTENTIAL AS AN OBJECT OF INVESTIGATION AND CONTROL IN THE SOVIET UNION

G. M. DOBROV

Department of the History of Science and Technology, Academy of Sciences of the Ukrainian SSR, Kiev

B Y "scientific potential" we mean the ability of a scientific system, whatever its form, to solve the problems of scientific and technical development presented to it. Scientific potential is a complex of manpower, informational, financial, technical and organizational parameters. These parameters can be controlled by appropriate organizational pressures (Table I).

Ensuring the rapid growth of scientific potential is one of the most important aims of science policy. In the Soviet Union, and in other countries with a planned economic system and a single State science policy, there are strong tendencies to include in the planning of the productive forces the scientific planning of science itself. Indeed, the principal task of the science of science is the generalization of the study of science, with the aim of acquiring such knowledge about science itself as can be used to organize the optimization of the scientific process as a whole.

In recent decades, the amount of scientific information in the world has been doubling every 12 to 15 years, scientific manpower has been doubling every 10 years, and the money spent on science has increased still faster. It is clear that these rates of increase cannot continue much longer.

We are convinced of the necessity for, and the possibility of, scientific and technical progress in all countries. The problem of scientific potential faces countries with a high level of scientific development in a form different from that facing the underdeveloped countries. Nevertheless, in both cases, this problem is basically one of radical improvements in the use of the available scientific potential.

Table I

PARAMETERS OF SCIENTIFIC POTENTIAL

Definition:	Scientific potential is the complex of parameters that define the ability of a scientific system to solve future problems of science and development.			
Main components:	*Supply of manpower*	*Supply of scientific information*	*Technical and financial resources*	*Form of organization of the system*
Groups of parameters:	Total numbers	Availability of new scientific ideas within the country	Financial support of science	Strategy of scientific development
	Qualifications of available manpower	Availability of information on world science	Availability of general equipment and new instruments	Organization giving optimum use of available scientific potential
	Resources and reserves of scientific manpower		Technical level already achieved in industry, and future possibilities	
	Age-structure			

The present world population of scientists is estimated as 2·7 million. The accuracy of this estimate is limited by the difficulties of definition and by the imperfection of world statistics. Nevertheless, we believe that statements by Auger (1963) and Price (1963) are incontrovertible—namely, that 85-90 per cent of all the scientists who have ever lived are still alive. We know also that during the present century the number of scientists in the countries of Western Europe has doubled every 15 years, in the United States every 10 years, and in the Soviet Union, every 7 years.

In 1917, the Soviet Union had 10,000 professional scientists; in 1941 about 100,000; and there are now about 700,000. This amounts to 29 scientists per 10 thousand of population. There are also now about 4 times as many other people involved in the sphere of science (including technical and scientific personnel). As a sphere of activity, science in the Soviet Union has expanded 2 to 3 times faster than all other fields of professional activity. Over the 25 years from 1940 to 1964 the total number of people employed in the national economy has increased 2·35 times; in industry, 2·36 times; in the health services, 2·71 times; and in science, 6·91 times (see *Narodnoe Khozaistvo SSSR v 1964 Godu*, 1965).

An especially important characteristic of scientific manpower, from the point of view of scientific potential, is the number of scientists with higher degrees. In the Soviet Union, this category comprises "candidates" (equivalent to doctors of philosophy in Great Britain) and "doctors of science" (equivalent to British higher doctorates). The numbers of such highly qualified people control scientific development, because they make up the majority of those taking an active part in the scientific process. In the period from 1950 to 1965, the number of people with higher doctorates in the Soviet Union has increased from 8·3 thousand to 14·8 thousand, and the number of candidate degrees from 45·5 to 134·4 thousand (see *SSSR v Tsifrakh v 1965 Godu*, 1966).

What controls these rates of increase? If we accept the premise that in the United States doctors of philosophy play the same role in the scientific process as doctors and candidates do in the Soviet Union, it is possible to compare the annual rates of replenishment of the most skilled scientific workers in the Soviet Union (Dobrov and Klimenjuk, 1966) and the United States (Berkner, 1965). These data (Fig. 1) show that in the war years (1941–1945) the production of doctorates fell much more in the Soviet Union than it did in the United States. There was also a temporary decrease in the Soviet Union in 1957, when higher standards were introduced. In the 1960's, the output of doctorates in the Soviet Union has continued to increase exponentially, whereas in the United States it has already developed a logistic curve, indicating signs of saturation. The upper dotted line in Fig. 1 refers to doctors of philosophy being recruited from other countries and trained in the United States—the "brain drain", as it is called (Bernal, 1964; Editorial, *Hommes et techniques*, 1965). It should be stressed that in the Soviet Union the problem of providing science with skilled personnel is being solved entirely without the importation of scientists. We have no "brain drain".

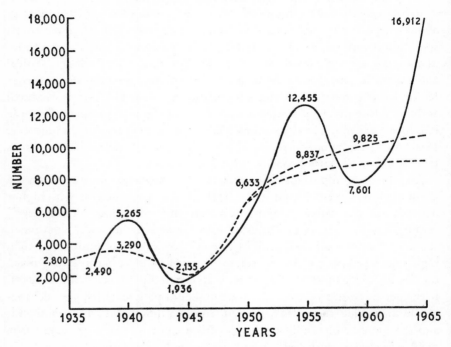

FIG. 1. Growth of highly skilled scientific manpower trained per year in the Soviet Union and United States, 1935–1965. ———, doctors and candidates of science in the Soviet Union. ––––, doctors of philosophy in the United States (the lower curve being the numbers excluding those from other countries).

Naturally, the rates of increase of skilled scientists vary from field to field. The branches of science being developed in the Soviet Union may be grouped as follows (see Fig. 2):

(1) Engineering, physical, mathematical, chemical and medical sciences. This is the most rapidly developing and, at the same time, most numerous group. No less than half of the total increase of skilled scientists occurs in engineering and medicine.

(2) Humanities (history, economics, philosophy, philology and pedagogics).

(3) Geographical and veterinary sciences, and architecture and the study of art.

Differences in the rates of increase to some extent are bound up with the position occupied by the different groups of sciences in general scientific progress.

The high rate of increase of skilled scientific personnel during the past 15 years could not keep pace with the rate of increase of the number of

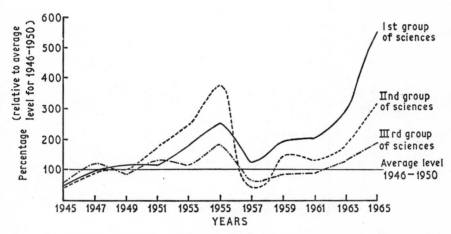

FIG. 2. Rates of increase of the numbers of candidates of science in the Soviet Union, 1945–1965. For composition of the three groups of sciences, see text.

scientists generally. Because of this, the "density" of the most skilled scientists has altered (see *Narodnoe Khozaistvo SSSR v 1964 Godu*, 1965, p. 699; *SSSR v Tsifrakh v 1965 Godu*, 1966, p. 138) from 33·1 per cent in 1950 to 22·7 per cent in 1965. There is an increasing shortage of the highest categories. This seems to be also a world trend.

However, in the past 5 years, large-scale efforts have been made in the Soviet Union to ensure the necessary increase of highly skilled scientists, in accordance with the needs of the country's scientific potential. Accordingly, the rate of increase has been doubled in less than 4 years. It is twice the total rate of increase, for all categories of degree in science.

The age-distribution of the scientific population merits special attention in assessing scientific potential. There are many examples in the history of science to support the thesis that "science is a constantly young organism.

It has a vital need for young manpower''. On the basis of the dependence of creative activity on age, found in studies made in the Soviet Union and in the United States (Lehman, 1954), it is possible to estimate the age-

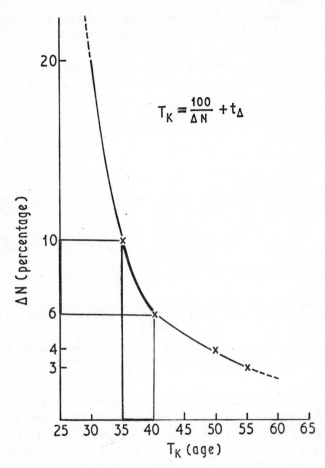

$$T_K = \frac{100}{\Delta N} + t_\Delta$$

FIG. 3. Average age of the scientific team (T_k) at different levels of annual replacement of staff (ΔN) by scientists of various ages (t_Δ, mean age).

structure of specialists in the Ukraine (see Academy of Sciences of the Ukrainian SSR, 1965, p. 119) as near the optimum. We should add that the mean age of scientists in the Siberian Section of the Academy of Sciences of the Soviet Union—the country's largest scientific centre—is only 33 years.

In the present conditions of scientific development, the training of a sufficient number of young doctors of science is not an easy task. The length of training tends to increase. Evidence has been obtained (Dobrov, 1966a, p. 106) that the increase in the number of people in the Soviet Union with doctorates since 1960 is being achieved by increasing the fraction of scientists above the age of 40 years. The task of rejuvenating our scientific manpower is considered to be an important aim of our national science policy.

Since the tendency towards collective scientific work is steadily increasing, the age-structure of scientific teams merits special attention. In the collectives (the department, laboratory, scientific institute or academy) the important task has to be solved of harmonizing the experience, knowledge and skill of the senior men with the special qualities introduced by their young colleagues and students.

Figure 3 shows the relationship found between the mean age of the team (T_k), the mean age of the annual recruitment of new manpower (t_A) and ΔN, the percentage replaced annually. We have:

$$T_k = \frac{100}{\Delta N} + t_A$$

In order to keep the mean age at the optimum (35–40 years) and to replenish with 25-year-olds, it is necessary to replace 6–10 per cent of the staff annually. But a net annual rate of increase of manpower of $7 \cdot 2$ per cent would give a doubling of scientific manpower every 10 years. Such a high rate of increase cannot continue indefinitely. Hence, to form communities of scientists that are stable and self-regulating in age there must be not only replenishment, but also the exchange of personnel with other spheres of useful activity (such as education, production, or information work). The Soviet Union has the possibility of solving this problem in a planned way. The close functional relationships between scientific centres, universities and industry which have been developed in recent years help in this direction.

In analysing the role of "invisible colleges" in the scientific process, on both the international and national scales, the age-structure of such communities is important. We can begin to estimate the "age" of some branches of science, and to find out how the age of the transmitters and creators of scientific information relates to the time-scales of the problems themselves. (See Goldsmith and Mackay, 1966).

An important aspect of scientific potential is the optimum recruitment of young people into science. Essential features of this in the Soviet Union are:

(1) The high educational level of the population. In January 1966, 34·6 per cent of the total population had had secondary education. This is 54·2 per cent of the employed population.

(2) A widely developed, public system of higher special education, with a high proportion of natural sciences and engineering. In the academic year 1965/1966 the Soviet Union had 3,859 thousand university students, 1·67 per cent of the population. In 1965, 170 thousand engineers graduated from institutes after 5–6-year courses.

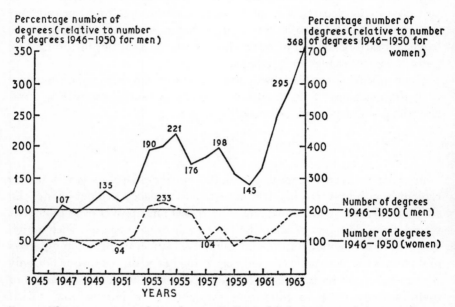

FIG. 4. The increasing numbers of scientifically qualified women in the Soviet Union, 1945–1964. ———, dissertations by men. ————, dissertations by women.

(3) The participation in scientific activity by talented people irrespective of their race, nationality and sex. The last point requires comment. In the Soviet Union 37·6 per cent of the total scientific manpower is, in fact, woman-power, and 44 per cent of those involved in science and its support are women. These figures describe a situation strikingly different from that in science in most other countries.

Data (Dobrov, 1966a) on the part taken by women in the scientific process in the Soviet Union from 1945 to 1964 are shown in Fig. 4, and indicate the significant part played by women in replenishing the resources of scientific manpower.

At the same time, all countries have to face the problem of selecting the most gifted people, at all stages in the training of scientists. Selecting, training and putting gifted people effectively to work are extremely important elements in the growth of scientific potential.

Because scientific investigation is becoming more and more sophisticated and expensive, the rate of increase in scientific manpower has to be exceeded by the rate of supply of technical equipment. We consider that the level of technical equipment used for research in scientific institutions should be at least two orders higher than that in the corresponding branch of industry, where the results of given scientific investigations ultimately will be made available.

The importance of a sound analysis of the organizational, financial and technical aspects of scientific potential is obvious, but we shall make a mistake if we confine ourselves to these alone in the science of science. This would be to behave like an art critic who, in speaking about a painting on a canvas, considers only the quality of the linen. An approach to scientific activity as a specific information process should help to provide a deeper knowledge of the nature of scientific processes. From this point of view, science might be considered as a complex, dynamic system created to collect, analyse and transform information to acquire new truths and new practical applications (Glushkov, 1966). Thus, an important component of scientific potential is the input of new ideas and methods into a given scientific system.

The system that has been developed in the Soviet Union for the flow of scientific information offers favourable possibilities for the science of science analysis of stores of new scientific results. There is the massive collection of documents in the State service for the registration of new scientific results (in existence since 1956). There is also the material of the All-Union Institute for Scientific and Technical Information, where copies of reports of completed investigations are collected. The emergence in our country of such stocks of information, the importance of which is obvious, has followed from the existence of a single State scientific policy, and the complete absence of industrial secrets, since scientific information is not private property. We therefore have available a level of information that is incomparably higher than that in the usual flow of publications: as a result, the repetition of known data, the duplication of information, and the other usual deficiencies of the flow of information are comparatively low.

Some of the characteristic results of the analysis of this flow of information are as follows.

(1) The whole stock of information doubles approximately every 3 years, and in physics, mathematics and mechanics every 2 to $2\frac{1}{2}$ years (Fig. 5).

(2) In physics, mechanics and chemistry there is a close correlation between the proportion of papers in each of these subjects in the

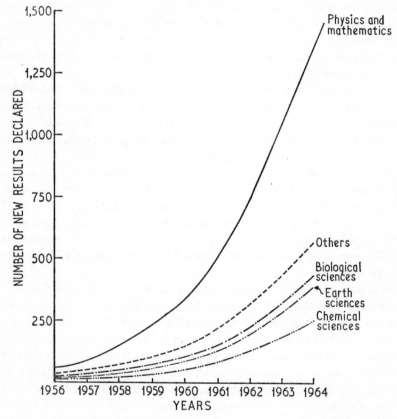

FIG. 5. The increasing number of declarations about new scientific results published in the Soviet Union, 1956–1964, according to the branch of science.

information stock and the numbers of scientists taking a degree in those subjects.

(3) In the information stock we find the same tendency to multiple authorship that was noted by Price (1965a, p. 88) for the *Science Citation Index*. But the actual figures are essentially different: for the period 1950–1960, single-author publications fell from 53 per

cent to 38 per cent, and in our stock of documents for the period 1956–1964 they fell from 97 to 85 per cent.

We regard as an important problem of the science of science analysis the detailed study of data about tendencies in the changes of the "lag" periods —the intervals of time between the formulation of new ideas and their publication, diffusion and realization. This problem is of interest from many aspects, and it has also an immediate connexion with the national science policy of the Soviet Union. The Five-Year Plan (1966–1970) states: "it is essential to increase the effectiveness of scientific research and the applications of its results. To this end, is is important to concentrate scientific efforts and material resources on solving the principal problems of science and engineering . . . to consolidate the experimental base of research institutions . . . to supply them with the newest scientific and laboratory equipment" (*Pravda*, 1966).

The second important information component of scientific potential is the process of supplying research workers with information about other people's work, both inside and outside the country. The need to investigate this aspect of scientific potential is shown by a constant increase in losses of information, in the duplication of research found in all countries and in the lack of utilization of important results. From half to three-quarters of all inventions declared appear to be repetitions of old work, and the size of the stock of unused scientific information increases nearly in proportion to the square of the number of scientists engaged (Glushkov, 1966, p. 17).

Generally, the present situation of science as an information system may be defined as follows: world science knows more and more about the secrets of nature and the new possibilities arising from this knowledge, but at the same time uses less and less of what is already known. This situation is influenced not only by the characteristics of science, but also by private, commercial interests, military secrecy, and so on. The economist W. Leontief has drawn attention to the incomplete use of scientific potential in the United States, and to the loss by the non-use of knowledge which may eventually have a more harmful influence on the rate of economic growth than even the immobility of capital and un-employment (Leontief, 1960). This aspect of scientific potential is significant for the sociology of science, and we have undertaken a study of the mechanism of the flow of scientific information and the tendency for its use to decrease. (For the results, see Dobrov, 1966a, b; Dobrov and Smirnov, 1966; Glushkov, 1966; Academy of Sciences of the Ukrainian SSR, 1966.)

It should be noted that the method of analysis of the *Science Citation*

Index (Garfield, 1963, 1964; Price, 1965 b) opens up interesting prospects for the quantitative exploration of the information component of scientific potential.

We must conclude by emphasizing that studies of the flow of information in scientific systems, made with increasingly sophisticated methods, are providing new understanding of how science works and form a basis for the assessment of scientific potential and for deciding on appropriate measures for planning it.

SUMMARY

The author maintains that, in the conditions of the Soviet Union, the principal task of the science of science is the generalization of the study of science, with the aim of acquiring such knowledge about science itself as can be used to promote the optimization of the scientific process as a whole.

The study of scientific potential is considered to be the central problem in the range of science of science investigations. Scientific potential is defined as that complex of manpower, informational, technical and organizational parameters of any science system that determines its ability to solve future problems of science and development.

Evidence is brought forward to show:

(1) That the principal components of scientific potential can be estimated quantitatively.

(2) That in countries with planned economies and a single State scientific policy the growth of scientific potential can be planned and guided.

REFERENCES

Academy of Sciences of the Ukrainian SSR (1966). *Pervyi Simpozium po Primeneniyu Koli-chestvennykh Metodov i Ispol 'zovaniyu Vychislitel 'noi Tekhniki v Issledovaniyakh po Istorii Nauchno-tekhnicheskogo Progressa (First Symposium on the Application of Quantitative Methods and Computers in Research on Scientific and Technical Progress)*. Kiev: Naukova Dumka.

Academy of Sciences of the USSR (1965). *Organizatsiya i Effektivnost Nauchnykh Issle-dovanii (Organization and Efficiency of Scientific Research)*. Novosibirsk: Nauka.

Auger, P. (1963). *Current Trends in Scientific Research*. Paris: UNESCO.

Berkner, L. V. (1965). *The Scientific Age: The Impact of Science on Society*, p. 3. (3rd edn.) New Haven: Yale University Press.

Bernal, J. D. (1964). The brain-drain. *Labour Monthly*, **64**, 4.

Dobrov, G. M. (1966a). *Nauka o Nauke. Vvedenie v Obshchee Naukoznanie (The Science of Science: Introduction to the General Study of Science)*. Kiev: Naukova Dumka.

Dobrov, G. M. (1966b). Model' potoka tekhnicheskoi informatsii (A model of the flow of scientific information). *Nauchno-tekhnicheskaya informatsiya*, **6**, 26–27.

Dobrov, G. M., and Klimenjuk, V. N. (1966). Trends in the number and structure of manpower for science (Ukrainian). *Ukrainski Istorichnyi Zhurnal*, **4**, 110–117.

Dobrov, G. M., and Smirnov, L. P. (1966). Statisticheskie issledovaniya nekotorykh zakonomernostei nauchno-tekhnicheskogo tvorchestva (Statistical studies of certain regularities of scientific and technical creativity). In *Puti Povysheniya Effektivnosti Nauchnogo Truda* (Trends in the Growth of the Efficiency of Scientific Research), part I, pp. 43–51. Novosibirsk: Nauka.

Editorial (1965). *Hommes et techniques (Paris)*, 21, 251, 1051–1061.

Garfield, E. (1963). Citation indexes in sociological and historical research. *American Documentation*, 14, 289–291.

Garfield, E. (ed.) (1964). *The Use of Citation Data in Writing the History of Science*. Philadelphia: Institute for Scientific Information.

Glushkov, V. M. (ed.) (1966). *Primenenie Elektromo-vychislitelnykh Ustroistv v Issledovaniyakh po Istorii Nauki i Tekhniki (Application of Computers in Research in the History of Science and Technology)*. Moscow: Nauka.

Goldsmith, M., and Mackay, A. (ed.) (1966). *The Science of Science*. London: Penguin Books.

Lehman, H. C. (1954). Men's creative production rate at different ages and in different countries. *Scientific Monthly (Lancaster)*, 55, 321–326.

Leontief, W. (1960). Introduction, p. 8, to *The Research Revolution*, by Silk, L. S. New York: McGraw-Hill.

Narodnoe Khozaistvo SSSR v 1964 Godu. Statisticheskii Eghegodnik (Popular Economy of the USSR in 1964. Statistical Annual) (1965). Prepared by the Central Statistical Board of the USSR. P.548. Moscow: Statistika.

Pravda (1966). Direktivy 23 s'ezda KPSS po pya'tiletnemu plany razvitya narodnogo khozyaistva SSSR na 1966–1970 (Directives of the 23rd Congress of the CPSU on the five-year plan 1966–1970 for the development of the economy of the USSR), 10th April 1966.

Price, D. J. de S. (1963). *Little Science, Big Science*. New York: Columbia University Press.

Price, D. J. de S. (1965a). Regular patterns in the organization of science. *Organon*, 2, 243–248.

Price, D. J. de S. (1965b). Networks of scientific papers. *Science*, 149, 510–515.

SSSR v Tsifrakh v 1965 Godu (The USSR in 1965 in Figures) (1966). Prepared by the Central Statistical Board of the USSR. P.138. Moscow: Statistika.

[For discussion, see p. 212.]

NATIONAL RESEARCH PLANNING AND RESEARCH STATISTICS: THE CASE OF HUNGARY

Alexander Szalai

Department of Economics and Law, Hungarian Academy of Sciences, Budapest and United Nations Institute for Training and Research, New York

H UNGARY is not one of the great powers of science, industry or technology. It is a relatively small country with a population of 10 million. Its modern development was hampered until the end of the first world war by the prevalence of an essentially feudal system of agricultural production; between the two world wars a semi-feudal, semi-capitalistic rule, more or less tinged by fascism, put a strong brake on modernization and led the country finally into war and devastation on the side of Nazi Germany.

In spite of this sorry past, Hungary is by no means a country without long-standing traditions in research, especially in disciplines where pencil and paper could serve as the main tools of scholarly investigation. In mathematics, theoretical physics, or for that matter in economics, sociology and psychology, Hungarian talent has made considerable contributions to learning. Although unfavourable political and socio-economic conditions led to a continuous loss of prominent Hungarian scientists by emigration to happier countries, and this long-lasting "brain drain" involved scholars of the stature of John von Neumann, Leo Szilárd, Paul Wiegner, Albert Szent-Györgyi, Karl Mannheim, Eugene Varga—to name only a few—Hungarian science somehow maintained its standards of excellence in some of its better-developed branches even during the most difficult periods of its recent history. And after the second world war, when conditions for research became more favourable, rapid development started on a rather broad front.

At present, 0·8 per cent of Hungary's active population is engaged in full-time or part-time professional research work. (In 1965, 39,384 persons were so occupied—42 per cent as research workers and academic teachers participating in research, 37 per cent as research assistants, 21 per cent in research administration. Total expenditure on research amounted to 1·5 per cent of the national income in 1965.)

The institutional framework of scientific research in Hungary (and I include the social sciences in my definition of science) has reached its present size over a comparatively short period, roughly over the last 15 years. Before the end of the second world war, limited possibilities for professional research were available only in universities, colleges, libraries, museums and similar educational or cultural institutions which were poorly subsidized for research purposes, and in some indispensable governmental research services, such as meteorological and hydrological stations, geological survey centres and public health establishments, all of them overburdened with routine work. Neither the Hungarian Academy of Sciences nor any other scientific organization had the resources to maintain research institutions. Only a few privately-owned electrotechnical and pharmaceutical factories maintained research laboratories of any size.

Even this modest institutional base was almost completely destroyed during the second world war. Most of the scientific equipment was wrecked by the German occupying forces and by the Hungarian fascists, who fled with them. The rest was destroyed during the siege of the capital. But reconstruction efforts began with unprecedented energy immediately after the liberation. In a hungry and inflation-ridden Budapest, when many government officers were still housed in patched-up tenements, one of the first public buildings to be reconstructed, and on an enlarged scale, was the university's biochemical research laboratory. Shortly afterwards the first industrial research institutes were established, employing by 1949 almost 500 persons, and in 1965 well over 10,000. The reorganization of the Academy of Sciences in 1949 was followed by the rapid development of a network of basic research institutes. Their number grew from four in 1950 to 38 in 1965. The more immediate research needs of industry are served primarily by 50 research institutes belonging to the ministries of the heavy and the light industries and concerned mostly with applied research and development. There are, furthermore, 17 agricultural, 13 medical and 11 other research institutes outside the educational network of universities and colleges—a total of 129 institutions having research as their main or only function. There are also 691 university or college chairs, laboratories, clinics, and so on where a certain amount of research activity is performed, in close connexion with educational activities. The number of industrial plants, agricultural establishments, public health centres, governmental offices and similar institutions equipped with more or less sizable research laboratories or sections is 103. Hungarian national research statistics are based at present on a yearly survey covering (as of 31 December, 1965) 923 "research units": 129 research institutes having research as their main or only function, 691 units within the education network of universities and colleges, and 103 minor but still sizable research laboratories or sections which form part of diverse productive, administrative or service institutions. On such an extended data-collection base the 1965 survey covered probably well over 80 per cent of the nation's total research effort.

In a socialist country, where the institutional and material resources of research are provided in the main directly by the government, in government-owned institutions, a rapid and large-scale development of national research facilities, such as took place in Hungary, cannot be planned or carried out efficiently unless research activities are regularly observed and recorded on a country-wide basis. Hence the need for the creation of national research statistics.

The first national statistical survey of research was made in Hungary in 1953 by the Central Statistical Office. Since 1957, the data for national research statistics are collected annually by the Council for Science and Higher Education, in collaboration with the Central Statistical Office and several ministries. Needless to say, it took some time before these statistics reached their present more or less standardized form. For instance, in order to determine what part of the staff, equipment and expenditures of medical research institutions could reasonably be attributed to research activities, careful comparisons had to be made between manpower requirements, layout, specific costs and so on in the clinical sections of medical research institutions and the corresponding departments of ordinary hospitals not specifically equipped for research. It was also important to find out by systematic time-budget studies how different university and college faculties divided their time between teaching and research, or how much time and manpower in various industrial and agricultural research establishments was devoted to such non-research tasks as routine testing, quality control, or productive labour (for example, the manufacturing of instruments or of special chemical substances, plant breeding, and so on).

As in other countries, much thought and discussion went into determining what constituted a research topic ("theme"), as a basic planning and registration unit describing the work carried on in research institutions. Without at least an approximate definition of such a unit, it is impossible to say how many research tasks are undertaken, when they were started, when completed, and so on. Officially, the Hungarian research administration defines the term "research topic" as follows:

"A research topic (research theme) is a specific research goal, the attainment of which will add one, and just one, new and hitherto unavailable elementary research result to available knowledge, and which can be reached directly on the basis of available knowledge and methods, without requiring any preliminary or intermediary results constituting in themselves new research achievements."

This definition sounds rather intricate, but it is theoretically sound. The attainment of a specific research goal requires usually a series of operations which do not in themselves yield any new scientific achievement, even if the sequence of operations is compressed or shortened. The same operations can be performed individually or more or less routinely in many combinations, according to the state of the art. This is why a research topic, as the fundamental unit of research planning and registration, has been defined as a minimum task whose solution goes only a single step beyond what can be obtained by performing routine operations according to the state of the art.

It may happen, of course, that the intended scientific result cannot be reached unless several intermediary problems are solved, the solution of each of which constitutes in itself a new scientific achievement. In such cases, each of the intermediary goals is considered for our purposes to constitute a separate research topic, and what appeared originally to be a single research topic is revealed as constituting an interrelated group of topics.

Unfortunately, it is not always possible to apply this definition satisfactorily. In practice, neither the operational requirements of a given research project, nor its phases and precise boundaries, are very clear, and in most institutions the administrative techniques of recording research processes have not reached a level where the definition can be applied uniformly and unequivocally by the suppliers of data. Hence, indications of the numerical distribution of research topics in Hungarian statistics are only approximations.

The use of such categories as "basic", "applied" and "developmental" research presents a somewhat similar problem. Here, however, the basic definitions are fairly well established and the terms are interpreted in Hungary more or less according to international usage.

In the final analysis, the numerous problems relating to the classification of different categories of research and the division of the research process into measurable units are more likely to be solved by the systematic execution and comparison of a large number of case studies than by further theoretical discussions. Several such case studies have been undertaken in Hungary for the purpose of improving present methods of planning and registering research, many of them representing a transition to the sociological study of research activities.*

When the first attempt was made, in the late forties, to introduce research planning on a national scale in Hungary, it was thought that it would be more satisfactory to centralize top-level decision making for all sectors and branches of academic, governmental, industrial, agricultural and other research into a single body. As in most other socialist countries, the Academy of Sciences was entrusted with the task of planning and controlling the total national research effort, as an institution directly responsible to the Council of Ministers. Although considerable official powers were transferred to the Academy and its administrative apparatus was greatly expanded, the whole scheme did not work very well. Academies, by their nature, are scholarly bodies that are not well suited for carrying out such wide-ranging administrative duties as are involved in the planning and control of the national research effort. It became evident, also, that industrial research—the quickest growing and predominant sector of the national research effort—forms such an integral part of industrial development in general, that its planning and control must be handled by the same authorities which direct industrial development. Also, it proved by no means easy to superpose the authority of the Academy of Sciences on the research activity carried out in the universities. So, during the late fifties, the outlines of a new, less centralized, organization for top-level decision making on matters of national research policy slowly emerged. The Academy of Sciences retained full control over a powerful network of basic research institutes and a number of special research establishments, which it established and sponsored within the framework of higher education, and continued also to act as an adviser to the government on matters of science policy; its authority, as the highest forum for the discussion of general principles in national research planning and of ideological questions concerning scientific development, remained unchallenged. However, a new body, the Council for Science and Higher Education, directly attached to the Council of Ministers, took over the task of working out detailed organizational and budgetary recommendations for the implementation of government policies in the field of science

---

*The system of Hungarian national research statistics is described in more detail in Szalai (1966).

and higher education. This new body was also responsible for the establishment of a National Long-Range Research Plan delineating focal research topics and problems which should have priority treatment in the assignment of financial and manpower resources. (The National Long-Range Research Plan was developed in close co-operation between the Council for Science and Higher Education, the Academy of Sciences, and the National Planning Office.) As a third body involved in decision making on national research policies, the National Technical Development Board was given special powers to work out detailed directives for industrial research and to finance research projects out of special funds in connexion with long-term plans of industrial development. But, within the framework of these arrangements, the Ministry of Education regained more or less full operative control of the research done at the universities, and the Ministries of Heavy and Light Industry, Metallurgy and Engineering, Transport, Construction, Health and Agriculture similarly acquired full responsibility for the direction of research in their own professional sectors, though naturally under the control and co-ordination of the National Planning Office.

Nobody in Hungary would pretend that this somewhat eclectic "pluri-centralism" represents an ideal solution for the difficult problem of efficient decision making on national research policy. It is also no mean task to strike the right balance between centralization and de-centralization or sectoral and institutional autonomy, between tight administrative control of an operation involving a considerable fraction of the national budget and a flexibility of planning and financing well adapted to the peculiar needs of science and research. As a matter of fact, the organization of national research planning is as yet in an experimental stage in Hungary —as probably everywhere else. Many changes can be foreseen in the structure of decision making on research policies in connexion with the economic reforms to be implemented in coming years. As a result of these reforms, for instance, socialist industrial enterprises will have far more freedom than they have had before in deciding about their own development and investment policies, and this necessarily will have an impact on the whole of industrial research. On the other hand, the increasing weight of research within the national budget and the growing impact of research policy decisions on the national economy as a whole might require the creation of a top-level governmental authority to deal with questions more or less affecting all sectors of research activity.

One of the more interesting experiments in the governmental financing of industrial research is represented by the National Technical Development Fund, created a few years ago under the surveillance of the National Technical Development Board. A regulation was put into force according to which, in every branch of industrial production, a certain percentage of the yearly gross production value has to be reserved for purposes of "technical development" (mainly applied research and development, but also the improvement of production techniques by the acquisition of licences, high-level professional training and so on). The percentage of the gross production value reserved for such purposes varies according to the specific development needs, and especially the research needs, of the branch of industry in question. (It is highest, at present, in the pharmaceutical and electronic industries and lowest in such traditional industries as textiles or woodworking.)

By far the greater part of the resources thus accumulated and made available to the National Technical Development Fund serves to finance directly applied research and development projects in enterprises in those branches of industry from which the funds were levied. The National Technical Development Board has available also a certain sum for financing long-range research projects of a more basic character. Hungarian industrial research institutes are maintained mainly through the support of the National Technical Research Fund.

In connexion with this levy on industrial production for purposes of research and development, some rather interesting investigations have been carried out under the aegis of the National Technical Development Board to establish "indicators of research demand", by which the percentage of the gross production value to be spent on research and development can be determined equitably for different branches of industry. Specific costs of research, rates of product and process obsolescence, the times needed for the completion and marketing of new products, and similar operational characteristics, differ greatly from industry to industry, and it is a rather complex task to determine how to make best use of limited funds.

However, research planning based on aggregate data of sectors and branches of national research activity represents only a first approximation to the solution of the tasks which face the planners. To improve the efficiency of national research expenditure and investment, much more needs to be known about factors determining the quantitative and qualitative aspects of the output from that peculiar "black box", the *research workshop*, where research activity actually happens, within the institutional framework of an academic research institute, a clinic, an industrial laboratory, or a pilot plant.

As a matter of fact, very little is known about the social and operational character of the research process. There are, also, very good reasons why relatively few large-scale studies have been undertaken on it until very recently. It is, first of all, very difficult to study research work in progress. Part of the process takes place in the mind, often half-consciously, or outside working hours, and thus remains unverbalized. Another part consists of numerous routine activities and attitudes whose specific function in the research process is difficult to define before results have been reached, and equally difficult to reconstruct afterwards.

Secondly, even though research has a scientific purpose, only rarely can it be considered as an activity performed in a scientific manner. Apart from very general logical and methodological principles, we possess very little precise knowledge of how research should be organized and carried out so as to maximize the probability of obtaining results. Consequently, a form of apprenticeship, analogous to what used to exist in the traditional arts and crafts, remains the best way of acquiring professional research skills. The apprentice, after acquiring some basic scientific knowledge which is not yet sufficient to qualify him for research, joins a good "master" or experienced research worker, whom he helps at first with routine tasks. By keeping his eyes open, by remembering his "master's" instructions and by following his example, which sometimes cannot be put into words, he gradually learns the tricks of professional research and, more important, acquires a "feeling" for research from a combination of knowledge, experience, success and failure.

Thirdly, the research worker and his work generally have a certain prestige in society, and he is apt to put up resistance, in defence of his real or imagined privileges, to any external "control" or "investigation" which might "interfere" with his work. There are, in addition, other types of ritual resistance which prevent careful sociological investigation of research work or of the research laboratory.

In a socialist country, where research is financed almost entirely out of State-controlled funds and carried out in conformity with comprehensive plans, research institutions and groups should, at least in theory, be more readily accessible to sociological investigation, in spite of the difficulties that have just been discussed. In any event, the central planning of large areas of scientific research, carried out over an extensive network of research institutes, should have a stimulating effect on sociological investigations of the general conditions of research and the mode of operation of research institutions.

A certain number of studies on the organizational structure of research teams, their communication and operation patterns, and the criteria of their efficiency have been carried out recently in Hungary. My own investigations on the time-budgets of research workers have included observations on how much time they spend during their working hours in face-to-face contact or direct communication with various members of the "group" or "team" to which they belong, or to which they seem to belong according to the criterion of joint authorship in a number of research reports, professional publications and so on. Results of these investigations tended to show that collective research and team-work are not as common in large research laboratories of the natural and engineering sciences as might appear from the increasing number of research papers with several authors that they put out. There can be many reasons for joint authorship of a research paper other than the collective execution of the research work in question. For instance, co-authorship may merely imply that the research has been divided up among several specialists who had no more contact with each other than workers on an assembly line—each working essentially alone and in a sequential division of labour between persons having highly specialized skills.

These multi-dimensional time-budget studies (multi-dimensional because they considered not only the time dimension of research activities, but also their social dimension as far as contact and communication with co-workers were concerned) were admittedly too limited in scope to be really conclusive. But they indicated rather strongly that in terms of the time devoted to joint activities, or the frequency of informal contacts, there seems to be no great difference between those branches of research where collective authorship is the rule and those where it is not. In many cases, when no serial division of labour between diverse specialists accounted for the publication of a collectively signed research report, it was found that a "star-like" structure replaced the usual "chain"; for example, an experienced senior research worker had a number of junior colleagues of diverse but rather narrow specialization working for him who assembled all the "details". These junior colleagues, however, had little contact with each other.

To be sure, small face-to-face work groups, composed of two or three research workers, do exist, and are even rather frequent in institutionalized research (even as elements of such chain or star-like structures as described above), but real research collectives—real "teams" consisting of half a dozen or a dozen people working together in close and continuous contact —are probably much rarer than one might think from the enormous amount of joint authorship in the research literature of the natural and engineering sciences (and more recently also the "hard" behavioural sciences).

The actual role and efficiency of teamwork in research, the value of different types of group organization for different types of research work, the optimal communication pattern of research workers within various frameworks of specialization and of division of labour—these are only a few examples of problems about which we shall have to know much more before we can develop relatively reliable and economic methods of research planning. Without more insight into what really happens within the small "black box" of the research workshop we cannot hope to answer in a satisfactory manner questions of high relevance for "macro-planning" on the national level—such as to what extent the bottleneck in the supplying of research with highly competent and specialized professional manpower can be relieved by increasing the proportion of technical and administrative assistants in the personnel of research institutes (how much of the research worker's actual workload could be transferred to less costly and more easily available manpower?), or to what extent investments in instrumentation (or in automated instrumentation) can increase the efficiency of research work and reduce its specific costs.

If we do not develop this type of "micro-research" on research (research on the intricate operational structure of the single research workshop), to acquire solid knowledge about all important aspects of that multi-faceted activity which goes on within the "black box", where the concrete and detailed results of scientific research are forged, we can hardly hope to get very far in the improvement of our methods for the macro-planning of research on the level of decision making about national research policies.

REFERENCE

Szalai, A. (1966). Statistics, sociology and economics of research in Hungary. *Social Sciences Information*, 5, part 4, 57–69.

GENERAL DISCUSSION

RESEARCH AND DEVELOPMENT IN PLANNED ECONOMIES

Shimshoni: I understand that there is a considerable attempt to centralize information systems in the Soviet Union, and I wonder how well this works. I gather that a large central organization has been set up, having many departments, with mechanical assistance. This centre should be a focal point for storing and disseminating information on all subjects. On the other hand, there is the view that, with all due respect for modern methods of information storage and retrieval, human behaviour is such that it is better to decentralize and have subject-orientated centres of stores of information. I wonder what your experience has been?

Dobrov: Our information system is a highly centralized one, as you say. The All-Union Institute of Scientific and Technical Information (VINITI) is the central institute of scientific information. One of its main tasks is publishing abstracts, and this is carried out very successfully, but the function of providing an operating information service is not so well suited to a single central body and can be decentralized, in my opinion—as is the information service in the Soviet Union (for a description, see Sviridov, F. [1967]. *Ciba Fdn Symp. Communication in Science: Documentation and Automation*, pp. 182–196. London: Churchill).

Weinberg: A basic question about the way Soviet science policy is made concerns the mechanism of making choices. From your paper I had the impression that the attempt is to try to maximize scientific output without constraint, but obviously there must be constraint, and I wonder how the choice is made.

Dobrov: As far as the actual mechanism is concerned, the Academy of Sciences of the USSR and the State Committee of Science and Technology together prepare a proposition which is presented to the government. As far as our decision-making criteria are concerned, we have three measures —the rate of growth of science, the rate of growth of techniques, and the rate of growth of industrial production. We try to maintain a correlation whereby the rate of growth of science is more than the growth of techniques, which is more than the growth of production:

$$\frac{dS}{dt} > \frac{dT}{dt} > \frac{dP}{dt}$$

(where dS/dt are the number of scientific discoveries per year; dT/dt are the numbers of patents per year; and dP/dt is some measure of annual productivity).

In our plans, we adopt the criterion of growth of production and we try to maintain this correlation; but this is only one possible approach.

Szalai: We have experimented with the following principle in Hungary, which may help with this problem of allocation. We found it very difficult to decrease the amount of money given to any branch of science in comparison to a previous year, so we tried the following policy. Suppose that we are spending 1·3 per cent of our national income on research in all sciences. There is a certain division of that sum between life sciences, physical sciences, and so on. Then we say that we shall continue that division linearly as the gross national product grows, so that every branch gets the same proportion of the 1·3 per cent. But if this percentage itself is increased, as it was from 1·3 to 1·4 to 1·5 per cent, the increases to the branches correspond only to the increase in gross national product and the difference arising out of the extra increase to 1·4 and 1·5 per cent goes to selected branches having an established priority for extra-rapid development. The decisions as to which branches should get such priority treatment are high-level political decisions, and are mostly taken by the Council of Ministers, and by the Central Committee of the governing party in Hungary.

Dalyell: I have been comparing many of the things that Professor Dobrov has said with what Mr. Carey said about the situation in the United States. Would one be right in thinking that many of the pressures which in the United States are carried out either through the President or through the Congress, in the Soviet Union belong to Gosplan and the Council of Ministers? To what extent are the big decisions determined by Gosplan, because my understanding was that Gosplan had a very considerable amount to say in the big decisions?

Dobrov: The main part of the proposals are worked over by the State Committee of Science and Technology. The general approach to the development of science in the Soviet Union is worked out by the Central Committee of the Communist Party, which decides on the general approach to science and its future developments, in relation to other problems of the State. This is a political task, not only a scientific task. Two other institutions of the government—Gosplan (the State Planning Commission) and the Supreme Soviet of the USSR—have the function of allocating money to science.

Carey: Roughly how extensive is research into research at the micro-level in Hungary, Professor Szalai?

Szalai: About eight or ten papers are published each year on this kind of investigation. Over the last six or eight years, fifty or sixty studies have been published, of which I would say fifteen are very good, twenty-five medium and twenty very bad. But it is a beginning. For instance, we have very extensive and detailed time-budget analyses of different "mixes" of research: of education mixed with research (in academic research units), of production mixed with research (in industrial research units), and so on. In the Hungarian national research statistics you will find a conversion of academic research manpower figures based on "full-time research manpower equivalents" for teaching personnel, clinical personnel, and so on, spending only a specific fraction of their working time on research. So we have made some advance.

Freeman: I believe that in your measurements of research and development in Hungary you exclude quality control, testing and information services. Does this mean that your definitions of research and development correspond fairly well to the National Science Foundation definition, or to the Frascati definitions of the Organisation for Economic Co-operation and Development?

Szalai: In 1957 when we began making the first systematic statistical survey of the national research effort in Hungary we took the National Science Foundation definitions as a starting point. They had to be adapted to a certain extent to circumstances in a socialist country, but our definition may be roughly equated with them. This was done deliberately, because we were interested among other things in comparisons with the highly developed apparatus of research in the United States. Categories like "basic" and "applied" research mean about the same thing in American and Hungarian research statistics. According to Hungarian usage, development has a somewhat different cut-off point from research, but even there the definition holds roughly.

Ackoff: We have done the sort of work mentioned by Professor Szalai and have tested its validity, using three different methods. First, scientists were asked how much time they spent in various activities; secondly, they were observed by others, using the ratio-delay technique; and thirdly, scientists were given random signal devices and they recorded their activity when the signal was given. The scientists were very accurate in recording their activities, but their subjective estimates of the time spent in various activities were frequently out by as much as several hundred per cent. To cite one instance, on personal and social activity during working hours, the average estimate of the scientists was less than 1 per cent; the actual amount was close to 10 per cent. (See Martin, M. W., and Ackoff, R. L.

[1962–3]. The dissemination and use of recorded scientific information. *Management Science*, **9**, 322–336.)

SOME ASPECTS OF RESEARCH AND DEVELOPMENT EFFICIENCY:
CZECHOSLOVAKIAN STUDIES

Nekola: The investigation of the efficiency of research and development is one of the most complex problems of the science of science. It is closely connected not only with the economics of science, the sociology and psychology of scientific work, the information processes used in science and the logic and methodology of scientific knowledge, but also with the economic conditions created by society for the use of science.)

An adequate expression of the efficiency of science and technology must be based on a survey of their complex social and economic consequences. Many factors influence research and development activities. Hence, conclusions should be drawn very carefully from a mechanical comparison of the financial input and the economic effect achieved within a given time-period. In particular, one must note that scientific results are also expressed as "information" and in the course of its application, are not used up but are in fact further added to, in the majority of cases.* The following facts should be considered in the complex appraisal of the effects of science.

(1) In practice the major part of new scientific knowledge is realized indirectly, as well as directly, and in every case with a certain time-lag between a discovery and its application. The length of this time-lag depends on many factors (generally of a socio-economic character) and can hardly be foreseen. Furthermore, the degree of realization of scientific knowledge (which represents only the *potential* efficiency of science) is dependent not solely on science itself—that is, on the efficiency of scientific work as such—but mainly on the nature of social life, and the degree to which society is capable of absorbing and utilizing scientific knowledge as a factor in its further progress.

(2) The growing complexity of the process of acquiring new knowledge and the size of the ever-increasing stock of knowledge means that the majority of new scientific achievements, particularly in recent years, have originated as a complicated synthesis of the estimated requirements of society and the initiative of scientists. A new achievement is never solely

---

* This special feature of science was fully characterized by the President of the Czechoslovak Academy of Sciences, Academician F. Šorm, in his opening report at the conference "Problems of Realization of Scientific Results", held 23–24 May, 1966, in Prague (not yet published).

the product of present activity, but is always the result of long-term activity, depending on earlier research and on the traditions of many branches of science.

(3) Scientific results can be realized only partially in actual innovations; many results provide the basis for the further advancement of science and future discoveries, and in this way find eventual practical application. Here a process is involved that was characterized by Academician Šorm as a gnoseological function of science, which represents an accumulated stock of scientific knowledge that acts as an incentive for further progress in scientific activity and consequently also in social practice.

(4) New scientific discoveries create new individual and social requirements and suggest ways in which they may be fulfilled. Science helps to overcome differences between the two poles of social activity—our requirements, and the resources for fulfilling them—as well as providing new sources of such controversy by disclosing structurally new, previously unknown needs of society. Thus science helps to determine the future course of social and economic development.

(5) Many scientific discoveries have no direct economic objectives but are directed towards other social areas (such as the health services, improvement of the environment, protection of the atmosphere and surface waters from pollution, and so on). Even though progress in these areas has indirect economic effects (often of great importance), its economic contribution towards the further development of the productive forces cannot be adequately assessed and quantified.

(6) Some research tasks are concerned with special aims which do not correspond to the general social development. The interests—either real or assumed—of individual countries or territorial and political groupings, however, compel the development of such research. These are mainly research programmes related to arms-production, defence capability, and so on, which, in certain conditions, are given priority regardless of their economic effect. For instance, in a number of countries a large part of the funds for research and development is allocated, directly or indirectly, to research connected with defence. Potential and often actual exploitation of their achievements for non-military purposes results from "spin-off" from these projects, however.

(7) Scientific knowledge plays a significant part in raising the general cultural level of the society. Scientific activity promotes many desirable human characteristics, including the intellectual capability of the society at large, and thus becomes a growth factor of general education and consequently of social development as well.

The facts mentioned, together with the very intricate problems of the possibilities and limitations of quantification in science, show that one-sidedness and mechanical simplification in judging the efficiency of science fosters neither scientific nor social and economic development.

Even if we concentrate only on the economic efficiency of research and development, it must be investigated from several aspects, in view of the dynamics of development and the characteristics of its consequences. In particular, it is essential to examine which scientific branches are connected directly with the development of the economy—or in a broader sense with the development of social practice—and which are connected indirectly. In some cases efficiency may also be expressed quantitatively. It is also useful to estimate, on the one hand, the time-lag in the application of a discovery and, on the other, the time-period during which new discoveries will serve contemporary and future social needs.

The efficiency of research can be greatly enhanced by well-conceived orientation, the satisfactory skill and structure of research teams, international collaboration in science, in addition to sufficient equipment (including computers), an adequate experimental base (pilot plants, prototype and test workshops, experimental and model laboratories, and so on), an efficient information process and the concentration and co-ordination of research and development activity.

Great significance must be attached also to the general socio-economic conditions for the development of science and the speedy application of its achievements (see Kožešník, J. [1967]. Výzkum a praxe [Research and social life]. Rudé pravo, 15th December 1967).

The problems encountered in assessing the efficiency of science and technology can themselves be an aid to the orientation of research and development. Even negative results are of positive value for the society and for the subsequent development of science, just as an ostensibly incorrect trend in research and development may lead to revolutionary discoveries; this fact is closely linked with the element of chance in research.

The orientation of research and development follows closely from the general conception of the nature of a given field. Efficiency usually depends less on the correctness in selecting a particular task than on the strategy of the branch as a whole. Decisions in the orientation of research and development must be based on knowledge acquired at home and abroad, on the world development envisaged and on the analysis of the status and tendencies in borderline areas.

The evaluation of the prospective use of so-called "spin-off" results— often of great importance in the industrial exploitation of research—is no less significant for increasing the efficiency of science than a correct orientation of the main policy of research and development activity.

The dynamics of the development of the particular branch must also be taken into account. When we assess the effects of a problem or line of research we tend to analyse it in isolation; in a full evaluation, however, efficiency must be examined in relation to the main trends in science and technology. No research and development project is ever isolated; it is a product of the research trends of which it forms part, and it represents simultaneously a nucleus and a basis for future discoveries. From this it also follows that a correct science policy can be determined only if the conception, analysis and prognosis of the future development of science and of its consequences for socio-economic development are of a sufficiently long-term character. The longer the time-period for which a research policy is worked out, the higher should be the degree of its usefulness.

Economic efficiency is reflected in the "economy of time", which can be quantitatively expressed in applied research and technical development as savings in labour. Other important economic effects obviously have to be taken into consideration as well. When evaluating the efficiency of the applied research and development carried on in socialist production conditions, it is essential to take account of the total use of labour, from the following points of view:

(i) Annual savings, both direct and indirect, in the entire cross-section of the economy;

(ii) Savings that can be achieved by non-recurrent capital investment in the total economy;

(iii) The frequency and range of application within the economy;

(iv) The expenditure on applied research and development proper.

The total economy of time may be determined on the basis of the effects which society attains by applying new research results. In some conditions, specified beforehand, it is possible to select certain criteria for quantification—for example, coefficients that determine the efficiency of research and development activity. On the basis of our earlier results we present here one way of expressing the efficiency of research and development projects, by means of the coefficient of research and development tasks (k_{tv}) and according to the following formula:*

---

* This formula was developed in *Study on the Problem of Efficiency of Research and Development* (See Nekola, J., and Řiha, L. [1966]. Science in growth—the Czechoslovak case. *International Social Science Journal* (*UNESCO*), **18,** no. 3).

$$k_{tv} = \frac{\sum_{i=1}^{n} (V_{is} - V_{in}) + k_n[(nI_{ts} - N_{vs}) - (nI_{tn} - N_{vn})] + n \sum_{j=1}^{p} k_{nj}(I_{sj} - I_{nj})}{N_{vn} - N_{vs}}$$

$$= \frac{\sum_{j=1}^{n} \Delta V_i + k_n(n\Delta I_t - \Delta N_v) + n \sum_{j=1}^{p} k_{nj} \cdot \Delta I_j}{N_v}$$

where V_{is} and V_{in} are the average annual total production costs using existing and new techniques for alternative units of equipment, i. We use the sum of the effects only in those cases where technically new equipment makes it possible to obtain savings in various sectors of the national economy —such as the use of tractors in agriculture, transport, the building industry, etc.; I_{ts}, I_{tn} are once-only (investment) costs for alternative units of equipment, using existing and new techniques; N_{vn}, N_{vs} are costs of the development and applied research on new and existing techniques (if N_{vs} is unknown, the value N_{vn} only can be considered); I_s, I_n are evoked and indirect investments in the main branches of the economy; j gives the sectors of the economy where indirect (evoked) investments occur; k_{nj} is the standard coefficient of the effectiveness of additional investments, determined for the given sector of the economy.

The application of the efficiency coefficient can be illustrated by a simplified example. Let us assume that a 400-Mw energy unit (boiler, turbine, generator) is to be developed which in comparison with the present 200-Mw unit could decrease employment per one installed Mw in three shifts by about 0·2 worker, and also reduce depreciation by decreasing the capital investment costs per unit of output. On the grounds of the analysis of other data let us assume that the total savings for the 400-Mw equipment amount to 0·008 Czechoslovak crowns (Kčs.) per 1 kilowatt hour; the total annual savings in production costs for the 400-Mw unit amount to Kčs. 19·2 million (0·008 Kčs./kilowatt hour × 6,000 × 400,000 kw). However, this represents the savings on production costs only. We must also take into account that if we do not develop this unit we should have to install two units each with an output of 200 Mw, which calls for a higher consumption of labour, material and services. Therefore, two 200-Mw sets will require higher once-only costs (capital investment) per unit of output. Provided the savings in this capital investment reach Kčs. 300 per 1 kilowatt of power installed, the total savings of once-only, capital investment costs will be Kčs. 120 million.

However, there are other savings on capital investment. In the calculation of savings in production costs we have supposed the replacement of two 200-Mw units by one 400-Mw unit to enable the saving of 30 grammes of specific fuel per 1 kilowatt hour—that is, of about 120,000 tons of coal in one year. If we suppose that it will not therefore be necessary to increase coal production further, a capital investment saving of about Kčs. 12 million can be made.* From this rough analysis we can conclude that by making use of research and development results, savings of about Kčs. 20 million in production costs and Kčs. 133 million in capital investment can be made. Let us assume that the costs for research and development will come to Kčs. 70 million. It is necessary to consider also the indirect (evoked) costs for research and development. In view of the fact that we are considering a complex installation, let us assume for simplicity's sake that there are no indirect costs of development but that it will be necessary to develop highly heat-resistant materials, the research and development of which will cost the supplier Kčs. 5 million. On the other hand, costs related to secondary targets need not be considered. (In our example they will concern research and development on various methods of cleansing air (dust and soot collecting, removal of sulphur, and so on.)

These data lead us to the following conclusions:

Savings on annual production costs including depreciations will be Kčs. 19·2 million.

Savings on direct, once-only (capital investment) costs will be Kčs. 120 million.

Savings on indirect, once-only (capital investment) costs in the sphere of operating costs will be Kčs. 12 million.

Savings on indirect once-only investment will be Kčs. 1 million.

Direct expenditure on applied research and development will be Kčs. 70 million.

Indirect expenditure for applied research and development will be Kčs. 5 million.

If these figures are put into the formula for calculating the efficiency coefficient, the following result is obtained. (The uniform coefficient

---

* There are other kinds of savings in once-only (capital investment) costs. For example, in the production of a 400-Mw unit it is possible to save 4,000 tons of steel and also other metals, in comparison with the production of two 200-Mw units. The total capital investment savings on this simplified example amount to about Kčs. 20 million. With regard to the life of the equipment one can include a part of such capital investment only. For example, for a 20-year life of the equipment of the steel mills and so on, a saving of about Kčs. 1 million might be estimated. Other savings come from releasing the saved capital investment for application in other branches of the economy.

standard for all indirect capital investments is expected to be 0.15; for all direct capital investments $k_n = 0.2$; the production of twenty 400-Mw units ($n = 20$) is assumed.)

$$K_{tv} = \frac{20 \times 19.2 \text{ million Kčs.} + 0.2 \ (20 \times 120 \text{ million Kčs.} - 75 \text{ million Kčs.}) + 0.15 \times 20 \times 13 \text{ million Kčs.}}{75 \text{ million Kčs.}}$$

$$= \frac{384 \text{ million Kčs.} + 465 \text{ million Kčs.} + 39 \text{ million Kčs.}}{75 \text{ million Kčs.}}$$

$$= 11.84$$

The question may be asked, what level of efficiency coefficient of research and development is adequate for society? Our present experience does not allow us to make a proper judgment of this yet. Only further analyses of the applied results will enable such a judgment to be made.

The efficiency of science is the result of a many-sided process. I have tried to point out some of its features by emphasizing that besides economic aspects, we must not lose sight of the wider contributions of science, the appraisal of which is extremely difficult, but which exert a permanent influence on the development of social life.

SCIENCE POLICY IN DEVELOPING COUNTRIES

SCIENCE POLICY MAKING IN LATIN AMERICA, WITH SPECIAL REFERENCE TO ARGENTINA

R. L. CARDÓN

Advisory Secretary, Consejo Nacional de Investigaciones Científicas y Técnicas, Buenos Aires

THE CONCEPT OF SCIENTIFIC POLICY

SINCE the expression "scientific policy" is in some ways ambiguous, it is convenient to begin by stating the sense in which I shall use it. The word "policy" is often used to refer to "any method of acting with the aim of accomplishing certain ends". This seems to be its most common English meaning, and also that used in other countries besides Great Britain. However, in the Latin languages, "policy" (*politica*, in Spanish; *politique*, in French) strictly refers to all that concerns the State (the successor of the Aristotelian *Polis*) and the management of public affairs. "Policy" thus understood admits a series of subdivisions, according to the nature of the matter concerned. In other words, the policy of a State is composed of several policies, which are naturally interdependent (see UNESCO/CASTALA, 1965a).

Strictly speaking, therefore, scientific policy includes the activity of the State in relation to science and the active participation of government in its promotion, in the development of research and in the use of the resources provided by science for the community's welfare and progress. This, of course, presupposes that the State or government has acknowledged the existence of "science and research" as an element of significance for the State and of basic interest for the community; that it is aware of science as a factor of power, prosperity and progress; and that, in consequence, the State has decided to use its power and influence in this field. Thus, science becomes an integral part of government activity (in the same way as, say, education and public health). Thus, scientific policy begins to take shape.

Thus understood, a scientific policy presupposes or implies, as every policy does, defined *goals* (even if they are rather general) that the government pursues in relation to science; *methods and procedures* that the government uses to attain such goals; and *agencies* that carry them out. Any policy also has an underlying doctrine—namely the *principles* that determine either the selection of the goals or the adoption of methods of accomplishing them.

The expression "scientific policy" is ambivalent, as a UNESCO document says, since, on the one hand, it includes the purpose and the means of promoting the expansion of scientific activities (*policy for science*). For this, it attempts to create or improve an operational network or infrastructure for scientific and technological work, by means of an investment of human resources. On the other hand, it includes influencing the goals of research workers, in order to guide their work according to national objectives, which are generally of an economic and social nature (*science policy*) (UNESCO/CASTALA, 1965*b*). It is clear that there can be a policy *for* science without a policy *of* science in this second sense. But probably no country follows a vigorous policy of promoting science— which implies allotting a significant part of the national budget to research —with a total lack of motivation of an extra-scientific nature. Therefore, the objectives of a scientific policy are closely related to those pursued by the government in other spheres of its activity (economic, social, military or international).

This is true of highly developed countries as well as those striving towards full growth. The latter countries consider, or should consider, science and technology and their applications as essential means of overcoming their lack of progress, as a source of better standards of living and as a means of attaining the goal of self-supporting development. This can be done through a systematic study of natural resources and the procedures best suited to their exploitation; through the scientific analysis of problems of public health and nutrition, as well as those of an economic and social nature; and through the study of the best methods for achieving effective modernization.

It is perhaps useful to point out that countries in the early stages of development should first attempt to establish a policy *for* science. That is, the State should encourage in a general way the expansion of scientific activities, the creation or multiplication of centres for such activities, an increase in the number of people working in science, and the provision of adequate environmental conditions for the development of scientific activity that is both permanent and of considerable volume. Only when this is achieved—when a certain "critical mass" is attained (mainly measurable by the number of qualified research workers employed)—can a *science policy* as such be devised. To do otherwise would be to attempt to operate in a vacuum.

MAJOR DECISIONS IN SCIENTIFIC POLICY

The second stage of our discussion is to state the fundamental kinds of decisions that should be made in scientific policy. We believe that they are the following:

(1) To determine the proportion of the national income or State budget (as a whole, or of the budget of public investment, according to the criterion adopted) that should be assigned to research and development—in other words, the total amount of public expenditure on scientific research.

(2) To determine the distribution of this sum among the different branches of science. This may require a further decision, of what proportion to assign to basic research and, consequently, what to applied research (a third level might be set up concerned with orientated basic research). The allocation of funds according to branches of science, or specialties within them, can be taken to different levels, and can include also the allocation of given amounts to clearly established research subjects. This problem is related to that of the allocation of resources among the different agencies, who are responsible for the research itself.

(3) The third question is implied in the second. It concerns the establishment of *priorities* for the national scientific effort and, therefore, for the use of the available resources. The "vexing priorities" (as James R. Killian, Jr. has called them) appear as an inevitable consequence of the disparity between the human and material resources available and the requirements or possibilities of scientific research. It is at this point that the economic, social and other objectives that the State pursues, with the assistance of science and technology, operate particularly. Here, too, the most difficult problems and most serious conflicts arise. The research worker very often claims absolute freedom (he wants money, and wants to spend it according to his own judgment); and governments, for their part, may make the great mistake of requiring tangible results, in very short periods of time (and the situation is complicated further by the prevailing belief that such results can be obtained by concentrating efforts at a few strategic points, forgetting that this can be done only on the basis of a certain general development of scientific research). For the same reason, it is in this field that a dialogue is most necessary—that is, mutual understanding and co-operation between the representatives of the scientific com-

munity and the government, the planning bodies and the administration.

(4) Decisions on which methods to adopt to promote national scientific development (for example, whether to send a large number of young research workers abroad for training, and how the problem of absorbing them by local centres will be faced) and what type of organization is desirable for scientific research in the country. Evidently, there are several possibilities, related to governmental control of the system, to the kind of agencies to be established, to the degree of centralization, to the role of the universities, and so on.

(5) Closely related to all this is the creation of favourable conditions for scientific development, ranging from the consolidation of an adequate social and economic status for the research worker, to the diffusion of a psychological attitude of evaluating science and scientists (the so-called "national scientific conscience"), to the development of a system of administration and government of the scientific agencies that harmonizes with the nature and requirements of their task. All these elements help to create a social climate within which scientific vocations are more easily multiplied, research becomes general as a professional activity, and environmental obstacles are reduced. At the same time, such a climate is favourable for a better handling of scientific problems and the finding of solutions through research.

(6) We need also to discover how to ensure a certain co-ordination of the national scientific effort, in order to avoid unjustified and useless overlaps, to encourage the co-operation and exchange of experiences among the different bodies, and, whenever feasible, to co-ordinate efforts and concentrate resources on objectives of fundamental interest. A by-product of the utmost importance arising from such dynamic co-ordination is that fields of study which are vital not only for their own sake, but also because they serve as essential supporting points for solidly based scientific development, are not neglected.

(7) Finally, decisions must be made on the mechanisms and procedures to adopt to make the results of research known and to promote their application, so that the full benefits of the expenditure of large sums in support of scientific and technological research are gained.

HOW DECISIONS ON SCIENTIFIC POLICY ARE MADE IN ARGENTINA

State of research in Argentina

I begin with a brief sketch of the situation of scientific research in Argentina. It is a country with a relatively low illiteracy rate (8·6 per cent in 1960). Secondary education is fairly well developed (32 per cent of the population in the 13–18 years age-range enrolled in 1957–1959), and so is university education (10 per cent of the population aged 19–22 years enrolled in 1957–1959). The number of professional people is large, particularly physicians (1 per 800 inhabitants in 1957). These rates in all cases are the highest of the region.

Like other Latin American countries, Argentina has no ancient scientific tradition. Nevertheless, since the second half of the nineteenth century the country profited from the work of eminent European scientists (such as Burmeister, Bonpland, Kunz, Lorentz, Hanke, Haumann, Berg, Gould and others) and produced scientists of high repute (Ameghino, Hicken, Holmberg, Agote, Miguel Fernandez, Mazza, A. Posadas). The natural and medical sciences, and later chemistry and biochemistry, attained high levels; progress has been slower in the physical, mathematical and astro-nomical sciences and in technology, although there are outstanding names in each of these disciplines, including a few with international reputations. Biology and experimental medicine—and in a certain sense, Argentinian science in general—received a great impulse from the work of Bernardo Houssay, creator of a school of continental standing, whose work found international acknowledgement in 1947 with the award of the Nobel Prize (the only one awarded to a scientist in Latin America).

During the past 10 years, scientific research has made significant progress, thanks to the creation of the National Council of Scientific and Technical Research and other agencies that promote, assist and carry out research work; to the foundation of new institutes and laboratories within the universities and independent agencies; to a significant increase in full-time research posts at the universities; and to a series of measures to encourage original scientific work.

The *National Council of Scientific and Technical Research* (Consejo Nacional de Investigaciones Científicas y Técnicas, CNICT) was created in 1958 to promote, co-ordinate and orientate scientific and technological research, and eventually to act as an advisory body in scientific and technological matters to the government. The *National Atomic Energy Commission* (Comi-sión Nacional de Energía Atómica, CNEA) came into being in 1950 but was reorganized in 1956. Its function is to promote and carry out studies in nuclear physics and its scientific and industrial applications. Its work also includes the exploration of the country's uranium resources, the con-struction and operation of reactors and the production of radioisotopes. The *National Institute of Agricultural and Cattle-Raising Technology* (Instituto Nacional de Tecnología Agropecuaria, INTA) was set up in 1956; it carries out and promotes research on agriculture and animal husbandry, as a means of improving agricultural practice. In 1957, the *National Institute of Industrial Technology* (Instituto Nacional de Tecnología Industrial, INTI) was created to stimulate, support and perform technological investigations concerned with the development of industry, with the participation of private enterprise.

Mention should also be made of the *National Commission for Space Research* (Comisión Nacional de Investigaciones Espaciales) set up in 1960; the *National Institute of Geology and Mining* (Instituto Nacional de Geología y Minería), set up in 1963; the *Commission of Scientific Research* (Comisión de Investigaciones Científicas), of the province of Buenos Aires, and the *Laboratory for Testing of Materials and Technologial Research* (Laboratorio de Ensayo de Materiales) of the same province. Although a review of the position of research in the military field is outside the scope of this paper, we should note the existence since 1954 of the *Board of Scientific Research of the Armed Forces* (Junta de Investigaciones y Experimentaciones de las fuerzas Armadas) as an organ of promotion and co-ordination, and the *Institute of Research and Experimentation of the Armed Forces* (Instituto de Investigaciones Científicas y Técnicas de las fuerzas Armadas), both dependent on the Ministry of Defence.

In addition to the agencies we have a network of universities, the national academies for the main branches of science (the oldest of which, the National Academy of Medicine, was formed in 1822, and was one of the first scientific academies in Latin America), many private scientific societies (such as the Argentine Scientific Society, started in 1872), and, much more recently, several scientific foundations that in some cases carry out research, but mostly encourage or stimulate it by awards, scholarships and other means. The number of active research centres in the country is estimated at 600, and there are about 3,000 scientific research workers (excluding the social sciences and humanities).*

Government expenditure on research and development has reached significant levels. Although all the necessary data are not available, from those that we have we find that in 1965 the money invested by the government in research, development and university teaching was 8 per cent of the national budget; expenditure in research and development alone may be estimated at something less than 4 per cent, if it is accepted that uni-

---

*This estimate is based on a total teaching and research staff in the universities of 5,219 persons (1966), which excluded the Schools of Law, Economics, Philosophy and Letters; and a total of some 2,500 scientific and technical workers in official bodies such as CNEA, INTA and INTI.

versities use 30 per cent of their budgets for those activities. In relation to the gross national product, the sums are 0·41 and 0·84 per cent, respectively.*

Scientific policy in Argentina

From this outline it can be seen that the organization of scientific research in Argentina, its infrastructure or operational network, the number of research workers and the money spent on research have all reached significant proportions, and are at the critical point of development where a defined and consistent national scientific policy is both possible and desirable. Nevertheless, it cannot be said that a national scientific policy exists in Argentina in the sense that I have defined it. Its goals have not been clearly established, and government action lacks continuity in this field, neglecting fundamental matters and not being fully integrated with the rest of government policy.

This is partly a consequence of the lack of a central agency specifically charged with defining or elaborating such a policy and responsible for its execution (although probably such an agency was not created because of insufficient consciousness of the need for such a policy). There is nothing in Argentina that can be compared with the ministries for science that exist in Great Britain, France, West Germany and other countries, or with the Conseil National de la Politique Scientifique in Belgium. Nor have we any agency equivalent to the State Committee for Science and Technology of the Soviet Union, or to the Special Assistant for Science and Technology and the President's Science Advisory Committee in the United States.

Since a National Council of Scientific and Technical Research exists in Argentina, one might expect that it would play such a role. In practice, however, it does not. The law does not expressly assign the responsibility for defining national scientific policy to the Council, and it has shown no disposition to undertake such a responsibility. It has acted primarily as an agency promoting and assisting research, and its action in giving general orientation and co-ordination has been occasional and of limited scope. Besides, the Council lacks the legal powers fully to comply with these other purposes theoretically assigned to it. The connexion between the

---

*These sums, which amount to $80,120,000 and $163,800,000 (United States dollar quotation, 1965), may seem low, but the low wages and cost of living in Argentina should be taken into account. In fact the rates are exactly the minimum rates obtained for Argentina if a rate is assigned to each country based on the ratio of its gross national product to that of the United States (the rate there amounting to 3 per cent) (see UNESCO/CASTALA, 1965c).

Council and the government, in our opinion, is insufficient. The Council depends directly on the President of the Republic, and its law of foundation says that the Council should advise the government on problems of a scientific and technical nature *whenever such advice is requested*. In fact, the Council is very seldom consulted, and besides, it has not that "full access to all plans, programs and activities involving science and technology in government" that is included in the mandate of, for example, the Special Assistant in the United States. There is not the two-way communication there should be between the Council and the departments concerned with economics, industry and public health, nor with the sectors of private enterprise in such areas. As a result, science in Argentina has not become an element of sufficient influence in the national policy, or in the country's conduct and development, and the requirement for this development has not found the necessary response in the organization and development of scientific activities.

It should be stressed that the Council's work in promoting and stimulating research has been important and very fruitful. It has, directly or indirectly, caused a substantial change in the conditions of scientific work in Argentina. The Council has done more (if not exclusively) in the development of a *policy for science* than a *policy of science*. Perhaps, at the time when it was set up, this was the wisest and most desirable thing to do, but it seems necessary now to go a step farther, to complete the work it has done in matters of policy *for* science and to enter further the sphere of a policy *of* science. Besides, this is the process that seems to have occurred in countries where scientific policy has been institutionalized to a certain extent.*

The adoption of decisions

No particular agency or authorized body determines the allocation of resources to research and development in Argentina, and what is done is not done systematically. Expenditure is determined *a posteriori*, through the aggregation of the budgets of several agencies and through the expenditures authorized for the different government departments, and as a result of a series of independent initiatives and isolated decisions which are not

---

*A document prepared by the UNESCO Science Policy Division states that the principal task of the body planning a country's scientific policy is "to plan the development of research" (UNESCO/CASTALA, 1965d, p. 6). Although CNICT did not do this in an organic manner in Argentina, it undertook "measures of a national character" which the same document describes as a further task of such a body (pp. 7–8). The Council has also played an important role in promoting science through scholarships and grants. A description of its work is given in UNESCO/CASTALA (1965e).

submitted to final review or co-ordination, from the standpoint of national science policy.

However, the significant size reached by expenditure on research and its application in Argentina shows that the government has acknowledged science as a matter of State interest. But the requirements of scientific development and the intensity of the efforts that the nation should make to achieve it have not yet been evaluated.

We thus answer implicitly questions (2) and (3), concerning the distribution of the total budget for research and development among the different branches of science and technology; among the different types of research (basic or applied); or among the so-called "tactical" or "strategic" research activities which differ according to their more or less immediate relation to the needs of development. In practice, the appropriation of budgetary funds for the different branches of research is made through credits opened for the various scientific agencies of the government (CNICT, CNEA, INTA, INTI, and so on) without any total study or statement of priorities based on a comparative analysis or plan of State interests regarding research (and this, as we have seen, does not exist). But we cannot conclude that the allotments are made arbitrarily or without some sound basis. Thus, for example, there are good reasons why the National Institute of Agricultural and Cattle-Raising Technology can count on much larger funds than those available to other agencies. In any case, we believe that the system allows too broad a margin for improvization and for the influence of factors foreign to the aims of scientific development or to the national progress to which it is supposed to contribute. Whether an institution gets larger funds sometimes depends on personal contact, the influence of executives, their skill in negotiation, or other similar factors. Such variables can never be eradicated completely, but an adequate organization and a well-established policy should try to reduce their influence to a minimum.

The scientific and technological State agencies (particularly the four previously mentioned, which are all autarchic or decentralized, plus the national universities), are quite free in the adoption of plans and the selection of projects, and in their working methods and ways of fostering or organizing research. The government assigns a sum to them and leaves them to decide its proper use. This means that immediate decisions on research expenditure are made, in most instances, by the scientific institutions. Exceptions occur when special programmes have been set up or administered directly by a ministry or government Secretary, or carried out by some office directly dependent on them.

By law, certain limitations are imposed when an institution is assigned a mission and given its terms of reference. But the scope is wide (particularly in the case of the CNICT), as is the range of possible action. The CNICT, for instance, may grant fellowships and subsidies, create or support institutes, organize services, contract scientists, sign covenants, carry out scientific exchanges with foreign countries, and so on. The limitations usually arise, not from the government's desire to influence decisions on the type of research sponsored or the manner in which this may be achieved, but rather from the insufficiency of funds and, more usually, from the imposition of inadequate bureaucratic criteria (regarding the remuneration of scientific and technical personnel, the purchase of research equipment, and so on).

A certain orientation regarding the implementation of a "policy of science" has been assigned to the CNICT by law. Article 1 of the law of foundation of the Council says that "in the distribution of the funds appropriated for the fulfilment of its specific goals, the Council may establish an order of priorities consonant with the needs of the country in what concerns research and the actual situation of the different sectors of scientific activity". Further, in detailing the Council's functions, the law includes that of "promoting and subsidizing" such studies and research that it deems are especially required for the advancement of science, the carrying out of government plans, or for any other reason of overwhelming collective interest" (article 2, item D). It must be stressed, however, that article 1 says that the Council *may*, rather than *ought to*, establish an order of priorities and that, in any case, the Council itself shall determine this. Likewise, it is the Council which shall decide which are the studies and researches of preferential interest to which article 2 refers.

I have already indicated that co-ordination of research is not really ensured in Argentina. This task has been assigned in theory to the National Council of Scientific and Technical Research, but it has neither the legal power nor the adequate structure to fulfil it. Undoubtedly, co-ordination was envisaged when the law prescribed that one representative of the Ministry of Education and Culture and one from the research organization of the military forces should be on its Board of Directors. In fact, this has had very little effect. Notwithstanding, some co-ordination is achieved by the Council—for example, when it brings together the country's principal research workers in a certain field and invites them to elaborate a national programme for the advancement of their specialty (which has happened in five or six cases). Also, indirectly, because of its structure, the Council supports co-operation and co-ordination through contact among the research workers from scientific institutions and universities who are on its standing or temporary scientific committees. But the Council cannot take *decisions*—and there is no other organization which could—to co-ordinate the plans and activities of the scientific agencies, to avoid duplication and to make sure that important goals for national scientific development do not remain neglected.

Decisions referring to the other points mentioned (paragraphs (4), (5) and (7), see p. 225), are in the hands of several scientific organizations, each with its own jurisdiction. The National Council (CNICT) is concerned with measures to create better general conditions for research throughout the country. As for the dissemination and practical application of the results of research, in my view the National Institute of Agricultural Technology is the institution that has most systematically and widely endeavoured to fulfil this very important task.

It is possible that the situation described will undergo some alteration in the near future. Apart from the recent announcement by the Secretary for Culture and Education of the creation of an Under-Secretary for Science, there are indications that the government is considering modifying the by-laws of some institutions. There has been mention also of promoting and supporting more technological research as an aspect of industrial policy.

For the present, it would be useful to make a general revision of the existing situation: agencies, spheres of competence, programmes, methods, resources; an examination of the productivity of the structure that has been built up over the years and whether this really corresponds to the needs for scientific advance and national progress.* It is my opinion that one fundamental innovation should be to ensure greater and more systematic co-ordination of the activities of the agencies and a closer relationship between the projects of scientific development (which should be more clearly formulated), the national development programme and the real needs of the country in the economic and social fields—including, for example, all that relates to public health. From the government is required a more energetic pursuit of science. All this presupposes a different and higher level of decision making.

It is unnecessary to add that such an integration of agencies, plans and

---

*In 1965 the Argentinian government signed an agreement with UNESCO to make, with its co-operation, a study of the national science policy and the organization of research in Argentina. The responsibility for the study has been given to the CNICT, and it might offer an excellent opportunity to make this general revision of the existing situation which, in our opinion, is of paramount urgency.

methods into some sort of national system for research and development, can and should be carried out without leading to undue interference by extraneous factors in the management of strictly scientific matters.

Such a system should be able to provide the drive for creating environmental conditions favourable for scientific work and for the dissemination and use of the results of research—two objectives of scientific policy that up to now have not been given sufficient attention in Argentina. It would also be advisable to establish rules and procedures to ensure the dissemination and exploitation of the new scientific and technological knowledge obtained in laboratories and universities.

As for the nature of the body or authority to be set up for carrying out these functions, it would be preferable, in my opinion, at least at present, to have a *Council for National Science Policy*, rather than the new Under-Secretary. This solution has been adopted successfully in countries such as Belgium, Canada and Sweden.

Such a Council should be made up of the main scientific and technical agencies of the State, together with representatives of higher education, industry and departments of government having a direct relation with scientific and technological research. This body would not require a very complex or large organization. It should not be concerned with setting up or supporting scientific centres, administering or financing research programmes (except in very exceptional cases), granting fellowships, or whatever other measures are within the competence of purely scientific and technological agencies, which the Council for Scientific Policy ought to support and co-ordinate, but never replace.

State of research in the industrial sector

The situation of research in the industrial sector in Argentina is probably similar to that in several other Latin American countries. Argentina is an industrialized country—not highly so, but industrialized nevertheless. About 35 per cent of the gross internal product for 1965 came from industry (in 1950 it was 28·7 per cent), and it absorbs 60 per cent of the employed manpower. Production is diversifying a good deal. Steel output was 1,368,000 tons in 1966, compared with 244,200 tons in 1959. Automobile production was about 200,000 per year, and at present uses only 5 per cent of imported parts.

But Argentinian industry, to a large extent, is dependent on external factors. Both capital and management are frequently foreign; these are merely branches or subsidiaries of North American or European firms. This is true for the automobile, petrochemical, pharmaceutical, meatpacking, electronics and electrical-appliance industries. There are, however, several exceptions.

Generally speaking, industry of foreign origin has had no interest in creating or supporting research laboratories within the country, and prefers to use exclusively the "know-how" and techniques acquired and developed in their laboratories in their own countries. Some important firms set up laboratories during the second world war, undoubtedly due to the difficulty in communicating with their central laboratories, or to the fact that some of them ceased to exist. But, once the war was over, the local laboratories were dismantled or reduced to a merely routine function. Most commonly, the laboratories of the Argentinian subsidiaries of large foreign enterprises have limited their activity to problems of adaptation, analytical work and quality control.

All this is undoubtedly logical and justifiable in terms of the organization of the companies and their profitability, but it is not favourable for the scientific and technological development of Argentina, nor for her economic development, since it leaves local industry—and, in consequence, one of the basic sectors of the economy—in a condition of excessive dependence. This is aggravated by the fact that many firms with Argentinian capital also produce on the basis of foreign patents.

As I have said, the National Institute of Industrial Technology is giving an impetus to industrial research, operating mainly at the level of small and medium-sized companies. The activity of other official organizations could also be cited. But the predominant picture is that which I have described. It may thus be concluded that, to a considerable extent, decisions concerning research in industry in Argentina are made abroad.

Role of the universities

Finally, I shall briefly state how the problem that we are considering is being met in the universities. I shall refer only to federal universities, since in private universities—apart from these being of very recent creation in Argentina—the adoption of decisions on scientific policy does not present any conflictual aspect, since their scientific development is the exclusive responsibility of their own authorities.

Scientific research in Argentina is based in large measure on the activity of the universities. They not only provide the professional background and constitute the principal stock from which new generations of research workers ordinarily come, but together possess the largest network of laboratories and research institutes in the country, particularly for basic research. The activity of the CNICT is to a large extent carried out in collaboration with the universities. Nearly 40 per cent of the State's expenditure on research is channelled through the national (federal) universities.

Traditionally, Argentinian universities have enjoyed very wide freedom in their activity and, above all, in the adoption of curricula and research programmes. They have had also very broad discretion in the use of funds and in their administration (they were autarchic bodies with a purely formal connexion with the Ministry of Education). The University Bill of 1955 left the election of authorities and the designation of professors and other staff members entirely in the hands of the university community. In 1966 this law was derogated and the Rectors were appointed by the government, becoming directly dependent on it. At the same time, a committee was established to draft a project for a new university statute, whose text has not yet been published. However, the highest representatives of the government have again declared that, according to its historic tradition, the Argentine University shall be "autonomous in its function, based on the principle of liberty of teaching and of scientific research", but, at the same time, "articulated with the rest of the nation, at the service of its institutions and its needs". The mechanism to ensure the attainment of this last objective has not been explained. Concerning the scope of the "autonomy"—or, rather, "autarchy"—it has been stated that it shall include the appointment of professors by their peers—that is, by the university faculties. To maintain full and responsible academic liberty is a firm and unanimous aspiration of the Argentinian scientific community, and of all university and cultural circles in the country.

SUMMARY

(1) In the author's opinion, the expression "national science policy" strictly involves actions of the State taken to promote research and development and to take advantage of their results for the benefit of the country. Consequently, it presupposes some degree of centralization at the highest level for making fundamental decisions, such as the assignment of resources to research and their distribution among different branches of science.

(2) Up to the present, such decisions have not been taken according to general objectives or pre-established principles in Argentina. They are not the responsibility of a central body invested with a specific power. The National Council of Scientific and Technical Research has not the legal or practical capacity thoroughly to fulfil that task, in spite of its prominent position, its prestige and influence and the importance of its work.

(3) The promotion and support of research and development is done by several government organizations, which adopt their programmes and spend their funds with a large degree of freedom. The universities have traditionally enjoyed very ample autonomy in all aspects of their activities. Industrial research is not widespread, which in large measure is due to the recentness of industrialization and to the fact that many bigger enterprises are branches of large foreign companies.

(4) In spite of the real achievements made during the last 10 years, some serious inconveniences derive from the situation referred to in paragraph (2). Although considerable, the resources available do not cover the requirements of national scientific progress, and their allocation to different agencies is not entirely satisfactory. Neither is there sufficient co-ordination among those agencies and between their programmes and the national economic development plan or trends. Control of productivity in the present "system" and the forecasting of future needs and perspectives are still more unsatisfactory. This situation makes advisable the creation of a new body specifically responsible for defining and supervising the execution of the national science policy.

REFERENCES

UNESCO/CASTALA (1965a). Conference definition of science policy. *Conference on the Application of Science and Technology to the Development of Latin America*, Document 2.4.2, pp. 3–4. UNESCO.

UNESCO/CASTALA (1965b). Report of Commission IV (Scientific and technological policies and instruments for their materialization), *Conference on the Application of Science and Technology to the Development of Latin America*, Document 3.4, p. 1. UNESCO.

UNESCO/CASTALA (1965c). Trends of overall expenditure and methods of financing the development of science and technology. *Conference on the Application of Science and Technology to the Development of Latin America*, Document 2.4.4, p. 13. UNESCO.

UNESCO/CASTALA (1965d). Highlights of the subject of scientific and technological policies and instruments for their materialization. *Conference on the Application of Science and Technology to the Development of Latin America*, Document 2.4.1. UNESCO.

UNESCO/CASTALA (1965e). The National Council of Scientific and Technological Research and the organization for research in Argentina. *Conference on the Application of Science and Technology to the Development of Latin America*, Document 2.4.10. UNESCO.

See also:

Cardón, R. L. (1966). *La ciencia en Argentina en los últimos diez años*. Report for the meeting of Directors of Research Councils and other organizations responsible for national scientific policy in Latin America, Buenos Aires, 1966. Montevideo: UNESCO.

DISCUSSION

Carey: Are there any inter-American joint bodies in science or technology which enable the countries of Latin America to collaborate?

Cardón: Several institutes in the field of basic research have been established with the help and initiative of UNESCO, such as the Latin American Center of Physics in Rio de Janeiro, the Latin American Center of Mathematics in Buenos Aires and the Latin American Center of Biology in Venezuela; more recently it has been decided to establish the Latin American Center of Chemistry in Mexico. UNESCO also has a liaison office in Montevideo for helping scientific activity in Latin America. The Organization of American States has a Department of Scientific Affairs, which carries out several programmes in this field and has also set up an Advisory Committee for Scientific Policy in the continent. The development of scientific activity and the application of science and research in economic development was one of the subjects included in the Conference of Presidents of the American countries held at Punta del Este in Uruguay this year (1967). But so far, it seems to me that there are more recommendations and plans than effective realizations.

Carey: Is American financial assistance, going through the Alliance for Progress, and directed to strengthening science and technology in the countries of Latin America, having a beneficial effect?

Cardón: The Alliance for Progress has not done very much in this field, at least in Argentina. I think that the most significant contribution that Latin America has received from the United States comes from the private foundations, especially the Ford Foundation in the case of Argentina. Another interesting initiative came from the National Academy of Sciences. Dr. Harrison Brown has proposed a joint committee between the National Academy of Sciences and the National Research Council of Argentina, in order to select subjects of research appropriate for development on a co-operative basis. This is just at the beginning for Argentina, but I understand that similar projects with Brazil and Peru are in a more advanced state.

Szalai: I am looking for developing countries with good national research statistics, as India has, for instance, thanks to Dr. Rahman in great part. Have Argentina or the other Latin American countries comprehensive statistics on the national research effort, or, at least, on research in the university sector and the industrial sector?

Cardón: The Research Council of Argentina has a special bureau, the Scientific Register, in charge of such activity. It collects and publishes a certain amount of information in this field. I have no information about an equivalent service in other Latin American countries.

King: The Organization of American States is about to hold an important seminar for the Latin American countries, concerned with the concept of establishing science-policy planning teams in relation to economic plans. This approach, which has strong support in some countries, such as Mexico, is an interesting attempt to relate scientific research and development to economic planning.

The similarity between Argentina and Canada struck me very much in Dr. Cardón's paper, Canada being at a more advanced level in many ways. Both have need for indigenous agricultural research and possess industries mainly based on the import of technology and even of entire firms from North America and Europe. There may be much experience in the development of Canadian science which would be appropriate for the attention of the research councils in Latin America.

Cardón: I agree entirely.

SCIENCE POLICY IN INDIA

A. RAHMAN

Research Survey and Planning Organization, Council of Scientific and Industrial Research, New Delhi

INTRODUCTION

DEVELOPING countries may be divided into two categories: those which had a scientific tradition in ancient and mediaeval periods and have now developed considerable scientific and technical potential, and those which neither had the tradition nor have been able to develop the potential. India belongs to the former category.

There is, however, a sharp break between her earlier scientific tradition and her modern scientific development. The latter is limited, without deep roots in history and society, and its organization is patterned on nineteenth-century concepts of science and technology, primarily those of Great Britain. The organizational pattern, under the impact of influences from other countries, has lately been undergoing change.

The major problem in India, as in other developing countries, is the need to change the outlook of scientists and to integrate science and technology with society, and thus to end their present isolation. Science can no longer be looked upon merely as a number of disciplines or independent fields of specialization: in the advanced countries there is a new awareness of the wider role of science and technology. In India, and other developing countries, outdated outlooks, social conservatism or administrative dominance may effectively prevent science from assuming a wider role in society. Consequently, there is an urgent need to evolve a new image of science and to develop the machinery necessary to support this image.

This paper deals with seven elements of science policy: (1) surveys and studies for evolving science policy, (2) the planning of science and technology, (3) national science policy, (4) national budgeting of science, (5) implementing agencies, (6) co-ordination and evaluation of research, and (7) international collaboration.

HISTORICAL DEVELOPMENT OF SCIENCE IN INDIA

The part that science could play in the development of India was realized by the leadership of the country long before independence. In 1939, the Indian National Congress appointed a National Planning Committee and invited leading scientists to help to formulate plans for economic development and social betterment. A study group dealt with the problem of general education, technical education and scientific research. It recommended that programmes of industrial and educational development should be closely linked with programmes of scientific research, and that the different sectors of research should be closely co-ordinated. In addition, Jawaharlal Nehru, the late Prime Minister, emphasized the importance of a scientific outlook and the need for science to be used in solving the problems facing the country.

After independence, India deliberately set herself the task of transforming the economic structure, through a process of planning, which was seen as the only way by which the country could be put on the road to self-sustaining growth after centuries of stagnation. The new government took an active part in encouraging research in the universities and in establishing a chain of research laboratories. The significance attached to scientific research in independent India can be judged from the creation of a Ministry of Scientific Research and Natural Resources, directly under the Prime Minister.

In 1958, the government passed its Scientific Policy Resolution, to indicate its concern with the development of science for raising the standard of living. The Resolution has often been restated. Its impact will be discussed later (see p. 247).

PRESENT ORGANIZATION OF SCIENCE AND TECHNOLOGY IN INDIA

The organization of scientific and technological research in India falls into six categories (see Fig. 1):
(1) Councils, such as the Council of Scientific and Industrial Research (CSIR), and the Indian Council for Agricultural Research.
(2) University research, supported by the University Grants Commission and other agencies.
(3) Departmental laboratories, directly under the various ministries or their departments.
(4) Defence Research Laboratories.
(5) The Atomic Energy Commission.
(6) Research supported by industries or endowments.

The pattern of organization within each category varies widely, while between the different groups it differs even more. Since my purpose is to draw attention to national problems, differences on various aspects of science policy among the groups will not be discussed here. It may be mentioned, however, that each organization, irrespective of the category to which it belongs, is a discrete entity depending solely upon its administrative affiliation to the ministry under which it functions. Administratively there may or may not be co-ordination between different organizations, but at the scientific level no co-ordination is evident. Some form of co-ordination between various organizations and groups is clearly necessary in order to achieve a total perspective of science and technology, national requirements and the available or potential resources.

The Scientific Advisory Committee to the Cabinet performs several functions, but how far they cover the wide range of problems falling within science policy, and how effective it is in discharging them, is not known, in the absence of published records of its deliberations and decisions.

SCIENCE POLICY IN INDIA

Organizations for studies for the development of science policy

In India, the studies necessary before a science policy can be developed have yet to be made. The lack of machinery for collecting information and for making such studies is surprising, in view of the importance attached to science and technology by the National Planning Committee of the Congress, government policies, the rapid expansion of facilities for education and research, a ministry specifically in charge of scientific research, and the Scientific Policy Resolution. Yet few data for science-policy decisions were available until recently, and decisions either were made *ad hoc*, or were based primarily on departmental considerations.

In 1963, the Council of Scientific and Industrial Research (CSIR) made a beginning by setting up a unit for the Survey and Planning of Scientific Research to carry out policy studies. In the course of these it became evident that background information was required from other organizations, to develop the necessary perspective for the CSIR. In 1966 the Unit was made a separate organization within the fold of the CSIR—the Research Survey and Planning Organization.

Apart from the work of this organization there is little organized study under way. Some research institutions have now begun to study their own problems, particularly under the impact of economy measures. Bodies such as the Institute of Public Administration have started to sponsor

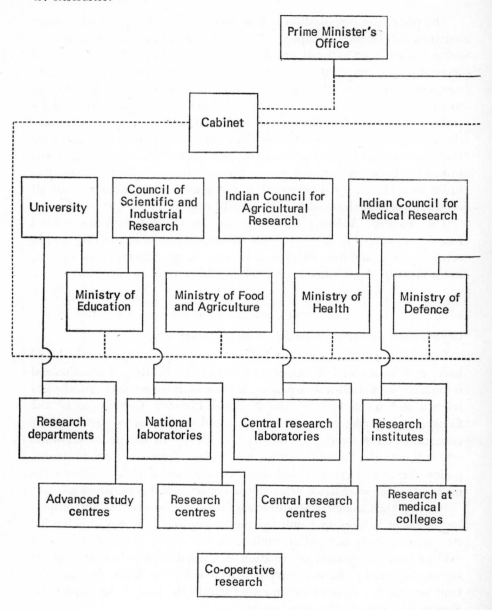

FIG. 1. The organization of scientific research in India.

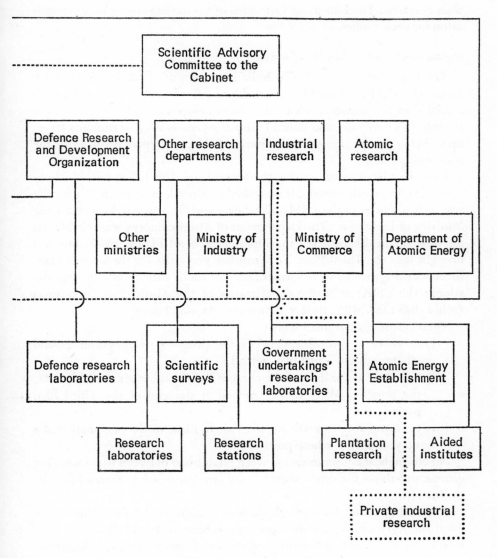

- - - -, line of co-ordination. ——— line of administrative control.

research on the specific problems of administering scientific and technological institutions. Data are being collected also by the University Grants Commission, most of it, however, dealing with education rather than research. The Education Commission has made a strong recommendation for such studies.

Organization for the planning of science

The Planning Commission in India has evolved a complex process for formulating its Five-Year Plans, in order to draw on as much expertise as is available in the country. About two years before each Plan runs out, the Planning Commission asks central ministries and State governments to set up working groups of experts in different fields, to prepare projects for the succeeding Plan.

For scientific research during the Second and Third Plan periods there was only one working group. It was asked to formulate schemes only for the research activities of the CSIR and other scientific organizations under the Ministry of Education. The Department of Atomic Energy was outside the purview of the Plan during the First and Second Plan periods, but was brought into the Third Plan. To formulate proposals for the Fourth Plan, three working groups were formed, one for each of the following organizations: the CSIR; scientific departments of the Ministry of Education (other than the CSIR); the Department of Atomic Energy.

Their terms of references were:

(i) to make a critical review of the progress of programmes and schemes of the Third Plan period;

(ii) to assess, in the light of the current trends and other available data, the position likely to be reached at the end of the Third Plan period; and

(iii) to formulate proposals for the Fourth Plan, in the perspective of a 15-year period where possible.

No channels of communication were established between these working groups and those for other sectors, nor any information channel for coordination.

A working group for agriculture was established by the Ministry of Food and Agriculture, and its report was submitted to the Planning Commission as a part of the overall programme of agricultural development. (Besides the central agricultural research organizations, there are a number of agricultural research stations managed by the State governments, where some research is done. Their development schemes and progress are scrutinized by a panel of experts of the State agriculture

244

planning groups, and are included in the State agricultural pro-grammes.)

In the case of irrigation and power, research is conducted at State research stations financed by the Ministry of Irrigation and Power. Two high-level expert bodies advise the Ministry on and formulate research programmes—the Central Board of Irrigation and Power, and the Central Water and Power Commission. The former is an advisory body, and the latter an implementing agency, for all major irrigation and power schemes. In addition, the State Electricity Boards have been recommended to estab-lish research laboratories. Research programmes are formulated and scruti-nized by the Central Board of Irrigation and Power and recommended to the Ministry for inclusion in its proposals to the Planning Commission.

The Ministry of Health set up a working group which in turn set up a number of sub-groups, including one for postgraduate medical education and research. The working group, however, felt that since the bulk of medical research is carried out in the medical colleges, there was no need to set up a separate sub-group for it.

For other sectors, such as Posts and Telegraphs, All-India Radio, Civil Aviation, Transport, Railways and Mines, research and development proposals are considered with the general programmes of the particular ministry or government department concerned, no special sub-group or working group being set up. This may be due to the fact that research and development are a very small part of the total activity of these sectors.

Research in universities and other academic institutions is considered to be part of the general programmes of State Ministries, and of the Ministry of Education through the University Grants Commission.

In 1956 the first attempt was made at a co-ordinated study of the scientific research programmes of the government agencies. The Planning Commission set up a panel of scientists, given the specific task of integrating programmes of industrial development with those of scientific research and advising the Planning Commission on measures necessary to ensure the implementation of its recommendations.

The first panel made specific recommendations that were forwarded to the implementing agencies. There was neither follow-up action nor a study to evaluate the extent to which the recommendations were imple-mented. It is, therefore, difficult to gauge the success of the panel in bringing about closer co-ordination between programmes of industrial development and scientific research. The second panel met in 1960 and considered only the recommendations of the working groups for the CSIR and the Ministry of Education.

The planning of scientific research may be attempted at three levels. Problems at the first, institutional level comprise the selection of research topics, the organization of research projects and research teams, the allocation of funds for different types of research, and sustaining the infra-structure, such as libraries, documentation services, workshop and extension services. In addition, the peculiarities of individual research workers, their working conditions, inclinations and aptitudes must be taken into account, to make full use of their creative capacities.

The problem of the planning of research at the second level is one of co-ordination between organizations working on complementary problems, or separate institutions working under one organization, and of acting as a two-way filter between the national and institutional levels.

Problems of planning at the third, national level include translating national requirements into scientific and technological problems, estab-lishing priorities for different sectors of research and allocating resources to them, and generating the necessary scientific and technological potential, in terms of the organizational and institutional framework, man-power and equipment, to sustain and develop research activity to meet national objectives.

To make planning effective and efficient, a methodology must be developed appropriate to each level, which may require intensive studies under Indian conditions. Further, to prevent the system from becoming too rigid, channels of communication are needed between research workers and policy makers on the one hand, and between institutions, organizations and national bodies on the other. This interaction is essential for the vitality and growth of science. Other countries—depending upon their tradition, and social, economic and political structures—have evolved channels of informal, as well as formal, communication with considerable benefit. Countries like India, which are now developing science and technology, have to do the same and make national planning a two-way process—specific and detailed thinking at the level of research workers and institutions interacting with broad general thinking at the national level.

National policy-making body

Different countries have evolved different national science policy-making bodies to suit their conditions and to meet their requirements. Their roles are continuously changing, in the light of experience and the new responsibilities that they are asked to shoulder. India has no central body at present with responsibility for formulating a national science policy, though the need for such an organization could hardly be over-emphasized. National science policy is a statement not only of the desires of a community, but also of the procedures necessary to achieve the desired objectives. Science policy, therefore, must state national objectives explicitly, in order to identify desirable actions and allocate responsibilities to each implementing agency. Viewed thus, the policy-making body must be closely integrated with study groups on the one hand and budgeting and implementing agencies on the other, if science policy is not to remain a mere expression of goals. This is evident from the study of developments since the Scientific Policy Resolution of the Indian government in 1958.

The Resolution stated: "Science has developed at an ever increasing pace since the beginning of the century, so that the gap between the advanced and backward countries has widened more and more. It is only by adopting the most vigorous measures and by putting forward our utmost efforts into the development of science that we can bridge the gap. It is an inherent obligation of a great country like India with its tradition of scholarship and original thinking and its great cultural heritage to participate fully in the march of science which is probably mankind's greatest enterprise today".

To attain those objectives, the Resolution emphasized measures to be taken, such as promoting science in all fields; maintaining an adequate supply of scientific and technical manpower and research equipment; encouraging individual initiative in research and other measures designed to secure for the people of India the benefits that can accrue from the acquisition and application of scientific knowledge. The government decided to pursue a policy of offering "good conditions of service to the scientists and according to them an honoured position by associating scientists with the formulation of policies".

In 1963, when a conference of educationalists and scientists was convened to review the implementation of the Scientific Policy Resolution, it had no statement before it on specific items of the Resolution, nor any data on how the national policy was being implemented. Consequently, discussion was limited to a general level. It did not result in refining the total perspective, nor in putting forward specific suggestions for implementation.

The Scientific Advisory Committee to the Cabinet, established in 1956, tries to advise the government on policy for the development of science and technology. But no information is published on how it discharges its duties, and judging from developments since its formation, the Council has been able to function only in a limited manner. This may be because it is purely an advisory body, without the staff to carry out specific studies and without links with the budgeting and implementing agencies.

It is highly desirable that India should have a national policy body, to discharge the diverse functions discussed above. The exact nature of the organization and its structure, functions and associations should be adapted to Indian conditions and requirements. Thus one important function would be to evolve a strategy of scientific research and development, but this need not be a mere imitation of what is done in other countries.

Whatever type of organization is developed for India, it is essential to build up both formal and informal channels of communication and to draw the scientific community into the formulation and decision-making process, and the implementation of policies and programmes. Scientists could also be used effectively in the evaluation programmes and the feedback machinery for assessing the implementation of policies.

Organization desirable for a national budget for science

India has no consolidated budget for science, like many other countries. The budget-making machinery at present is co-ordinated administratively only, and the process is partly modern and partly traditional. It is divided between many organizations, such as the CSIR, the Indian Council of Agricultural Research and the Department of Atomic Energy, on the one hand, and between scientists and administrators on the other.

The government machinery itself has become more complex, under these demands and pressures. In place of the empirical attitudes and deductive reasoning of the administrators, the belief is gaining ground that solutions should be based on systematically gathered quantitative data, scientifically assessed. "Science now has entered into the affairs of government both as an object and instrument of policy and as a means of thinking about policy".

There is no uniformity in the procedures for allocating funds to the various sectors of science. The budget is voted by Parliament for central organizations and by the State legislatures for State institutions. The degree of autonomy and the extent to which each organization can take decisions in financial matters varies. It is now realized that these methods of financing and the system of control of the research organizations are not conducive to full development of their research potential. Recently, there have been distinct trends at two levels. First, greater autonomy is being given to organizations, and secondly, there is greater decentralization of powers to laboratories within each organization. Some of the recent decisions of the Council of Scientific and Industrial Research could be cited here in illustration.

It may also be desirable to channel allotments through one organization, even though the departments financing research may be different. This may help in determining proper priorities, consonant with national objectives. It would also help to rectify imbalances in the development of science in the country. Such an organization could also help to initiate scientific studies in areas of potential development, as indicated by long-term plans.

Realizing the importance of a national budget for science, the then Minister for Scientific Research, Professor Humayun Kabir, at the second conference of scientists and educationalists in 1963, which was convened to review the implementation of the government's Scientific Policy Resolution of 1958, expressed the general opinion of the scientists present:

" . . . The major problem is, however, the allocation of funds between different councils. This is done on an *ad hoc* basis and it is being increasingly felt that it would be desirable to have some kind of an Advisory Body which could include representatives from each of the Research Councils, the Defence Science Organization, the Atomic Energy authorities and the University Grants Commission, strengthened by the addition of a large number of independent scientists of eminence. Such an Advisory Body would enable the government to have independent advice on the recommendations of the Heads of the different Research Councils . . .

"Apart from the advice on allocation of funds, such an Advisory Body would be in a position to advise government on the relative priorities in research and where best they can be carried out; it would certainly be an advantage for the government to have the advice of an expert body before it takes any decisions. Once the allocation to an authority is made, it should be free to distribute its funds among its laboratories and other agencies at its discretion".

It would clearly be in India's interest to develop a national perspective for science and technology and to work out the relative priorities for different areas through objective studies of the problems. On the basis of such an approach, a national budget for science and technology could be worked out, either through the national science policy-making body itself or by a separate body responsible to it. This approach would cut across departmental practices and would make possible the balanced development of different sectors of science and technology in relation to national development.

Implementing agencies

In countries with well-developed scientific and technological traditions, research organizations and laboratories have been in existence for some time, whereas the concept of national science policy is a recent one. Consequently, the tendency has been to co-ordinate activities of existing bodies, to make them the implementing agencies of the national science policy. In socialist countries with centralized planning this has been relatively easy; and in other countries it is being achieved by subsidizing or sponsoring research in those areas which need to be supported most strongly.

Six groups of institutions (see p. 240 and Fig. 1)—the research organizations, such as the CSIR; the Atomic Energy Establishment; departments under the ministries; defence research; research in industry; and university research—between them constitute the national implementing bodies. With varying degrees of sensitivity, they have given shape to the research programmes and have implemented national policies such as the Science Policy Resolution.

Working methods, however, vary very much. These differences, and the lack of proper co-ordination among the organizations, are due to the absence of a central co-ordinating agency working within the framework of a national science policy. These implementing agencies should be co-ordinated, in terms of objectives and tasks, within such a framework, in order to break down rigid compartmentalization and to allow the more efficient use of facilities. The proper planning, financing and evaluation of research might then become possible.

Machinery for review and evaluation

With the growth of organizational machinery for research and the increasing financial investment in research comes a greater need for reviewing policies and programmes and evaluating the way in which they have been implemented. In order to be useful, review and evaluation need to be continuous, to give constant feedback to policy makers and to make research organizations sensitive to rapidly changing circumstances. The machinery for review and evaluation must depend on systematic studies of the problems involved. The speed and accuracy of such studies would determine the effectiveness of the feedback and its usefulness to policy makers.

Many countries have developed machinery to collect data continuously and to carry out special studies to enable the policy- and decision-making bodies to review and evaluate the achievement or otherwise of objectives.

This continuous feedback has a considerable effect in countries that have recognized its significance, accelerating the progress of science and technology and bringing the organization of research into line with national requirements.

In India, the machinery for review varies from organization to organization. The CSIR, for instance, periodically reviews its activities, and special committees also look into particular problems—for example, the Bhabha Committee on electronic research. Such reviews are useful, but limited. Their limitations are clear if we consider existing national policies. The Scientific Policy Resolution, for example, was passed in 1958, but it is difficult to discover how each research organization has implemented it, if at all, because hardly any data are available. In their absence, the two conferences held on the Resolution have remained ends in themselves, without leading to further refinement and development of the Resolution or suggestions for concrete steps in specific spheres.

In addition to such broad reviews, research should be evaluated at the institutional level, in terms of the objectives set and the resources used. This is rarely done, with the result that research programmes drag on for years and the investment of resources is heavier than any possible results could justify. There is, therefore, an urgent need for machinery for both review and the continuous evaluation of programmes at the institutional level.

International collaboration

International collaboration in science and technology is increasing in importance, and in fact is now part of the foreign policies of many countries—both donors and recipients. Science being an international activity, scientific research in every country needs to build up its own framework of international relations. These fall into several categories:

(i) International agencies such as UNESCO, WHO and FAO.

(ii) International scientific unions.

(iii) Relations with national scientific academies and societies.

(iv) Bilateral arrangements between research institutions working in the same area.

(v) International scientific conferences.

(vi) Contact between individual research workers investigating complementary areas.

A country may aim at the exchange of information or personnel, joint research programmes, or the giving or receiving of scientific and technical aid. For developing countries scientific and technical aid received—

whether foreign exchange, equipment or experts—is of particular importance, but for a country like India, which has characteristics of both a developed country and a developing country, the entire range of international co-operation has significance.

National scientific organizations in India are either directly affiliated to international organizations, or act through national committees or commissions, which also decide India's representation to the international organization of the United Nations. Cultural agreements signed by the government and operated by the Ministry of Education are designed to increase exchanges of information and of personnel collaborating in research programmes, and to help in giving or receiving aid. National organizations such as the CSIR or the Atomic Energy Commission have made bilateral arrangements with national organizations with similar objectives in other countries.

At the moment a complete picture is not available. It would be useful to have more information on different types of international collaboration and the countries concerned. In addition, a national policy on international collaboration and machinery for its implementation at the national level are desirable.

SCIENTIFIC AND TECHNOLOGICAL INSTITUTIONS IN INDIA

It may be useful to supplement this outline of the institutional framework of science policy and the machinery for decision making with a brief idea of the scale of science and technology in India.

There are 74 universities and institutes of higher learning that award degrees. The total enrolment in various faculties during 1965–1966 is shown in Table I. That is, the student population at graduate level in science and technology during 1965–1966 was roughly 449,130. There is a rapid rise in numbers every year. The growth rate since 1950 for various courses in different branches of science has been between 9·6 per cent for the B.Sc. and 16·6 per cent for the M.Sc.

The CSIR—one of the three main research councils—has 50 national research laboratories, co-operative research associations, organizations and units employing 3,451 scientists and technologists and 4,351 technical personnel. It had a total budget of 173·2 million rupees in 1966–1967.

The Indian Council for Agricultural Research is being reorganized. The agricultural institutes under it and under State governments and the veterinary and fisheries institutions number about 117, and there are over 700 agricultural centres and stations.

There are about 44 medical research institutes. In addition, about 90

Table I

ENROLMENT IN FACULTIES OF SCIENCE AND TECHNOLOGY IN INDIA, 1965–1966

Faculty	Graduate	Post-graduate	Research	Diploma certificates
Science	251,372	20,888	3,412	257
Engineering and technology	74,216	1,540	278	2,364
Medicine	55,812	3,336	93	3,800
Agriculture	22,405	2,797	261	205
Veterinary science	5,561	423	50	60
Totals	409,366	28,984	4,094	6,686

research institutes are supported by defence science organizations, State governments and other organizations.

The Atomic Energy Commission has a smaller number of institutions than the research councils, but its financial involvement is quite heavy: and it employs about the same number of scientists and technologists as the CSIR, if not more. Government support for research in 1965–1966 was 840·65 million rupees, 0·45 per cent of the national income.

This brief comment reveals the considerable, strong base for science and technology in India. The institutional framework for science and the machinery for its execution have been described. The question which poses itself is why, with this base and organization and the involvement of the government on this scale, is India still a developing country?

The question becomes still more significant when it is looked at in terms of the time-scale: India had an early start as compared, say, to Japan. India has over 400 scientific societies, the earliest going back to 1779, and over 600 scientific and technical journals, the earliest having been published in 1820.

The answer to the question may lie in the point made by Professor Ackoff (see p. 84), namely that science is a subsystem of society and has to be examined as such. This means that there has to be a meaningful interaction between science and technology and society. Science and technology can neither be promoted nor be developed in a climate which is anti-scientific or apathetic to science, nor in a cultural desert. Unless society begins to absorb the values of science, and begins to imbibe technology, investment in science and technology is not likely to bear fruit and the institutional structure may remain floating on the top. This fact is pertinent not only for India, but for all developing countries.

CONCLUSIONS AND SUMMARY

In the past decade, advanced countries have seen an almost total transformation of scientific research from the level of individual effort to the level of a national industry. This transformation has a profound effect on the character of research and its organization, in so far as factors other than purely scientific and technological ones have influenced the choices of research and the ultimate social, economic and political values that determine the scale of support for research.

In India, the transformation has just begun. Consequently, the necessary framework for research in terms of national policy, planning and co-ordination of resources, and the necessary machinery for implementation, review and evaluation, have yet to be fully developed. But they are urgently needed. Since independence, India has made a considerable investment in scientific and technological research, has built up an extensive machinery for research, and has created a potential which is creditable. The full use of this potential and return from this investment will be possible only when the transformation from the traditional heroic concept of research to the view of it as a national industry is made.

To hasten this transformation, India must take steps already taken in other countries, such as:

(1) The creation of machinery for collecting data on research and development and its organizational problems, for its analysis, and for the preparation of documents for science policy making and other decisions. This must be done at institutional, organizational and national levels.

(2) The creation of a body to formulate a national scientific and technological policy which is in step with social, economic and industrial programmes.

(3) A national budget for science and technology, channelled through a co-ordinating agency.

(4) Scientific research planned with regard to the requirements of economic and industrial development, effective links being made between the planning, policy-making, budgeting and implementing agencies.

(5) Implementing agencies to be brought within the framework of a national policy, to break away from the departmental and compartmentalized approach to research.

(6) The creation of reviewing and evaluation machinery at the institutional, organizational and national levels, to give continuous feedback to policy makers and to make research organizations sensitive to national requirements.

(7) Creation of national machinery to co-ordinate international collaboration, to review and to give aid.

The taking of such steps and the setting up of the necessary machinery need not lead to excessive centralization, even though support for research may come only from government sources. In this respect, recent trends in socialist countries may help us to avoid unnecessary centralization and bureaucracy, which can stultify research. Greater emphasis must be laid on co-ordinating the existing machinery, in order to overcome such pitfalls; the participation of the scientific community at various decision-making levels, with greater formal and informal channels of communication, will also reduce these tendencies.

Science in India can develop further only when this transformation is effected and when the necessary machinery is developed to make this possible.

BIBLIOGRAPHY

The reader is referred to the following publications:

Ahmad, A., and Gupta, S. P. (1967). *Opinion Survey of Scientists and Technologists*. RSPO, CSIR Survey Report No. 9. New Delhi: Council of Scientific and Industrial Research.

Ahmad, A., Sharma, K. D., and Gupta, S. P. (1966). *Foreign Assistance to Scientific Research in India*. RSPO, CSIR Survey Report No. 7. New Delhi: Council of Scientific and Industrial Research.

Chowdhury, P. N. (1966). *A Study on the Conservation of Foreign Exchange by the National Laboratories*. RSPO, CSIR, February 1966. New Delhi: Council of Scientific and Industrial Research.

Government of India (1959). Scientific Policy Resolution, March 4, 1958, New Delhi.

Husaini, S. H. M., Ghosal, A., and Rahman, A. (1965). *Research Efforts in Industrial Establishments in India*. S & P Unit, CSIR, Survey Report No. 5. New Delhi: Council of Scientific and Industrial Research.

Iyengar, M. S. (1964). Some observations on scientific policy resolution and its implementation. *Vijnan Karmee*, **XVI**, 3.

Mahalanobis, P. C. (1955). Operational research approach to economic planning. *Sankhya*, **16**, I & II (December).

Mahalanobis, P. C. (1966). Objectives of science and technology. *Symposium on Collaboration Between Countries of Africa and Asia for Promotion and Utilization of Science and Technology* (*CAAUST*), New Delhi, 1966.

Maheshwari, P. (1964). Indian scientific policy: science and government. *Minerva*, **III**, 1 (Autumn), 97–113.

Mukherjee, Dilip (1964). Indian science policy: organization and application. *Minerva*, **II**, 3 (Spring), 360–369.

Nagpaul, P. S., Bhatia, J. R., Rahman, A., and Bhargava, R. N. (1966). *Trends of Research in Electronics Engineering*. Current Trends Research Series No. 2, RSPO, CSIR, December 1966. New Delhi: Council of Scientific and Industrial Research.

Rahman, A. (1964). Planning of scientific research. Co-ordinator's remarks, *Symposium of the Association of Scientific Workers of India on Science and the Nation*, New Delhi, 1964.

Rahman, A. (1966). "Problems of Planning and Organization of Scientific Research in Developing Countries". Science of Science Fndn., London. Unpubl. lecture, May 1966.

Rahman, A., Ghosal, A., Sen, N., Rajagopal, N. R., Das Gupta, S. (Mrs.), Husaini, S. H. M., and Roy, A. K. (1964). *A Study of Expenditure in National Laboratories*. S & P

Unit, CSIR Survey Report No. 2. New Delhi: Council of Scientific and Industrial Research.

Rahman, A., and Malik, S. (Miss) (1966). *Current Trends of Research in Botany in India*. Current Trends Research Series No. 1, RSPO, CSIR, December 1966. New Delhi: Council of Scientific and Industrial Research.

Rahman, A., Sen, N., and Rajagopal, N. R. (1966). *State Support to Scientific Research in India —an Analysis of Trends*. RSPO, CSIR, Survey Report No. 8. New Delhi: Council of Scientific and Industrial Research.

Rahman, A., and Shama Rau, T. H. (1967). *Flight of Scientific and Technical Personnel*. Occasional Paper Series No. 2, RSPO, CSIR, February 1967. New Delhi: Council of Scientific and Industrial Research.

Rahman, A., Sharma, K. D., Sen, Uma (Mrs.), and, Malik, Sudarshan (Miss). (1967). *Science Policy in India*. Occasional Paper Series No. 1, RSPO, CSIR. New Delhi: Council of Scientific and Industrial Research.

Rahman, A., and Subbarayappa, B. V. (1965). Science policy in India—past and present. *Symposium on Collaboration Between Countries of Africa and Asia for Promotion and Utilization of Science and Technology (CAAUST)*, New Delhi, 1965.

Ranga Rao, B. V. (1967). *Scientific Research in India—An Analysis of Publications*. Occasional Paper Series No. 3, RSPO, CSIR, New Delhi. Reprinted from *Journal of Scientific and Industrial Research*, **26,** 4, 166–176 (1967).

Science in India (1966). 2nd edition, RSPO, CSIR. New Delhi: Council of Scientific and Industrial Research.

Second Conference of Scientists and Educationists (1963). *Proceedings*. Held at New Delhi, 4th and 5th August, 1963. Welcoming speech by Minister for Scientific Research and Cultural Affairs.

Sharma, K. D. and Garg, R. L. (1964). Planning of scientific research. *Symposium of the Association of Scientific Workers of India on Science and the Nation*, New Delhi, 1964.

DISCUSSION

Todd: Dr. Rahman has underlined one of the great problems of a number of countries that are described as developing countries, although it is a different kind of development from that of the Latin American countries. Whereas the latter were recently more or less empty countries, and appear to be developing towards a "United States" pattern, India has to achieve a reconciliation of an age-old cultural pattern and the new social pattern of scientific development, which is extremely difficult. As Dr. Rahman says, you have the machinery, but you are not wholly satisfied with the way it works.

Weinberg: I have talked to scientists in several Eastern countries, and one problem besetting these countries in the application of science to matters that are relevant to the society (perhaps a central problem, which one sees also in the Western countries but, for obvious reasons, it makes less difference) is whether scientists are willing to compromise their individual scientific aspirations, as visualized by them in terms of the disciplinary community to which they belong, with the larger aspirations and needs of the country. You mentioned that an urgent need in India is the rationalization of the irrigation system. You have many people who, if they set their minds to this, could help. Why do they not volunteer?

Rahman: A large number of people, if they were asked to shift their interest, would shift if the necessary incentive was given to them. Judging from discussions with my colleagues—this is not based on an analysis of data because the data have yet to be analysed—such a situation can arise only when scientists feel confident about their careers. There are instances where people have been asked to take up new work, and in a large number of cases they have been utilized by the senior scientists for their own work and have been left high and dry after having worked in a field which was new and interesting and of national importance. Consequently, there is some resistance, simply because of apprehension.

The second point arises out of incentives given to scientists. We have calculated that 70 per cent of those who join the administrative services receive a monthly salary of 700 rupees and above; but only 20 per cent of engineers, scientists and doctors receive this salary. 700 rupees is not a large salary in Delhi. Thirty per cent of those who join the administrative services have a salary of 1,500 rupees and above; the number of scientists, engineers and doctors receiving this salary is less than 3 per cent. For salaries of 2,000 rupees and above, the corresponding figures are 15 per cent and less than 2 per cent.

Weinberg: You said that there are 50,000 working scientists in India; presumably they have made their peace with the pay scale?

Rahman: No; they continually change from one job to another, depending on where they can get an increase in salary, sometimes totally disrupting the scientific work. But, and this is the main point, they will do a piece of research if there is suitable motivation. This is not usually possible, because of the administrative control and the nature of the decision-making machinery, which is totally dominated by the administrators, without taking into consideration any scientific data available.

If a study were to be made on decision making at various levels in a particular department, on the type of data available, on how much of it is being used, and on whether literature and technical notes are prepared when a decision is to be made, it would be found that in practice the technical expertise or information available within a department is often ignored and without effect on the final decisions.

Weinberg: Has India considered legally establishing a Science Adviser in each of the ministries?

Rahman: From the point of view of the institutions required, anything that is being done in advanced countries is also being done in India. But it is done only to meet the requirements of individuals who would like to have posts. The whole motivation for creation is entirely different from what it is in, say, the United States. Many of my colleagues in India may not agree with my rather harsh comments, but this is my personal feeling.

Weinberg: You give the impression that aggressive scientists in India do not have much influence. Is that really so? I have in mind Dr. Bhabha and his influence, which was considerable. Was he an exception?

Goldsmith: When I was in India I found that you tend to have the virtuoso of science—someone like Bhabha, who, in effect, ran an empire of his own and who built up, because of his considerable abilities and his private wealth, an emphasis on the establishment of research in atomic energy, which was not really related to the needs of India. Much of this empire-building is still going on, so that one has, as Dr. Rahman pointed out, individual scientists pursuing individual goals that are quite out of line with goals of the kind that the country needs to develop along the lines we have been discussing.

In addition, I found an enormous amount of frustration among the rank-and-file scientists. For example, I spoke with many physicists who had been trained abroad, both in the United States and the United Kingdom, and they were complaining of the things that Dr. Rahman has mentioned; that is, that they could not make an effective contribution in their fields of research unless they left the country, which they did not want to do. I suggested to some of them that they might take up botany, but this subject has no status. It is not easy to turn from one subject to another.

Foster: Dr. Rahman said that 50,000 scientists were employed in research and 250,000 are coming out of the universities each year with bachelors' degrees and above. This must mean fantastic unemployment of the white-collar worker. What a terrible system! No wonder those who are lucky enough to be employed hang on to their jobs, and are most reluctant to venture into new fields and new institutions. Since many of the 250,000 are, I believe, badly taught, the superficial diagnosis of the problem is surely very obvious. What can be done about it may be more difficult to determine.

Rahman: About 50,000 is the total number doing research, in both universities and government institutions.

The unemployment is high, and yet there is this paradox; a large number of posts in geology are available in different departments in the country, and yet according to the national survey, the maximally unemployed scientists are the geologists at the moment.

There are a surprisingly large number of research institutes; I could not believe that we have over 750 agricultural research centres, until I started collecting the facts.

Rexed: Dr. Rahman's paper was fascinating; it is a story of development out of step. Evidently in India a scientific community has been created which has not yet been integrated into Indian society. One possible explanation is that investment in general education has not been sufficient, because to create an understanding in a society for science and for the use of science, general education is vital, varied and broad enough for people to be able to grasp these principles and to see the interaction of scientific thinking with practical applications. My question is this: has there been a wrong priority decision in Indian society at large, putting too little emphasis on general education, to make possible all the other developments which would follow?

Rahman: I would answer by suggesting a hypothesis on which I am now working. There is a peculiar historical and social situation in India. The first period of scientific development in India in antiquity was associated with Buddhism, and the language was Pali; the second period of scientific development in antiquity was with Sanskrit as a medium of communication and Hinduism as the religion; in the third period, Persian became the language of communication and Islam the religion; in the fourth period, in which we live, English is the language of scientific communication, and it is associated with Christianity. At no period in history has there been any interaction between these traditions, to synthesize or lay down the basis of a scientific tradition. Even today, in India, *Ayurvedic*, the ancient system of medicine, *Unani*, the mediaeval system of medicine, and modern medicine, are considered to be competitive systems rather than three stages in the development of medicine. This failure to look critically at historical traditions and to allow them to interact with a view to evolving a scientific tradition, is to my mind the immediate cause of having a superstructure floating on top of Indian society.

Ackoff: There is one major difference in the evolution of science in Western and Eastern cultures. The fact is sometimes overlooked that the Renaissance was made possible in Western culture because of a change in attitude towards the hand—the emergence of the respectability of manual labour. In India this change has never taken place. For example, the doctor and nurse have low status in India because of the manual work that they do. Many practising engineers in India never touch a machine. Science is regarded as an almost spiritual activity in India. Do you see any hope of getting science and the hand together in India?

Rahman: That is what some of us are living for! But in asking the question you have answered it yourself. A very large number of the members of the staff of the Mechanical Engineering Research Institute did not know how to drive a car. When the new director took up his post he said that they must learn to drive, at the expense of the Institute, in spite of administrative objections. Either they come from poor families and cannot afford a car, or they come from families who have their own chauffeurs. The main point I have tried to submit is that science and technology cannot exist in a cultural desert; it has to be an integral part of the whole social system of the country.

Braun: It would seem to me that in the case of India—or any similar developing country—the insufficient interaction of scientific thinking with practical applications is not just the result of a wrong priority decision in national education. I am more inclined to believe that we are here dealing with a manifestation of the national culture pattern—the set of learned behaviours, values and beliefs that are widely shared in local society.

The orientation of the local value system exercises a tremendous influence on education, science, technology, industrial growth and work relations in general. If it prefers material progress, quantity, action, vitality and youth, and so on, we find that manual labour is well accepted. However, if it prefers spiritual progress, quality, contemplation and meditation, wisdom and age, we are faced with a low status of manual labour.

In nations with a large percentage of illiterate people, those who finish high school are a very small proportion of those who began schooling. In their last year of high school, it is natural and almost inevitable for these students to think of themselves as members of an elite group. Why then should a member of an elite lower himself to do manual labour? This trend produces the overcrowding of universities, research institutes and certain liberal professions and an ever-growing shortage of technicians and skilled workers. As long as society remains thus orientated toward speculation rather than achievement, the indispensable effort to bridge the gap between theory and practice, science and technology, knowledge and its application, is tragically shunned. The interaction of scientific thinking with practical applications can only prosper where there is a strong motivation to experiment. Experimentation, however, needs in addition to scientists also technicians, skilled workers *and manual labour* by all concerned.

Before any educational reform is attempted it would seem important first to encourage the social research necessary for the measurement of culture, which in turn can help to provide people with a better sense of where they are and a better prospect for making intelligent decisions about where they want to go.

Todd: One is facing in India what is, perhaps, essentially a social and hierarchical problem. Dr. Rahman's comment about those who do not need to drive a car underlines this. There is an absence in India of a "middle-class" on any large scale, and the part of the community from which these changes would come is arising only rather slowly. The main hope is that as it develops, this synthesis will occur. (See also p. 281.)

SCIENCE POLICY IN A SMALL COUNTRY— ISRAEL

Daniel Shimshoni

Department of Political Science, University of Tel-Aviv, Israel

THE choices of science policy take on a particular poignancy in a small country. In how many fields of science can the country be outstanding or even first class? Given problems of resources, communications and scale, can it be other than a provincial part of the world of science and technology, and therefore of society? (See, for example, Ben-David, 1962.)

Strong efforts in basic science are needed in a small country, as a window on the world, to maintain a high general level of education, and to allow many of the youth to find intellectual fulfilment in their own land. Unlike a larger country, the small country has difficulty in letting a market-place for ideas operate freely, where those areas of science that attract peers and graduate students demand more of the resources. Most "provincial" countries report that their basic science tries to follow current world fashions, that the reference groups of individuals are located abroad, and that goals are obscurely, if at all, related to local needs or aspirations.

In a sense, there is a technical "balance of payments deficit". Technology is imported as finished goods and as knowledge. A decision to achieve excellence in education and research, and to give each person an opportunity to go as far in school as his talents will take him, implies the risk of exporting intellectuals, at least in the short term, when opportunities and numbers may seem out of balance.

Technology faces a very small home market. Because of cost, few areas or even projects can be developed with any real chance of success. There are constant technological "make or buy" decisions, and these are often based on very imperfect knowledge. Communication in engineering is far less feasible than in basic science—because of the specificity of the knowledge, and the influence of competition and of national and commercial interests. A large development programme may be needed merely to know enough about a subject to make an intelligent purchase. Actual production, on an economic scale, can imply importing most products and producing only a few, mainly for export. This means taking risks at very large odds— hard for a government and harder for an industry.*

Given these kinds of problems, the way in which a small country decides on science policy becomes critical. It has to secure the benefits, despite its own limited scope, of a free play of enterprise and ideas. Great emphasis is needed on communications. The decision process needs to take account of the peculiar features of the social and economic structure, and of the accentuated small-country roles of inter-personal and inter-institutional relations.

Science policy for a small country is justified, it seems, in the sense that nationalism in the world is justified. A nationalist feeling can stimulate a people to try and to achieve. Here there is a similarity to regional develop- ment within a large or even a highly developed country; as, for example, in the less developed and less industrialized regions of the United States, where regionalism can stimulate local educational and technical advances.

The questions for science policy in Israel can be seen as a special case of those of a small country—an unusual location, far from European and American technical market centres, yet closer than they, in many ways, to the new nations of the world; marked heterogeneity in the cultural and scientific traditions of the inhabitants, with more than half of the popula- tion recent immigrants, and most of these from relatively backward coun- tries; some outstanding scientific achievements, and universities at a world standard, yet with more than 80 per cent of an age-group not qualify- ing for university entrance; an excellent climate and burgeoning agricul- ture; with other raw material endowments virtually limited to phosphates, potash and some clays, limestone, copper, and so far a very little oil. With all this there are challenging national goals and the relative unity of purpose of a free society which has not yet learned to make its collective talents equal to the sum of those of the individuals.

The approach and substance of Israel's science policy can perhaps now be assessed, some 19 years after independence. Among the applicable criteria are the formulation of goals and methods; the extent to which the diverse interests of a variety of groups and individuals are aggregated; and success in gaining acceptance of policies, and in actual achievement. Comment needs to be tentative, given the short perspective; and to be seen against

---

*Israel's gross national product in 1964–1965 was $3,590,000,000, less than the sales of some corporations, yet it comprised a diversity of scientific and technical endeavour that most corporations would try to avoid.

the background of the political, economic and social structures, of the actual problems faced, and of the major goals.

Some of these goals are within reach. Productive labour, and agriculture in particular, were established as a way of life. Today some 15 per cent of the population feeds the rest. The diffusion of the results of agricultural research has been spectacular, in some ways due as much to the qualities of the recipients as to those of the research itself. The important defence establishment has a highly developed technology. A great many services of the welfare state are provided, particularly in health, pensions and housing.

But many far-reaching problems remain. The country was able to be a haven for immigration, the population rising from less than one million in 1948 to more than 2·6 million in 1966. This was accomplished with heavy foreign investment, and economic growth based on building, services, and on relatively unsophisticated industry, such as textiles, whose export future is problematical. A high growth rate could not be maintained on this basis (for example, about 10 per cent per annum in real terms from 1960 to 1964, and 7 per cent per annum for 1964–1965 [Bank of Israel, 1966]). An economic recession occurred before the groundwork had been laid, through industrial research, for a shift to industries having the high technological content which could provide an export base.

The desalination of water (any further expansion of agriculture and the use of the arid Negev lands is dependent upon added water resources); possible uses of the oceans which lie on two sides; the social and physical implications of urban living, including air pollution and increasing demands on the transportation system; added search for oil and for new minerals—all these are aspects of the infrastructure which need considerable research.

A third major task is that of realizing the potential of the manpower which is growing up in the country, and even more important, of advancing the children of immigrants so that we achieve some of the ideal of equality. Today more than half of the children of school age either were born, or are the children of parents who were born, in countries in an early stage of development, mainly along the Mediterranean or in the Middle East. An unusual effort is needed to overcome their early difficulties in meeting the demands of a school system designed for a highly developed country—a lag which can show itself even before schooling starts, in vocabulary and in orientation to abstract concepts.

Looking farther ahead, there is already a shortage of university places in laboratory sciences and engineering. Yet, as shown in the Appendix (p. 269), a smaller percentage of engineering or science graduates are using their professional training than would be hoped.

Israel has not yet decided how to plan and co-ordinate the development of the university system, nor faced up to ways of making, overtly, decisions for basic science, although in fact these decisions are somehow made. Clearly, then, a further major problem is the development of the scientific and technical infrastructure in all its aspects, and most particularly those which concern people and their education.

These, then, are the broader problems with which science policy is faced: how to enlist social and technical resources so as to change the structure of industry and services, and to make them competitive in sophisticated areas of export; how to develop further the physical basis of the country's existence; and in particular, to decide the basic guidelines of the country's educational and scientific infrastructure.

Decisions regarding industrial research may illustrate some of the relations of science policy to the social and political framework. In brief, the need for a shift to industry having a deeper technological content was long recognized by a good many scientists and engineers in Israel. Plans were put forward and some concrete steps taken; yet the resources allocated were meagre, the social changes needed are taking place slowly, and no very considerable progress has been made in advancing industrial research or industry based on technology. A better preliminary analysis of the social environment would possibly have permitted a greater achievement.

Many contrasts in Israel have often been pointed out. Ancient intellectual traditions contrast with the ideology of labour and citizen defence. Higher education, until recently, was seen as leading back towards the old, middle-class urban values, and as such was believed to be detrimental to the new ideals, to practical accomplishment, and to nation building. Yet, high value is given to abstract thinking in higher education and research. It is no accident that pure mathematics is one of the outstanding departments of the Hebrew University. Only the Technion teaches engineering.

Anything that is said here may not apply to the future, for the present political structure and culture are beginning to feel the winds of change. The impact of technical education on the new generation; an inherent dissatisfaction with essentially hierarchical political and economic relations; a feeling on the part of younger people of strong cultural differences from many of the leaders—a group which with will, idealism (and the use of analysis, if at all, *post facto*), helped to build the nation: these differences have been accentuated by the present economic difficulties and by the simultaneous approach of retirement age for those who originally founded the State, and of middle age for the generation which fought the War of Liberation and which now carries much of the executive responsibility.

The older generation, not having the newer techniques of management available, substituted for them force of personality, determination and acumen. Their decision processes are based in no small part on trust in the proved loyalty, dependability and industry of those proposing alternative courses of action. Yet many of those working at the next levels are interested and competent in sophisticated analysis, which is thus superimposed on much politization of the economy and of management.

At the same time, a number of scientists and others of an individual, entrepreneurial bent have found little common language with civil servants and many others who have what might be described as an administrative or "bureaucratic" culture.

Government is highly centralized on the one hand and pluralistic on the other. It is centralized in the sense that proportional representation places political power in the hands of comparatively few people, in party secretariats and the Cabinet. It is pluralistic in the sense that the system implies the inclusion of several parties in the Cabinet. When these are "given" ministries, they look upon them as domains and impose their particular interests. Parliamentary government thus presents less of a unified government policy, despite collective responsibility, than can be had in systems where one party can achieve a clear majority.

In the mixed economy of Israel, the control and direction of a large part of industry is highly centralized. The government has been a dominant force through some of its large raw-material and transport corporations (even though these have organizational inertial forces of their own and often show greater independence than does private industry); but most particularly through its guidance and control of foreign investment and of the local investment which takes place through increasing pension and insurance funds. The Trade Union Federation, the Histadrut, owns through its holding company, wholly or partly, a good share of basic industry. Effective control of private industry is centralized in a very few investment companies and banking institutions, many of them closely linked with government circles, particularly for credit and administrative advantage. Government perforce nurtured industry in the early days of industrialization, but an excess of nurture, and the hierarchical relationships which emerged, tended to make the profits of a given industry perhaps more dependent on administrative relations, and on local rather than export markets. This environment did not develop the kind of manager who looks for competition abroad, based on new technology.

Such factors help to explain what turned out to be a serious lag in research for industry. The early policy of the National Council for Research and Development, set up in 1959, was based on a few research associations, grants to universities and to industry, and a proposal to form a development corporation to fund prototypes or pilot plants based on local research results. There was an early shift from the research-association approach towards the idea of central, multi-discipline, multi-industry central laboratories (the first of these is now being set up at the Technion), and to increased industrial research grants.

In the event, the funds allocated for industrial research were minimal compared with the annual growth rate of $6,000,000 originally proposed (Shimshoni, 1959). In 1963, total national expenditure on industrial research was only $3,800,000, of which half came from the government. The founding of the central industrial research laboratory was held up by the Treasury for over a year, and the ministerial economic affairs committee rejected the idea of a development corporation until 1965, when private capital took up a controlling interest on favourable terms.

The small size of government allocations stemmed in part from euphoria associated with a ten per cent annual rise in gross national product, and in part from a lack of contact, on the part of those deciding, with the nuances and demands of a technological industrial culture. While the Research Council in the Prime Minister's Office was aware of the needs, this Office was and is essentially non-executive for domestic affairs, and is occupied with the cares of foreign affairs, defence and the most pressing of current political questions. As a result, the Council was never effectively represented at the cabinet level, where in fact the economic and budget decisions are made.*

Industry, for its part, had little interest or readiness for risk-bearing investments in research. Even as grants became available, comparatively little interest was aroused. Perhaps the booming 1960-1965 economy provided profits, or the hope of profits, without benefit of science. Other factors were the industrial culture of the older generation of manufacturers and the small scale of most plants. In any case, the proponents

---

*When the National Council for Research and Development was formed in 1959, Treasury officials recommended reliance on civil servants rather than on ministers as Council members. If there were more of a common language between the administrators and the scientists—entrepreneurs, this arrangement might have worked. As it turned out, action at cabinet level was needed. This possibility is now provided for by a cabinet committee on science and technology, formed at the time of the general elections in 1965. Recently this committee has begun to meet in earnest, apparently stimulated, in part, by the present economic recession.

of industrial research seem to have misunderstood the needs and psychology of Israeli industry, as they did those of the leaders of the government establishment. The Council did succeed, however, in some aspects of analysis, with concrete results.

For example, a simplified systems analysis of the pharmaceutical industry was made. Israel was shown to have excellent doctors, hospitals and medical schools, and its share of patients, organic chemists and microbiologists; yet the pharmaceutical industry was on a very small scale. By all counts, this was an industry very suitable for a country having few raw materials and looking for products of a high technical content. The analysis showed that the chemists and biologists could produce materials having a biological potential, technical knowledge being available for their testing. A medical profession of some reputation could develop them further. There was lacking in the system, however, the capability to carry out screening of potential drugs on any scale, and this seemed to be the missing link in the process of developing new drugs. As a result, a biological screening facility was recently put into operation.

Another example is an analysis of plant-breeding in agriculture. It was found that most agricultural development was being done within departments concerned with very specific families of plants, often with success, but there seemed to be too little effort in research in genetics as such, which could impinge on the work of those engaged in applied research. In this case, the recommendation was for more effort in a given area of basic science.

Staff work and technical forecasting could have been more helpful if the analysis of subsystems had been part of a more general and deeper study of the structure of the economy, in order to try to foresee, on a comparative basis, the activities most helpful for the future. This was not done, partly because of the absence until recently of cabinet level or other adequate inter-ministerial co-ordination; and partly because of budgetary limitations and civil service impediments to the attraction of high-level staff.

Whereas industrial research started very slowly, the problems of the general infrastructure were better served. The large goals were more in line with the pioneering needs of nation building, and more tangible. Natural conditions gave a clear mandate, and the decision process benefited from the adversary approach built into the pluralism of the Cabinet (see Shimshoni, 1965).

The approach to higher education and basic research is at an early stage of what has been, until now, a useful discussion, in that the government has accepted responsibility for higher education policy and, in the Sharef committee report (Committee on Higher Education, 1965), took an important first step in formulating the problems.

What can be learned from this brief experience? As we have seen, the formulation of the goals of Israeli science policy has been reasonably successful, while actual achievement lags behind. The founders of the Council understood the social structure of science in Israel only imperfectly but their sensitivity to it far exceeded their comprehension of the social structure of industry, finance and politics.

The objective factors available augur well. There is an awareness of national needs and purpose, capable individuals, a broad technical competence, an improving educational system, and strong basic science. Communications with the larger world are reasonably good. Changes based on social comprehension and change could make it possible to realize this potential.

APPENDIX
BACKGROUND DATA

Government

A single-chamber parliament (the Knesseth) is elected by proportional representation from the national lists determined by the several parties. The maximum term of parliaments is four years. The Prime Minister is a parliamentary leader who can form a government having a majority in the Knesseth. This has been by a coalition of parties, with little change since 1948 in leadership or in the proportions of electoral support. The government has consistently been predominantly labour, favouring a mixed economy (ownership by private enterprise, government and the Trade Union Federation—the Histadrut). Cabinet members need not be Knesseth members but usually are, and are responsible to the Knesseth. The Treasury is the dominant ministry in domestic affairs, by way of the budget, the Controller-General and the civil service commission. Cabinet members have a collective responsibility for government decisions on all issues except those involving "individual conscience".

The Prime Minister's Office comprises a personal staff and departments which do not have independent ministerial status (for example, the information services, the National Council for Research and Development—NCRD). There is a cabinet sub-committee for science and technology, formed in 1965, which has met several times, and whose secretary is the chairman of NCRD. It has not yet taken decisions and has now asked for information and policy proposals. The ministerial economic affairs committee of the Cabinet is a focus for government economic decisions.

The National Council for Research and Development was formed in 1959. In 1964 there were 35 members, who met annually or semi-annually. Of these, ten were civil servants, *ex officio*, and the rest were appointed *ad personam*—twenty-one from academic or government laboratories, and four from industry. A smaller executive committee, nearly all scientists and technologists, meets monthly. A headquarters staff of some twelve professionals does the staff work and at any given time works with some eight or ten part-time task forces or sub-committees.

The Ministries of Agriculture, Defence, Development, Commerce and Industry, and the NCRD, all operate their own laboratories. In principle, the NCRD makes budget recommendations to the Treasury on all non-defence government research and development. The main centres of decision on government research and development are the Ministries of Defence and Agriculture, and for industrial research, the NCRD and the Ministries of Development (chemical industry and mining), and Commerce and Industry.

Resources for research and development*

In 1964, about 45 per cent of non-defence research and development was supplied directly by government (of this 12 per cent was as part of block grants to universities); the universities provided some 30 per cent (assuming about 50 per cent faculty-time spent in research); foreign governments (mainly the United States) supplied 15 per cent; foundations provided about 2 per cent and industry only 8 per cent.

Industrial research and development is about 0·25 per cent of turnover—about half from government. Between 1960 and 1963, industrial turnover increased by 88 per cent, and industrial research and development expenses increased by about 45 per cent, largely due to increased government expenditure. Most industrialized countries report that 85 per cent, if not more, of research in industry is carried out in plants having more than 1,000 employees. In Israel there are only a few firms of this size. In 1963, fifteen plants having more than 500 employees reported a research and development programme; these accounted for over 40 per cent of industrial research.

All in all, about 1 per cent of the gross national product was spent on research and development of all kinds. Not including capital gifts, 15–20 per cent came from foreign sources, which provided almost half of all medical research funds. Approximately half of all research funds were spent on basic research.

Scientists and technologists

The proportion of scientists and technologists in the work force is among the highest in the world (over 1 per cent). The proportions engaged in research and development, however, and particularly in industry, show a different picture.

	Israel	United States	United Kingdom
Percentage of scientists and technologists engaged in research and development (1963)	16	33 (approx.)	36 (approx.)
Percentage employed in industry	18 (1961)	56 (1959)	41 (1959)

In Israel, only 6 per cent of research workers are employed in industrial establishments.

Some 15 per cent of the annual group of 18-year-olds pass the matriculation examination, and are qualified for the university. The indications are that more than 85 per cent of these enrol. The proportion of those studying science and technology, however, decreased from 45 per cent in 1955 to 26 per cent in 1963, which was still about 4 per cent of the relevant age-group. This decrease is explained by a large growth in places, and unselective enrolment, in the humanities and social sciences, with only a slow growth of facilities in science and engineering.

---

*Reports of the National Council for Research and Development for 1961–1962 (English) and 1963–1964 (Hebrew); and unpublished data.

National productivity and the balance of payments (Bank of Israel, 1966)

Between 1958 and 1963, at constant 1963 prices, the gross national product grew from $1,590 million to $2,643 million. The important surplus, or balance of payments, showed deficits of:

	1962	1963	1964	1965
Millions of dollars	479·5	434·7	569·3	521·1

(The 1964 figure reflects both a boom atmosphere and a large purchase of commercial ships and aircraft.)

In 1965, commodity exports were $400 million, and service exports, $350 million. Of these exports, agriculture was 22 per cent (80 per cent citrus fruit); industrial goods, 45 per cent; polished diamonds (imported raw from Africa), 32·5 per cent. Potash and phosphates are other important exports.

REFERENCES

Bank of Israel (1966). *Annual Report*, 1965. Jerusalem.

Ben-David, Joseph (1962). Scientific endeavour in Israel and the United States. *The American Behavioral Scientist*, 6, 4.

Committee on Higher Education (1965). *Report*. (In Hebrew.) Jerusalem: The Prime Minister's Office.

National Council for Research and Development (1961–1962). *Report*. (In English.) Jerusalem: The Prime Minister's Office.

National Council for Research and Development (1963–1964). *Report*. (In Hebrew.) Jerusalem: The Prime Minister's Office.

Shimshoni, Daniel (1959). *Research and Technical Development in Israel*. Herzlia, Israel. (Prepared for the Prime Minister's Office.)

Shimshoni, Daniel (1965). *Minerva*, III, 4(summer), 441–456.

DISCUSSION

Krauch: I was most interested to learn about the foundation of an institute for pharmacological screening in Israel. Even in countries with a strong pharmaceutical industry, such additional research activity is needed. Companies tend to limit the facilities devoted to screening and to be mainly "molecule-orientated" or "product-orientated". What is needed is "disease-orientated" research institutes. An analogous situation is the electronics industry. There are "social diseases" which could be cured by research and development, which so far is not provided by industry. Do you sponsor a similar effort between government and industry in electronics?

Shimshoni: Not so much in electronics. The principal example so far is a Center for Industrial Research—a multi-disciplinary development laboratory intended to serve the long-range needs of such industries as plastics and petrochemicals, textiles and food.

Freeman: What is your policy towards inviting foreign-owned firms to establish themselves in Israel and do research in such fields?

Shimshoni: Feelings in the past have been mixed about allowing foreign firms to establish research laboratories. I think that now we would be receptive to such proposals, and, indeed, some are under discussion. One motive is a desire to have more of the research process carried on within the country. For example, a motive in setting up our own drug screening was the fact that Israel received almost no feedback from the screening which took place abroad; nor do I know of instances where there have been substantial royalties from drugs tested by foreign pharmaceutical firms.

Weinberg: I gather that Israel has not so far elected to encourage companies to come in from outside and set up laboratories to exploit her cheaper manpower. As you know, many companies are doing this now in Europe. Union Carbide, an American Company, has a laboratory in Belgium. Would you consider such an arrangement advantageous or disadvantageous to Israel? It would staunch some of your "brain drain".

Shimshoni: I, personally, would not be averse to trying it. Again, we feel that the possibility of a "brain drain" is probably most serious in medicine. Part of the reason lies in the highly developed system of training for specialization in the United States and the high pay received by qualified specialists, which can be as much as six times the Israeli scale. In other fields of science, the experience seems to be that if one can offer a person a reasonable opportunity, he will come back to Israel.

Weinberg: I have been involved with Harrison Brown's Science Organization and Development Board, in connexion with the Latin American countries. One of the points under discussion there is how to encourage private firms from Europe and North America to come to Argentina or Brazil and establish local laboratories. There have been some successful ventures of that sort; for example, the Syntex group has such a laboratory in Mexico.

Cardón: This is certainly feasible. Some foreign firms have established research laboratories in Argentina—for example, Squibb and Pfizer. But in general they prefer to devote such laboratories to routine work, adaptation problems and quality control. In almost all cases they work with patents brought from abroad and are not trying to develop original research in the country. There is a feeling in these countries that this situation should be changed in the interest of the scientific development of the country, and also for economic reasons. One important component of the balance of payments of these countries is the large sums paid for foreign patents. But I do not know of any special measure that has been taken.

Rexed: Professor Shimshoni, in view of the high influx of untrained manpower into Israel and the problem of the acculturation of a big proportion of the population, have you considered developing mechanized educational techniques—for example, programmed instruction and language and other training laboratories?

Shimshoni: We have not used programmed or machine-aided learning very much. We have found that the vocabulary level by the age of six years, and the ability to handle abstract concepts, are far lower for immigrants from less-developed countries than for children whose parents came from more developed countries, and these differences show in the statistics of entering secondary schools and university.

The following kinds of measures have been taken: compulsory or free kindergarten from the age of three or four instead of five years for children from these backgrounds, and a longer school-day, with special help from teachers. There is also deliberate "reverse discrimination"—a more favourable policy towards the less advantaged in secondary school and university admissions and scholarships. These methods are being used in other countries too, of course.

Freeman: As I see it, the critical problem for science policy in relation to economic development is that not even the largest and most developed country can master all fields of research in science. Every country stands to gain from international exchange and import of knowledge and technical "know-how" in one way or another. The vital question is how to achieve the right "mix" of imported science, imported "know-how", indigenous research and development capacity, and indigenous science.

I am struck by the big difference between the position of Israel and that of India or Argentina. In Israel there was a deliberate science-policy decision to set up a technically advanced pharmaceutical industry, based on its own research and development capacity. I would ask two questions. First, what are the distinctive features in Israel that enabled this to be done, whereas apparently it cannot be done in the other countries? Is it the availability of the discipline specialists—and I think it probably is—who make it possible to put this missing link of research into the system and build a technically advanced industry? Or is it something else?

The second question is, how do you decide to go ahead and establish a technically advanced industry, based on indigenous research, rather than to take a licence for a drug? These seem to me to be critical questions for science policies in developing countries.

King: A third question is, how do you choose one industry rather than another?

Shimshoni: On this last question, ideally one should consider all possible choices simultaneously, but they do not suggest themselves simultaneously, and so are looked at case by case, or in groups. Because research workers are a scarce resource, one tries to look at areas where either there are problems or there is potential strength or a resource. For example, living on two oceans, we considered oceanography, and set up an oceanographic station on the Red Sea because of the great variety of marine life available, and the need for a first-class laboratory for foreign marine scientists wishing to work in our part of the world. Another interesting oceanographic question is why the Eastern Mediterranean has apparently been fished out and why there is very little marine life there.

In making choices, various people are engaged in a dialogue—locally or internationally—about what to do next. Usually, there are fewer good ideas that stand the test of this dialogue, than means to carry them out. The impact of personal "championship", and "advocacy", in such a dialogue should not be neglected. Examples where belief and persistence contributed are legion.

In answer to Mr. Freeman's questions, a pharmaceutical industry is possible in Israel because most of the scientific infrastructure exists—as Mr. Freeman said—in the availability of capable people in the needed disciplines. Secondly, the desire to ground industries in our own research is based on the importance of timing and of originality in the competition for export markets.

GENERAL DISCUSSION

SCIENCE POLICY IN DEVELOPING COUNTRIES

Goldsmith: From the three preceding papers—those of Cardón, Rahman and Shimshoni—it seems clear that in their countries there is a separation between scientific organizations and the political set-up. Although the politicians may agree to the establishment of certain organizations concerned with what they believe to be the interests of science, there seems to be no understanding by politicians of the real needs of science and of scientists, in terms of national goals, and the obverse seems also to be true. This might be linked up with the kind of comment that Dr. Rahman made, that unless one has a scientific and technological temper within a country, all one will get is an opportunistic approach to science. This is particularly true of the less highly developed countries, but I suspect that it is true even of the more advanced countries. We need to look at this more closely because there is not, certainly in Britain, a really adequate technological temper, which means that young people do not opt in sufficient number any more for science and technology when going to university.

Science-policy planning teams, to be sent out to developing countries, have been mentioned (p. 237). I wonder whether these are not likely to prove as "dangerous" as the provision of technical aid has so often been. Technical aid, as we know, has been given without real understanding of the requirements of the recipient country and of the way in which aid can be integrated with that country's needs. What has happened is that prestige and status have gone with the provision of large pieces of apparatus, but these have not been used. There may be a danger that unless we understand more clearly the socio-economic background into which a national science policy can be fitted, science-policy planning teams may come to be welcomed as a kind of salvation offered to a country, and this may produce all kinds of dangers.

King: One of the immediate problems raised by the situation of, say, Argentina, is whether it is necessary or useful for such a country to have a research effort. Is it not better, at a certain stage of development, to buy your technology and to concentrate on science for education and training, rather than to invest in research, especially basic research, in an elaborate way? I suspect that in many countries—certainly not India, where science

275

policy and development, from what Dr. Rahman said, exist as types of epiphenomena rather than as an assimilated part of the total system, but in many other places—science is being considered in terms of economic policy or of cultural policy rather than science policy. That may or may not be right. I suspect that a policy for science and technology is especially important for some developing countries even if, as part of this policy, research as such is not particularly stressed. Science policy is concerned as much with the application of existing information as with the creation of new knowledge.

Ackoff: Science has had a role in the development of Western culture that goes far beyond economic and intellectual development. It produces a general cultural milieu within which science-based decision making is accepted.

Rexed: Mr. Goldsmith's and Dr. King's points are important and are related to the point already made that science by itself is useless; it becomes free-floating. Science must be put into relation to something that one wants to do—science is a means to some end. Therefore it would be preferable if the science-policy team approach could be converted into the type of activity that the Organisation for Economic Co-operation and Development has been favouring in the Mediterranean countries—the pilot-teams project for developing local economies in conjunction with the scientific effort. One can go to any country and think of what its scientific development might do for it; but this must be seen in relation to the general situation in the country, its natural resources, how its industrial production is diversified and in what technological areas it has progressed. Only then does one discover how to construct its science policy. One does not have to decide whether to have a science policy or not—every country has one, implicitly or explicitly, whenever it does something in the scientific field. The pilot teams are a very fruitful form of help, because it is combined with expertise to review the situation as regards the research and development effort and at the same time, a national team is created which brings knowledge of the economic situation and possibilities of the different branches of industry and agriculture into a productive relationship. Dr. King, as leader of this experiment through the Scientific Directorate of the Organisation for Economic Co-operation and Development, could perhaps comment on the work of the teams in these countries—which include Turkey, Greece, Spain and Italy.

King: These pilot teams, consisting of natural scientists, engineers and economists, have attempted to provide a basis for science planning in the countries in which they operate, in order to develop the knowledge and skills required for the success of national economic and social plans. They all attempt to establish permanent links with national economic planning teams; they aim to encourage innovation and to facilitate technological transfer. The pilot teams consist exclusively of nationals of the country in question, backed up by consultants and experts from abroad. In some countries—Ireland, for example—the team has led to the reformulation of the country's technological aims, with recommendations for major institutional changes. In nearly all cases, as with the kind of work that Dr. Rahman is doing, the first task is a review of the existing situation. The teams obtain statistics and make a close assessment of the value of the existing scientific and technical effort and of its relevance, because in nearly all cases the scientific organization of the country is a copy of what has arisen in so-called more advanced countries, in a way not necessarily appropriate to the country itself. The teams seek to establish a model for science, based on the local environment and indigenous needs, and not a copy of a foreign system adapted to quite other circumstances.

Pilot-team studies have already been done or are nearly complete for Greece, Italy, Ireland, Portugal, Spain, Turkey and Yugoslavia. At a recent meeting, held to evaluate this approach, it was suggested that attempts be made to try out the technique in a Latin American country and in countries such as Egypt, India or Pakistan.

Rahman: I had a look at the national councils and policy-study units in a number of countries. In one country, I prepared a report on behalf of an international agency. My analysis of South-East Asia, West Asia and some of the African countries suggests that each country has either a supreme council for scientific research or a similar body. Its functions are laid down by law, but when it comes to its real operation, the isolation and the extremely limited function that it serves are apparent. Not to be too critical, it simply means allowing certain people to occupy certain positions as a label for something else.

King: I would add that in the really under-developed countries—not the type of country that we have been discussing—a large proportion of the scientists, having been trained abroad at sophisticated research centres, consider themselves as expatriates from the world scientific community with little interest in local problems. This can be a tragedy, both for the individual and for his country.

Rahman: My submission is that they may be expatriates and represent an extension of the science of the ex-colonial countries in their own country, but having acquired the methods and techniques and having gone through the process of looking at things from a different point of view, they have the

277

desire to continue in this outlook. Under the agencies of the international organizations, or in the internal politics of the country, organizations for the planning of science are being established, but not as part of the problem of social evolution and developing technology and science—rather as showpieces for them.

A further point can be illustrated by the specific example of Ceylon. A major effort was made, through the Ceylonese Association for the Advancement of Science, to bring about a scientific community and a science council and to develop research laboratories. An expert team from an advanced country undid all the effort made by the local scientists, and its recommendations—made in consultation with the administration—were that a consultant institute, like the one that existed in the country of the consultants, was all that Ceylon needs, and that nothing else is necessary.

Another point is that raised by Mr. Goldsmith. Science policy cannot be effective and science cannot develop unless there is a major effort to create a scientific temper, not only among scientists, administrators and politicians, but also among the general public. Any political issue that affects science vitally is scarcely debated in India; it does not affect the country. That is the crucial point, which links up with Mr. Braun's earlier remarks on the dissemination of science as a cultural force (p. 260). Unless that is done, these show-pieces will develop with a limited practical function. They may be used by people but they will not bring about a meaningful transformation in the situation, to come up to a level where we can look scientifically at the problem of selectivity, choice, meaningful investment, and so on.

The role and tradition of the administrator in India is a very interesting sociological problem that has not been studied. It is a question of the adjustment of the traditional social system, where the caste positions have been reorganized and reorientated to maintain certain power positions. We should try to look into changes that are happening, but not from the categories that have been built up in our minds on the basis of an unjustified hypothesis—for instance, the idea that Indian culture is fundamentally contemplative is widely held but not justified by the facts. I have evidence that the Indian cultural tradition was very much like any other tradition until the seventeenth century; the so-called "contemplative" attitude is a myth built up in a period of decadence after the conquest of India by England.

Cardón: I consider that in Argentina the level of education of the population, the general culture, the social and economic conditions and also the prevailing attitudes with regard to science and research, are rather favourable for its development. The sectors which have been most backward and from which the most serious obstacles to scientific progress have come are politics and administration.

Aron: I believe we are facing a problem which is well known in economics and is called the "imitation effect"—namely, the people in developing countries want to have and to consume more or less the same as the well-developed countries. In this case it goes even further. To import some elements of science brings prestige and status in the eyes of the people concerned, in spite of what could be called rationality. One aspect of a very general sociological problem is how to transfer what the developed countries have achieved to developing countries in an effective way that does not destroy the real development of the country concerned.

The worst aspect of transfer is the transfer of the administration without the transfer of the activity, as in India. The transfer of an advisory science group or an advisory board on science policy may be worse than nothing. As Professor Rexed said, there is always a science policy but it may be explicit or implicit; often it is better that it should be implicit. When it becomes explicit it is done by an administrator without scientific culture. Perhaps you always have a philosophy, but perhaps it is better when your philosophy is implicit! It is the same with science policy.

de Reuck: I should like to ask Professor Aron whether there are lessons to be learned from other areas—economic areas, for example—in the acculturation of a whole society which could be transferred into science?

Aron: Sociological studies could be done of what can be transferred more easily and what can be transferred only with difficulty. It is clear that it is easier to transfer a whole factory from one country to another than to transfer agricultural practice. In the case of science, the main danger is that if you transfer only one laboratory or only one type of higher education it will remain an isolated enclave that will not be disseminated through the whole society. However, beyond these very broad propositions, it would be dangerous to state general rules of application. To a large extent it depends where the initiative lies. Where the initiative in some high-level activity is in the hands of a few people, the others being only servants of the competent people, the transfer is relatively easy. When it comes to agriculture, where there must be a complete change in the outlook of a lot of people, the transfer is much more difficult.

King: How has Japan managed to inculcate a modern scientific industrial culture and at the same time run this in tandem with its indigenous, quite different culture?

Krauch: My impression is that the Japanese succeeded with this inculcation. They were able to preserve the basis of their culture, mainly an exceptionally strong ability to perceive the totality of a situation, taking into account the needs and desires of all the people involved. Scientific rationality was accepted and carefully implanted, without destruction of the cultural identity. This process was by no means an easy one. The Japanese experienced and experimented with a large number of ideas, belief systems, political, religious, social and scientific ways of thinking, more than any other culture in the world. Many of them belong to more than one religion and they are able to switch from one value system to another with ease. This might be the key to their success as designers of consumer goods. Better than anyone else, they can bring into accord the technical design and consumer needs and wants. (Compare Lifton, Robert Jay [1962]. Youth and history. Individual change in postwar Japan. *Daedalus*, Winter, 172–197. See also Yamada, Keiichi [1964]. *Philosophy and History of Modern Technology*. Tokyo.)

Aron: Japan—which is a miraculous case—is the only known example where the people who took the decision to Westernize their society started from below. They introduced first a system of general education. They sent missions to all the countries of the West and took what they saw to be the best in each field, taking some legal aspects from the French, some technology from the Germans or the English. Japan is the only case where a decision was made to transform the whole of society. At the same time, as Dr. Krauch points out, the Japanese were able to maintain many elements of the past in their family and religious life. But it is an almost unique combination.

Ackoff: Another example, which unfortunately is frequently overlooked, is Mexico. We have a great deal to learn from its incredible development. With less foreign aid than many developing nations have had and despite its installation of extensive social welfare and educational systems when investment capital was in short supply, it has been developing at a rapid rate. Anyone who visits Mexico cannot but be impressed by the dedication to national development and the long hours of hard work it extracts, particularly from professionals. Perhaps its welfare programme has produced this dedication. We should find out.

de Reuck: In Europe the example usually quoted is that of Turkey, but the case of Scandinavia is also interesting. It seems to me that high civilizations —like China or India—achieve cultural levels of such integrated complexity as to give rise to peculiar difficulties, when it comes to adapting themselves to scientific or technological ways, which less sophisticated cultures may not have to face.

Thus, Greece and Rome found no way of using or developing the benefits of science. Apparently science could not become a social force in the classical high civilizations of the Mediterranean: the collapse of the Roman Empire and a feudal episode were necessary preludes to the development of science in Europe. Only after this reversion to a neobarbaric level which was—compared, for example, with Chinese civilization—both socially and culturally relatively labile, did science take hold and transform the culture of the West. Now, Scandinavia was never part of the Roman Empire and never lapsed into feudalism. Sweden evolved directly from tribal society, and when the time came, took science without any great strain into her relatively plastic culture, which had not yet begun to harden into a highly civilized mould.

The Japanese, of course, had a high civilization, but in certain key respects, it presented a remarkable parallel development to the case of Europe, including a relapse into feudalism. Specifically, the Tokugawa period saw the gradual growth of a market economy and increases in agricultural productivity justifying comparison with the agrarian revolution in Europe. At least two important consequences followed: one was a social mobility unknown in China or India; and the other was a capital surplus which the Japanese invested in modernization.

Rahman: If Japan is compared with India, language emerges as a crucial factor. In Japan after the Meiji restoration, Japanese was chosen as the language of instruction. In India, English was chosen, although India already had more scientific societies, more scientific journals and more industries and universities than Japan had in the nineteenth century. The language gulf made it impossible for the new ideas to travel down, so that craftsmen could adapt old techniques and practices to modern technology.

de Reuck: In 1868 the Japanese had a large and restive middle class—merchants and manufacturers—which was rapidly growing, partly from landless peasants and partly from masterless *samurai* seeking new occupations. This may also have been important.

Rexed: We have never fully realized how important is the growth of general education for all these transitions and for the implications of the many innovations that science and technology bring. In all Western countries we have a population that can easily be transferred from one activity to another and can easily be retrained according to the needs of the situation. This is not so in a country where a broad general education is lacking. Japan had this advantage to begin with—this tradition of learning and education. That is surely one of the explanations of their progress. As Professor Shimshoni said earlier, even at the kindergarten age it is important to bring people up to a certain level.

Goldsmith: Professor Shimshoni, what effect has the use of the military system in Israel had in introducing some kind of technological temper to the new immigrants?

Shimshoni: It has been beneficial, but its relative impact has decreased as the civilian technical infrastructure of the country advanced, and the population generally acquired a modern technical culture.

Aron: Was military training not an essential part of their *civic* education, which is at the same time a part of the general development? I was struck in Israel by the impact of army education on people coming from Eastern countries.

Shimshoni: Yes, I think the army gave more a sense of belonging and of being an important part of the country than it gave specific technical knowledge. We have some technologies which owe their high standard almost entirely to the original military needs—such as aviation and electronic maintenance. Here the military set the initial high standards, which were taken over by the economy. But one can over-emphasize the importance of the military influence.

APPLYING FIRST PRINCIPLES

Aron: I speak as an observer of the social drama of the symposium. To start summing-up from general principles is clearly impossible, for a general reason and for a very special reason. Professor Ackoff has said that the complexity of a problem is a measure of our ignorance of it. So I find myself in an impossible position. Either I simplify; in that case I give the impression of being conceited, because I give the impression that I know the answer. Or I can be extremely complex; in that case it will not be a summing-up. So I would like to qualify slightly the proposition that the complexity is a measure of our ignorance. I would say that there are two forms of simplicity: the simplicity of complete ignorance and the simplicity of complete knowledge. In between there is the complexity of discovery, and perhaps we are in the process of discovering this.

Let me start with a very simple proposition which has been admitted by everyone here, without all the consequences being drawn from this first principle. The science of science is a social science and not a natural science. Therefore it is rather surprising that in this symposium, devoted to the science of science which, it was admitted, is a social science and not a natural science, the social sciences have been said not to be sciences. Perhaps this slip of the tongue has a certain meaning, because it was said also that it was more a philosophical exercise, and perhaps that is the beginning of the social drama. But I will come to that later.

The science of science is a scientific study of the socio-economic process which is the development of science and technology. This science was born out of a social process, which began with the mobilization of scientists during the war, their non-demobilization after the war, the big increase in the scientific budget which has taken place, and the need of the administrators to make a better allocation of resources—or at least to give the impression that they are making a better allocation. So this social science arises from these social phenomena and is orientated towards *action*.

This social science has four peculiarities, in relation to other social sciences; they are not unique, but they are more accentuated in this case than in the other social sciences. The first peculiarity is that a great number of natural scientists are interested in the science of science; this brings with it the professional attitude and outlook of the natural sciences, and this is all to the good.

The second peculiarity is that the boundaries of the field known as the science of science are rather undefined, because if you ask whether higher education is to be included, you may discuss indefinitely to what extent the system of education should be regarded as a part of the social system of science, which is the object of the science of science. If higher education is included in your object, why not secondary education or even the kindergarten? I have nothing against this, but it shows the difficulty of defining exactly the boundaries of the subject called the "science of science".

The third peculiarity is the uncertainty of the vocabulary, because of the number of professional people who have come into the field from different points of view, using different concepts. Quite clearly, on many occasions you can rightly use the language of economics, and when you try to measure the productivity of a certain investment in science, you are thinking as an economist. When you are studying the functioning of a laboratory or the relative efficiency of this or that research organization you are doing a micro-sociological study and you are using more or less the technique of the sociologist, good or bad; but it is another language, another approach, and quite clearly both are necessary.

The fourth peculiarity is what I would call the normative, or the practical, tendency of the science of science. There is a sort of permanent, almost inevitable, confusion arising from mixing up the science of science as a pure science with reflection about the policy of science, which is a sort of applied science of science. The fact is that for most of the meeting we have not discussed the science of science, but we have discussed a great deal how to make what we are doing in any case more reasonable, or more rational, or less stupid.

I believe that these four peculiarities of the science of science may be a good starting point for considering the science of science, and with greater modesty, our own discussion. In this social science, as in all social sciences, one part is descriptive: it deals with the organization of the policy of science in different countries—for example, with the relations between institutions, and with the scientific community as such. It is purely a description of what is going on.

The second part of our symposium was mainly a comparative description of the way the policy of science is organized and how it functions. The former may be compared with anatomy, and the latter with physiology.

That is probably a very bad comparison, but throughout the expositions we heard one element of, let us say, bureaucratic description, which was always clear, and one element of analysis of functioning, which was always obscure, and this is because, by definition, the manager and civil servant know the legal regulations and do not know, or do not want to know, the way they are actually functioning. Quite clearly, the science of science is not interested mainly in the question of what is the relative authority on paper of the Scientific Adviser to the President of the United States; but it would like to know how the different groups are acting, bargaining. And that is an object for a descriptive science of science, or for a descriptive sociology of the functioning of the organization of science. All the very illuminating studies of the Organisation for Economic Co-operation and Development are descriptive, with an element of polite analysis of functioning, required by the international character of that organization. Some small elements of normative advice are provided also in a marvellous way, because the advice is extremely clear in spite of the politeness, which is a great tribute to the skill of the people concerned.

The second part of our discussion, or the second part of the social science of science, should be the analytical and experimental science of science: namely, studying to what extent the organization in a laboratory is efficient, or how science is progressing, and so on. And this is done with the idea that from this scientific analysis may emerge some advice to governments, but without implying that the objective study is at the same time such advice. We mean only to point out that if people react in a certain way to science, the probable results will be this or that.

The main difficulty of the experimental and analytical part of the science of science is linked with the undefined character of the boundaries. If you really want to study the process of science you will have to do as Professor Ackoff suggested—make a general model of society. The process of science is a part of the general process of society, and this leads to traditional discussions among sociologists on whether to engage in micro-study, the limitation of the field, or macro-study, the effort to work out a general model.

Let me now make a few remarks about the descriptive part, which at this symposium we have considered in the form of a comparison between nations, or between organizations within nations. There was also some consideration of the comparison between the different organs of decision, and the relationships between them—namely the universities, industry, government agencies and government. These two comparisons were mixed up; namely, an effort was made to discover to what extent the different

10**

organs of decision had the same role or a different role according to the nation concerned. If I had drawn up a plan for the comparison, there would have been, of course, these three elements—university, industry, government—but taking into consideration the different status of those three elements in the different countries, it would have been possible to understand why a general result or a general proposition is extremely difficult to formulate.

As regards a comparison between nations, I shall limit myself to a few very primitive remarks, which may be necessary because the same words have not always the same meaning in different nations. First, when you try to make comparisons between government, industry, universities and government agencies using the American vocabulary, you fall into the danger of using words that have an exact meaning in the American context but very different meanings in the European context. Some of our discussions struck me as being based on a degree of misunderstanding which has gone beyond what was absolutely necessary. (A certain degree of misunderstanding is necessary in all discussion, but it should be reduced to a minimum!) Quite clearly, to put the question, "Where should basic research be sited, in a university or not?" has one meaning in America, but a different meaning in Germany or France where the universities are completely different. If you contrast "a government agency" in France with "a university", the difference is relatively limited. There are differences, but they are not the same as in the United States because French universities are all State-owned, and we, the academic staff, are all paid by the State. The result is complete anarchy inside the universities—but that is a special French trick! But in a discussion such as ours it is extremely dangerous, when making comparisons between institutions, to forget that the same words are applied to different realities.

My second remark concerns the danger of global comparisons between research and development budgets. As an example, it is agreed that this budget is specially big in the United Kingdom, yet the rate of growth of the economy has been lower than in Japan and Germany, where less is spent on research and development. This global correlation has little value because there is no short-term correlation between the amount spent on research and development, and economic goals. If you spend money on missiles there is no reason why you should increase the rate of growth of the economy. The notion of the research and development budget has been extremely useful at a certain phase of the development of the science of science, but it may be coming now to have a bad effect, in that people may believe that if they spend more on anything which could be described as research and development, they will necessarily get the social or economic results they want.

As regards the strategy of the nation, we came to agree on a few well-known ideas. They are familiar, but it is necessary to repeat them: the danger of imitation, the necessity to take into consideration the special circumstances of the nation concerned, the necessity of economic concentration, and consideration of science as one of the key factors in deciding what to do.

I now come to the second point about the different organs of decision, or the different elements that are decision makers. Professor Weinberg said in his paper that everybody is, in a certain way, his own science administrator. Of course, this is true; just as it can be said that everybody in a certain sense is a practical economist. By definition we are making choices; any scientist is making choices in the use of the scarce commodity called *time*. But without being a pupil of Hegel, I may say that quantitative difference may sometimes create qualitative difference. It is clear that my choice, let us say, between teaching the doctrine of Marx and doing research in the organization of research is an individual "administration" of science, but it is a relatively simple one. If it comes to the French Head of State having to decide whether he wants to produce the Concord or not, I would say that the number of variables and the consequences of the choice are so much greater that even I would admit that in *principle* it is the same, but *practically* it is something fundamentally different.

How does the decision-making machinery function? The impression I have received from everything I have heard is that whatever the institutional set-up, nobody knows for sure how decisions are taken; because first, you have social needs, then the scientific community and the pressure groups within it, also the State with the necessity of national defence, and also there is the vague notion of a few things which should be done, either for economic goals or for obscure reasons normally called prestige, for lack of a better word. Quite clearly, the functioning of any science policy is a mixture of all these different elements, much more complicated in practice than in the models of the organization.

On this point I want to distinguish between two meanings of the word "politics", which has been used with great generosity in this meeting. "Politics" may mean quite simply the taking of decisions; to quote Aristotle—"politics is when somebody gives an order and someone else obeys it". Thus, the head of a laboratory takes a "political" decision when he tells someone to do a particular thing and not something else. In that sense, there is policy of science at all levels from laboratory to university to government agency to the State. But when it was said that the decision to produce the Concord or an atomic striking force in France was a political decision, something else was meant. It meant—if I am right—a decision taken for reasons which are concerned neither with economic growth nor with the progress of knowledge. Generally, today, it is thought that when a decision is taken for the sake of pure knowledge, it is rational; when it is taken for the sake of economic goals, everyone is ready to accept that it, too, is a rational decision; when it is taken for national security, to a certain extent it is accepted, but with reluctance, that it is rational; when it is taken for outside reasons we call it prestige and we mean that it is irrational. I would not say that this is a definition of rationality and irrationality—although I have nothing against it—but I believe that as it is part of the job of a scientist to debunk, it is good that we should know what we mean when we say that going to the moon is irrational. In terms of the progress of science it is clearly irrational; in terms of economic goals, in all probability it is irrational; in terms of national security it is in all probability irrational; in terms of prestige—you have to measure prestige and you have to ask the President of the United States what he means by that. If he says that to go to the moon before the Russians would be a first-class victory and that he puts the highest value on that, you may say he is crazy, but he has a case.

Now I come to the last comparison; namely, to what extent do the different elements play the same role or not in the science policy of the countries concerned? A question I asked myself before this symposium, knowing that it would be a comparison between different nations, was: is there a fundamental difference between the way science policy functions (a) inside the Western world, between France, the United Kingdom and the United States, (b) between the Western world and the Eastern countries, and (c) between the industrialized nations and the non-industrialized or poorly industrialized nations?

As regards the United Kingdom, the United States and France, I do not believe that there is a fundamental difference either in the organization of the scientific bureaucracy or the way it functions. There are many differences because of the national set-up of the universities, but there seems to be the same mixture of pressure group, discussion, social needs, scientific community, and so on, which it is the pleasure of the sociologist to decipher and the despair of the rational man to observe. It is the way politics is functioning, starting not with national goals, but with demands.

I was amused to find, in the discussion of American science policy, that there was always assumed to be a demand coming from the public, as if the public was really the sovereign of the State. It was for me the expression of the national ideology of the United States, more than an expression of the way in which society really functions. Not that the public can be completely manipulated, but I would not say that public opinion knows exactly what it wants. Let me quote an example from French public opinion polls. The question was: "Are you in favour of the French atomic striking force?" There was a small majority for it. But another question asked: "Do you believe that France has the means to have a really efficient atomic striking force?" A large majority answered "No". Which means that an absence of consistency is not a peculiarity of politicians! I do not believe there is a fundamental difference between the United Kingdom, France and even the United States, leaving aside that the research budget of France may be more like the budget of General Motors than like the budget of the United States.

As regards the difference between Eastern and Western Europe, it is harder to gain even an impression. Clearly, on paper the centralization is much greater, but I am not absolutely convinced that in practice there is complete planning of science. And I suppose that there is the same inter-action between the scientific community and the political leaders. I am sceptical about the possibility of the complete planning of science, even in a planned economy. I believe that discussion between scientific people, and between scientists and government, is an integral part of any modern society, whatever the system may be.

As regards the third comparison, I find this much more difficult. Clearly, the institutions are more or less the same, but according to what we have heard, the differences from Israel to Argentina, or from Argentina to India, are so enormous that it would be necessary to make further studies to discover how it is possible to integrate the scientific community into the broader society, and to make the impact of science effective on society. This is a new aspect of an idea which arose many times in this discussion; namely, that science and technology are part of the general social process, and if they are not integrated into this, they may become, or remain, half sterile. How to cause science and technology to have a more complete impact *is* a social problem. The problem exists everywhere. Even in the Western countries, the technological temper is not the same from country to country. Certainly the United States is much more orientated towards technology and the application of science than the older countries of Western Europe. There are certain resistances to the "application" of science and technology, let us say, to secondary school or higher education, which are stronger in France than in the United States. But, between the social resistance to science in Western Europe and in India, let us say, there may be such a difference of degree that it may amount to a difference in kind.

Now, for the second part, on which the discussion was most exciting, because it was concerned with what we should do in order to know more. This was the only point on which there was some heated expression. Looking from the outside as a sociological observer, I had the impression that there were two camps. In one camp were the people responsible for the administration of laboratories, who said, and thought, that after all they did their job in a very sensible way and, without excluding the possibility of study, they would not learn very much from the science of science. In the other camp was the specialist of the management of science who, of course, played his social role perfectly by explaining how useful he could be to these purely practical men who had a knowledge of science, but not a knowledge of the science of management. The dialogue was so pure, so perfect, that it was a kind of ideal sociological experiment showing how every social actor normally acts in conformity with the roles of his profession, without even being aware of it!

However, the discussion was not as pure as I would have liked it to be, because there was a combination of two topics. On one topic the specialist of the management of science was right; namely that it is good to have experimental study of the degree of efficiency of an organization, whether small or large. But he made his case at the same time more exciting, both stronger and weaker, by combining the idea of experimental studies with that of a general model. Of course, it is much better to have a general model, but it gave the head of the laboratory the possibility of rejecting the rather obvious requirement of a scientific study of management by expressing scepticism about a general model or a general system theory. And as the two elements were confused, this gave the best possible social drama. Because two topics were discussed at the same time, each side was sure to be right and each was able to give wrong arguments. When the head of a laboratory said: "This cannot be measured," he meant only that one can measure it, but it will not *help me*, which is something different. To what extent a certain form of measuring will be useful can be decided only after experiment.

On the other hand, when you have before you a general model of the functioning of the whole society there are always two possible attitudes. There is one attitude which is individual; that is, admiration. But after admiration, which is the beginning of the reaction, there are two possibilities. The first is to say: "This would be useful if it were practical, but it is not". The second is to say: "Let us try". You may ask which side I am on. I would say—being also a social actor—that my spontaneous reaction would be to share a certain degree of scepticism about immediate usefulness; but, having an inferiority complex in relation to this sort of science, I am ready to admit that I am wrong, and that it is the right thing to do. I take refuge in a general proposition, which is that in science you must try. The wrong thing to do is to start with the proposition "You can't do it". After all, there *is* no general principle in the strategy of science, and what will be the right strategy in the science of science will be shown only by the development of the science of science.

Let me make one point clear. We should discriminate completely between the obvious necessity of experimental studies of laboratories, organizations, productivity, and cost-benefit analysis, and whether a general model is at present necessary or useful. I was much impressed by Professor Ackoff's model because it avoided what I dislike, which is to take the gross national product as an absolute measure of the quality of a society. When I saw that there were "intrinsic" goods and services in the model I found myself in my own job of philosopher with profound satisfaction. I believe that there has been immense progress in relation to the "gross national product" type of reasoning, which was very useful twenty years ago and has still a certain usefulness today, although it has become a shibboleth.

It has been said that the science of science is partly science and partly philosophy. I would agree with that, and I would add that the same could perhaps be said about almost any science, which always includes a minimal element of philosophy. It has been said, also, that the function of the science of science, and the analysis of science policy, is on the one hand to forecast technological evolution, and, on the other, to illuminate discussions and to make them more rational, or in any case *clearer* for the people who are taking the decisions. From this point of view, I believe that what we have done in this symposium, and what those interested in the science of science are doing, is extremely important. Let us take the example of Keynes' general economic theory. I am not absolutely sure that it was completely right, or that it was such a fundamentally new departure, but the Keynesian theory is one of the great developments of economic science of the twentieth century, because it changed the economic perception of the social actors. From Keynes' general theory, economic policy has not been deduced in a rational way, but it has grown from it, because the social actor now has a different perception of the world and a different perception of his function. I believe that the science of science, which we are trying to develop, may have, with time and patience, a function of the same sort;

namely to change progressively the social perception of the social actors and to improve the rational character of their decisions.

FUTURE TASKS OF THE SCIENCE OF SCIENCE

Szalai: I would like to draw attention to the fact that although the title of the symposium is "Decision Making in National Science Policy", we have in fact been discussing throughout national *research* policies. Quite apart from the problem of whether social science is a part of science—let us hope that a growing part is becoming a science—research cannot be simply identified with science. Research activity is a small part, although a growing part, of what we understand as scientific activity, and the great deficiency of our discussions has been that we have regarded research more or less as an entity abstracted from such things as education, and particularly documentation and popularization. We have also dissociated it from the arising of general cultural attitudes out of research, whereby even scientific words become part of daily usage. Furthermore, it is still true that only part of our knowledge about the world, even about the natural world, arises out of professional research. Most of our knowledge in the past arose out of the everyday experience of working people and peasants, sublimating through a long process into general culture, into knowledge, and into science. We have tended to neglect those parts of science, or scientific activity, or scientific culture, without which professional research could not exist.

I mention this only because the science of science is something much more general, much more philosophical than any of us, including Professor Aron, have said. It goes over into the sociology of knowledge, into philosophy, ethics and many other subjects. But it must be clear to us all that unfortunately at present, decision making in national *science* policy is mostly concentrated on decision making in national *research* policy, which is not the same. At least, it is thought that by putting "inputs" into research one can govern the whole of science policy; in fact, one can govern probably only a very small part of it.

King: I do not entirely agree with you. I agree that most of our discussion has been on *research* policy rather than on *science* policy, and this has equally been the case in national policy discussions and national decision making. But increasingly we have turned to the question of science's impact on other policies. We are not concerned so much with research in the classical sense of the natural sciences, but in the application of knowledge which may have to be produced by science for its own purposes, to the improvement of social and economic conditions.

Szalai: The popularization of scientific research is a tremendous problem, solved in no country.

Weinberg: Popularization is a highly important question to which the scientific community generally has not directed enough attention. This is particularly important in view of the fact that the survival of the scientific society itself depends upon a broad popularization. The question of their own survival should motivate scientists to do more in this direction.

With respect to the dissemination of information, on the other hand, a great deal has been done and is being done, and this is part of the scientific policy of all countries.

However, I would like to take up a point made by Professor Aron. Perhaps as a laboratory director I am simply acting my social role, and there is nothing I can do about it, but it seems to me that the essential issue in the argument is the question of values, and that we are trying to define what we mean by scientific values. My illustration in my paper of the individual scientist was by no means to deny that President de Gaulle's decision with respect to the Concord was a more difficult one than that of an individual scientist, but I was trying to stress the fact that for the first time scientists have injected into the scientific discussion the question of value in an explicit way. When I disagree with Professor Ackoff it is not that I deny the validity and usefulness of doing experiments and of making models, but it is that I feel so strongly that the primitive and most important input into his system is some kind of system of values. It is on this account that I would disagree with one point made by Professor Aron. He said that we would believe it to be rational if a decision in science was made on the basis of increasing our store of knowledge. Surely this is precisely the problem that we are talking about, because the question is not whether to increase the store of knowledge, but whether to increase one part of knowledge or another part, and what are the criteria—what is the value system—that we should develop in order to decide this? Because on one system of values, increasing this branch of knowledge is rational; on another system of values it is irrational.

Aron: I do not think we differ; quite clearly, in any evaluation of a decision there is an element of value, but in certain cases, when the mission or the goal is clearly defined, there may be a possibility of measuring the efficiency. Even when the values are multiple and heterogeneous, which is often the case, there may be a possibility of giving more or less weight to the different values, which means more or less measuring. To say that because there is an element of value, measuring is impossible, seems to me wrong.

293

But, of course, I would be the last to deny the obvious point that we are doing science for the sake of certain values.

I tried to make clear not what it should be, but what it is, that the ordinary man today calls irrational. I had in mind the dialogue, about which I know something, between civil servants and ministers. If the civil servant tells a minister that something will have an impact on the growth of industry or on economic growth, or if he says that microbiology today is of great importance and we should spend money on that, the civil servant and the politician will both be completely satisfied that it is a rational argument. If the Head of State says, "I want the Concord because otherwise there will be only an American plane to go to Martinique", the civil servant will have the impression that the argument is irrational. I did not want to say more than that. That is a purely social definition in the vocabulary of the civil servants of what they believe to be rational and what they believe to be of another type. And what they believe to be of another type they call political, which is unjust to the politician.

Carey: It seems to me that one cannot rationalize science in social terms unless one considers values. Professor Ackoff's earlier remark about "guts" is possibly most applicable to this problem of hypothesizing and articulating values which one tries to sustain, strengthen and achieve through science as a means or tool. But very few people in the United States seem willing to face the question. If we look at the allocation of money for science by categories, it *suggests* a reflection of values, but this would not stand up to close scrutiny. The question is, who is to play the role of statesman? This is probably hard to do within the constraints of the executive area of the American government. It is rather hard to do within the scientific community, which does not generally think that way. It seems to me that one has to look to the political arm in order to find the courage. Politics is a risky business, and if you do not take your chances in one area you have to take them in another. But I think that it is in the political area that values have to be worked out.

The Brookings Institution in Washington two years ago arranged meetings which provided neutral ground where members of the legislative branch of the United States Government could meet members of the executive branch, with the moderating influence of scholars to help the process. One meeting was devoted to the question: how can we better equip Congress to deal with science and public policy? I took the view that there was really nothing wrong with the way Congress dealt with science, if you measured it against the way the executive deals with science. On both sides there are faults and strengths. Congress was perfectly capable of making up its mind about the moon programme, or the Mohole; in "Big Science" it could make decisions reasonably well. It was not so clear about "Little Science", where everything was vague because the executive had been vague and so had the scientific community.

I suggested that a contribution could be made if the executive would produce an annual report comparable to the President's annual Economic Report, which is a "perspectives" report, analysing the behaviour of the economy in a multitude of dimensions and outlining economic expectations over the next year or two. This is not a decision-making paper; it is highly illuminating in terms of shaping the questions and defining what people ought to argue about. It becomes the subject of public hearings by a special Joint Committee of Congress, and there is an educative feedback from this through the press and other media. People think in broad perspectives about economic policy. I suggested a similar report for science policy. The meeting ended without any consensus on this idea; however, four or five Bills have been introduced in Congress which provide for such a report to be prepared by the President. None of these has yet reached the enactment stage, but it may happen, in one version or another. However, it is only a beginning.

Yet I think that the problem in science policy must be to suggest the social values to which science can be directed. Someone must have the courage to do it; he must be able to take dissent and argument, because people ought to argue about values. This is surely the critical next step. Systems approaches certainly could be used to improve the efficiency of decision making and policy making, but I am not sure that they *can* come to grips with the question of over-riding values, which tend to be worked out as a consensus from polarized view-points. When Professor Weinberg suggested in his celebrated piece in *Minerva* three general criteria, and came to the third, "social merit", it seemed to me that this was a very provocative hypothesis, but very little has been done by the philosophers on science and public policy to give that third criterion flesh and blood (Weinberg, A. M. [1963]. *Minerva*, **I**, 2 (Winter), 159–171; [1964]. *Minerva*, **III**, 1 (Autumn), 3–14).

I once attempted in a meeting of scientists and administrators to break down social merit into three categories—economic values, cultural values and political values—and I defined four sub-values within each category. On a very subjective basis, I added some relative weights. I then tested five different investment areas, both heavy and light, in science, against this framework, and asked those present to vote on these five areas.

To get an argument going, I arbitrarily assigned the following values, on social merit:

Economic values

Contributions to health and general welfare	3
Effect on technical innovation (including value for high employment)	10
Contribution to conservation of basic resources (water, food, energy)	10
Return on investment	2

Cultural values

Contribution to exploration	5
Enlargement of understanding of environment	5
Enrichment of education	10
Improvement of human relations	5

Political values

National prestige	2
International understanding	5
Problem solving in under-developed countries	3
Cold-war advantage (this assessment was made in 1965 and would not reflect the world in 1967)	15

Desalination scored 20 points out of a possible maximum score of 75; population control scored 21; weather modification scored 48; oceano-graphy scored 52, and the manned-landing lunar programme scored 37, all out of a possible total score of 75. From there on, the meeting became vociferous and heated. This kind of experimenting in ideas and values, though very tricky, may bring us closer to wisdom; I think this is the most critical part of the whole business.

Dalyell: Mr. Carey has suggested that dissent, argument and disagreement are essential. On one level I agree, but on the other hand, there is a tremendous price to be paid here, especially in a Western type of political system. It is asking a great deal of the politicians to get across their political colleagues and their civil servant advisers. If we give the impression that we are critical of politicians and the civil servants who work for them, we could be wide of the mark. The real difficulty arises with the politician's own colleagues. If you are asking that a minister should make himself unpopular in this respect—after all, by definition, nothing will be done *unless* he is going to risk making himself unpopular—you are asking a tremendous amount of him.

We perhaps tend to forget the "horse trading" which goes on inside any political party among a man's political friends, under any system. If a minister responsible for science objects to people in other ministries not doing their job properly—in order to follow Mr. Carey's idea, I think he may have to object—when his turn comes at the public-spending sub-committee of a Cabinet he may find that his colleagues will get their own back. This may not put the politician at a very high level, but do not let us imagine that great decisions are based on anything like pure reason—far from it. Decisions become a matter of *weight* inside a political party. In many ways this is extremely disappointing, but it does point to some of the difficulties that Mr. Carey was raising.

There is one other point. The appeal that should go out from this symposium is for honesty to confess to failure. Yet because, in our system, failure attaches to people rather than to ideas, defence mechanisms are built up inside politicians that make it difficult for them to do many of the things that this meeting has wanted them to do, and to expect to survive at the same time. This is not just a question of personal promotion or personal survival. If you are labelled with failure, and this is the risk that is run, you can be no more use and cannot serve any noble or other purpose.

It is primarily a matter of education; one has to have, surely, a well-educated electorate that values frankness and self-criticism almost above any other quality in a politician. Once we have that, we shall achieve many of the things that we want.

Ackoff: Well into this century, traditional philosophy of science, and science itself, insisted on separating the question of what ought to be and what is. It produced a concept of science that was essentially descriptive rather than normative. It was maintained either that science was incapable of investigating questions of ethics and value or, if it was capable, such investigations were inappropriate. Building on the philosophy of pragmatism, E. A. Singer, Jr. developed a comprehensive philosophy of science which incorporates the problems of values into the problems of science itself. Perhaps the most complete statement of this philosophy is presented in a recent book by C. West Churchman—*Prediction and Optimal Decision* ([1961]. Englewood Cliffs, N.J.: Prentice-Hall). A similar effort is to be found in *Operational Philosophy* by Anatol Rapoport ([1954]. New York: Harper) and in an article of mine, "On a Science of Ethics" ([1949]. *Philosophy and Phenomenological Research*, **9**, 663–672). There have also been a number of less philosophical attempts to do exactly what Mr. Carey is calling for. French economists and sociologists in particular have done significant work on the value of human life, because it has become apparent that in many cases public decisions demand weighing the value of human life against other things (see, for example, Abraham, C., and Thédié, J. [1960]. Le prix d'une vie humaine dans les décisions économiques. *Revue Française de Recherche Opérationelle*, **4**, 157–168; Thédié, J. [1961]. Report of discussion in session on economic decisions that could involve loss of life. *The Proceedings of the Second International Conference on Operational Research*, pp. 784–786, ed. Banbury, I., and Maitland, J. London: English Universities Press). They have faced this problem head on, as did British and American operational research workers during the second world war in evaluating alternative bombing strategies. Work of the same sort has been done on city planning (Ackoff, R. L. [1963]. Toward quantitative evaluation of urban services. In *Public Expenditure Decisions in the Urban Community*, pp. 91–117, ed. Shaller, H. G. Washington, D.C.: Resources for the Future, Inc.) and on the poverty programme (Anderson, Jacqueline [1966]. *Operations Research and Long-Range Planning*. Ph.D. Thesis, Case Institute of Technology, Cleveland).

Braun: Throughout this symposium, it has been sufficiently stressed how national science policy and cultural pattern are closely related. In certain instances, to improve science policy would be possible only through cultural change, a task that looks almost impossible—at least at first sight.

However, if we consider that the problems created by science and technology can be turned into either blessings or disaster and that its effects can hardly be confined to the nation that takes the decisions, we seem to have no other choice but to attempt the needed cultural change. With the aid of behavioural scientists and systems specialists, we shall have to study present methods of decision making in national science policy and develop better systems. No doubt, the interpretation of scientific and technological information for the benefit of government officials, politicians and the general public will have to be considerably improved. Altogether, the formulation of scientific policy and strategy will have to be surrounded by safeguards, similar to those in legislation, for a sound national science policy should not only provide for science and scientists, but also protect society from having to accept blindly the decisions of its scientific experts.

King: Despite our occasional genuflections to principles, we have been discussing mainly the practical, applied social science aspects of the problem of science policy. I am not sure that there is yet much fundamental research on this subject. I want to mention what seem to me to be major problems to be faced by science-policy makers, ministers, or the civil servants who are preparing for ministerial decisions.

We have first to make a clear distinction between two aspects—the management of science and the impact of science on various other elements of national policy—and the interaction between the two. Furthermore, there is a tremendous amount of work to be done, and many decisions to be made, with regard to science in relation to the probable explosive development of education in the next few years.

There is a great uncertainty in many countries on how ministerial responsibility for science should be arranged. There has been disagreement in different countries on whether the minister responsible for science should be in charge of a ministry, and therefore have a large range of subjects under his executive control as well as for policy making, or whether he should be a high-level person attached to the Prime Minister's Office or otherwise close to the centre of government, without executive responsibility, and hence able to act with impartiality over the whole field.

A number of the European countries fall between two stools. For example, in Germany the Wissenschaft Minister is responsible for atomic energy and space and a number of research councils; with this vested interest in part of the field and with rival ministries responsible for other applications of science, how can he be impartial in his approach to allocations? In Italy a Bill is before Parliament to copy this position and to give similar powers to a Minister of Science.

A further important problem which is not yet settled is the question of where to divide executive and ministerial responsibilities in the field of science. There is a spectrum of activity, from the primary schools, through secondary schools, universities, postgraduate work, government and other research institutions, industrial research, applied research, to development and production. It is obviously too much to be the responsibility of a single minister. In the United Kingdom we have made a division between science and technology. Many people doubt whether this is the right place to make the division, but most countries in carrying out scientific tasks have to decide where to make a separation, and this is a matter on which much more experience is required.

Another point of great importance is the question of whether to have central budgets. Professor Aron suggested that the central budget was probably useful for an initial period; afterwards it can become dangerous, not only for the reasons that he mentioned. It can also give a very false picture of the potential help which science can give to different applications in different sectors of the economy. This is a matter on which France and Belgium take one point of view and the Anglo-Saxon countries another. We want to know more about this, as with all questions of allocation or, as I would rather put it, deployment.

Another matter is the rapidly evolving concept of science policy. A purely practical social conflict arises in many countries between existing agencies, set up for scientific research for government interests, and created before any concept of policy existed, and newer central policy organs created because outsiders are saying that science is too important to leave to the scientists. A conflict of this kind occurs in many European countries; it is probably one of transition, but there is not yet a reconciliation on the part of many research directors. This needs a lot more looking at.

The question of the social sciences and the formulation of science policy is also unfinished business in many countries. Of course, this equating of science with natural science is the Anglo-Saxon heresy and is officially denied in other countries, but even there, where the allocation of resources, at least for research, covers all forms of knowledge, not only natural science, nevertheless the natural sciences tend to call the tune because of their obvious and dramatic results. There are very few countries where social scientists are on the national science policy councils, although we have just admitted that the basic concepts of science policy are socio-economic. There is an anomaly here which has not been resolved.

There are many problems concerning the scientific community and the desirability of the evolution of collective statesmanship. We have been discussing the question of how parliamentarians can have access to the basic facts and principles on which wise decisions of science policy can be made. The science of science has an important role here.

We have hardly touched on international co-operation in science. In the European countries, for reasons of their small size, there has been a tremendous but sporadic creation of organizations, from the relatively bureaucratic Euratom, to bodies like CERN (the European Organization for Nuclear Research), the European Space Research Organization, and many smaller co-operative schemes. All this activity is disorderly, sporadic and out of the control of governments. There is no sense of priority. Countries are not yet regarding international research co-operation as an extension of their national resources. A whole colony of problems for the science of science is connected with the efficiency and creativity of the scientific systems, institutions and individual laboratories, starting with institutional and other causes which inhibit or encourage productivity, and particularly high creativity.

Finally, there is a series of emerging questions which we shall have to face in the near future and in which the scientific and systems approach will be very important, such as the question of technological transfer to under-developed countries, the world food problem, which is the concern of agricultural policies, and many aspects of aid policy. Science has an inherent and probably leading role in many problems of this kind and could start new approaches, but by itself it is impotent. Equally, there are many other topics such as urbanism, water resources, advanced means of transportation, where we shall be dealing with multi-variant systems with socio-economic and technological characteristics in which the classical unique approaches of the economist, the behavioural scientist, the technologist and engineer, or the natural scientist, working separately, are bound to fail. The science of science should help us to build towards the application of scientific methods to an attack on such problems.

There is a very great need for a body such as the Science of Science Foundation, independent of governments, to encourage, through impartial research not aimed initially at specific applications, new methods of attacking many of these problems, and I hope that it will be a centre for the creation of knowledge for innovation in science policy.

Goldsmith: And now a closing word. In this symposium we have been concerned with a practical problem—decision making in national science policy. I stress the practical nature of the problem. But, as is clear, we have not yet the criteria to allow us to say that one decision is more valid in terms of, say, the national interest, than another decision for action. One of the difficulties we face is that people ask us: what is the practical importance of the science of science? The classical answer might be: what is the use of a newborn baby? Or, more significantly, we might answer that if we increase the level of the self-knowledge of science, we might use it to forecast its own future development. I agree with Professor Aron that we need to have more basic research; we need to establish our frontiers and philosophical principles. Of course, governments want help now, and scientists have become the new intellectual force in public affairs. Thus, prematurely, before the basic researches are even begun, the scientists are seeking to find urgent answers to enormously complicated questions. We need to foster *basic* science of science, before we can concern ourselves with *applied* science of science. I am most encouraged by our three days of discussion, especially because we seem all to agree that the scientists of science will begin to appear, and they will provide the studies to enable us to plan the advance of science in relation to the socio-political problems we have to face. I expect that the science of science will come to be seen as a significant advance of the second part of the twentieth century.

In conclusion, on behalf of the Science of Science Foundation, I want to thank Lord Todd, Tony de Reuck, and the Ciba Foundation for having provided the facilities for this meeting, and for enabling us to have so interesting a discussion, and Sir Solly Zuckerman for starting us off with his keynote lecture.

INDEX OF AUTHORS*

Numbers in bold type indicate a contribution in the form of a paper; numbers in plain type refer to contributions to the discussions.

---

* Author and subject indexes prepared by Mr. William Hill.

INDEX OF SUBJECTS

Printed by Spottiswoode, Ballantyne & Co. Ltd., London and Colchester

SOCIAL SCIENCE LIBRARY

Manor Road Building
Manor Road
Oxford OX1 3UQ
Tel: (2)71093 (enquiries and renewals)
http://www.ssl.ox.ac.uk

This is a NORMAL LOAN item.

We will email you a reminder before this item is due.

Please see http://www.ssl.ox.ac.uk/lending.html
for details on:

- loan policies; these are also displayed on the
  notice boards and in our library guide.

- how to check when your books are due back.

- how to renew your books, including information
  on the maximum number of renewals.
  Items may be renewed if not reserved by
  another reader. Items must be renewed before
  the library closes on the due date.

- level of fines; fines are charged on overdue books.

Please note that this item may be recalled during Term.